GER   LUDWIG

Practical

Handbook

DOGS

▶ The Reference Work for All Dog Owners
▶ With Portraits of the Most Beloved Breeds
▶ Including a Quick Finder from A to Z

GERD LUDWIG

Practical

Handbook

DOGS

Contents

What Dogs Need

2

3

Friends for Life

4   Feeding, Care, and Health

Sports, Games, and Travel

5

Quick Finder from A to Z

6

Foreword

Dogs and people need each other more than ever.

Dear Readers,

The dog has chosen its career. Its relationship to people has become more intensive, demanding, and stimulating. The changed role of the dog is a reflection of our changed needs and longings in a society in flux. Foremost is the desire for the closeness of a devoted friend that accepts us the way we are and that is always there when we need him. With a dog we may very well fall short of the detachment that we aim to achieve.

We can prove that dogs contribute to our well-being. People who deal with dogs are more well balanced and resilient, and less susceptible to heart and circulatory disorders. When we pet a dog, our heart rate decreases and our blood pressure goes down. The good that dogs do for us becomes especially evident with people who have psychological problems and can't open up to others. The animal almost effortlessly breaks through the armor of anxiety, vulnerability, and anger.

It is part of the pack animal's self-perception to fulfill its master's wishes. This surely has became easier, now that the dog's jobs are less demanding and more feasible than when it was the master of the herd and the watchdog that never let a mouse in the territory get away, or the draft dog that gave all it had, as if it intended to pull the whole world upside down. Today, its physical exertion is required almost nowhere but in dog sports; however, there is even more

headwork, deduction, thinking things through, and thinking ahead. For a dog this is often strenuous and confusing—and sometimes simply too much, specifically, when the dog is intended to replace an absent partner and we attribute human characteristics to it. Whether through ignorance or exaggerated love of animals, the results commonly include misunderstandings, defiance, and refusal to cooperate.

The dog adapts and fits in. It needs a solid place in the animal-human partnership, and has a right to appropriate living conditions and the fulfillment of its needs; often the psychological ones are more important than the physical ones.

This book will help you to meet your dog's expectations and understand and supply its needs. This is a well-grounded advisor for daily life; it describes the most common misunderstandings and problems, and offers practical suggestions to solve them. And it shows us how much dogs need us and how much we need them.

Gerd Ludwig

How to Find the Right Dog

Dogs enrich our lives. The relationship with a dog is more intense than with any other pet. In keeping with the dog's inherited pack mentality, it bonds closely with its owner. Closeness to the dog also signifies responsibility and readiness to compromise. What do you expect from your dog? In this chapter you will find out what kind of dog is right for you, and what you should look for at point of purchase. Sketches of the most beloved breeds will help you choose the right dog.

1

What Dogs Are Like

Breeding has developed dogs in many sizes, shapes, and colors. But whether Westie, Spitz, or Mastiff, all dogs are similar in nature.

NO DOG LIKES TO BE LEFT ALONE. The dog is a social creature; the pack, with its clearly established hierarchy, is the focus of its life, and provides the dog with security and protection. The needs of the group always take precedence; a public spirit and a willingness to cooperate strengthen the pack.

The dog's sociability paved the way for its partnership with humans. This partnership has lasted for thousands of years, since dogs and men first came together in prehistoric times. A lonely dog is a deprived dog. It needs to be with its human companions on a regular basis.

Dogs are born to run. As pack hunters they have the best physiological features for extreme endurance performance. Even breeds that we have bred these qualities out of—Dachshunds, for example—still exhibit an astonishing capacity for running. You shouldn't underestimate even a lapdog's will to run. Dogs become unhappy and sick if they don't get enough exercise.

The History of the Dog

With the exception of cats, herd and pack animals are the only ones that humans have been able to domesticate. They are the only animals that have the ability to fit into a living community. The dog is our oldest house pet; it had already lived with early humans for several thousand years before the other work animals and house pets came onto the scene.

The Dog Is Our Oldest House Pet

East Africa was the homeland of the first humans; from there they colonized the other continents through their wanderings. We don't have such reliable evidence about the early history of dogs. It's also debatable whether the DOMESTICATION (◐ p.262) of the early dog spread out from a single point or occurred in different places on the globe independently and more or less simultaneously. The 25,000-year-old paw prints in the Chauvet Cave in southern France are considered to be the oldest evidence of dogs. The earliest bone discovery of a dog that lived and worked directly with humans comes from a 14,000-year-old grave in northern Germany. More recent dog bones and skull fragments, between 9,000 and 11,000 years old, have been discovered in North America, Japan, Turkey, Great Britain, and other countries around the globe. The worldwide distribution of dogs in these early periods of development supports the supposition of several independent centers of domestication. There is discussion of four evolutionary lines of the domestic dog, one of which became the principal line. That is supported by present genetic research on over 60 dog breeds, which concludes that more than 70 percent of all present-day dogs are very closely related to one another. The dog has been living with us for at least 15,000 years, and all other house pets and work animals were domesticated much later—the goat around 9,000 years ago, the

sheep, cow, and cat 7,000 to 8,000 years ago, the donkey 6,000 years ago, and the pig 5,000 years ago. The horse is a latecomer, with a history of domestication of just 3,000 years; it was quick to make a career of service to humans with its versatility as a beast of burden and a means of transportation.

Searching for Ancestors

The wolf has long been considered the favorite among possible ancestors of the dog. As long as there were no conclusive evidence

 INFO

Dingos—Australia's Domestic Dogs Gone Wild

Dingos are as emblematic of Australia as kangaroos. These wild animals arose from domestic dogs that came onto the fifth continent with the original inhabitants around 10,000 years ago (◐ FERAL DOGS, p.263). Since then, wild dogs, which are about the same size as German Shepherd Dogs, have been living independently and free, but even today they show many of the characteristic features of their domestic dog ancestors.

and research into the ORIGINS (◐ p.39), coyotes and jackals were also possibilities. Wolves, jackals, and coyotes are found where we believe the first dogs lived. All three can mate with dogs and bear fertile offspring, and all are similar in physical build.

Not long ago the behavior researcher and Nobel Prize laureate Konrad Lorenz awarded the role of forebear to the golden jackal, for

▷

The wolf is the ancestor of our domestic dogs and the largest wild variety within the canine family (Canidae). *In Europe wolves have been persecuted for hundreds of years, and have survived in only a few areas of southern and eastern Europe.*

like the dog, this animal subordinates itself unconditionally to its boss. Subsequently the relationship behavior of several research groups came under greater scrutiny, with one unambiguous conclusion: The wolf is the direct ancestor of the domestic dog. The long-term studies and attempts at crossbreeding conducted by Dr. Wolf Herre in his Kieler Institute left no room for doubt. Wolves and dogs easily adapted to one another and mated, whereas jackals and dogs remained rather aloof, even when they brought offspring into the world together.

How the Wolf Turned into the Domestic Dog

Wolves and domestic dogs crossbreed with one another in nature; on the other hand, mating between jackals and dogs occurs quite rarely, or purely by happenstance. The wolf is indicated as the ancestor primarily by its way of life; domestic dogs exhibit the typical lupine pack social structure and characteristic behavior patterns among their human families.

There is also plenty of other evidence. The brain of a wild canine is larger than that of a domestic dog because the latter's adaptation to the carefree life with humans has required less mental activity. In comparison to the wolf, a dog's brain is consistently much smaller and lighter; a jackal's brain, however, never reaches the weight of a dog's.

There are also resemblances between wolves and dogs in their teeth and blood. Excavated bones some 400,000 years old provide evidence that wolves lived in the immediate vicinity of humans. Recent comparative genetic analyses suggest that dog-type ancestors existed as long ago as 135,000 years (❍p.127).

The Wild Community

Our domestic dogs belong to the family of canines; thanks to their exceptional adaptability, they spread out from North America and colonized all parts of the world except Australia. Australia does have a type of wild dog, which is known as a dingo. Ranchers there often consider them troublemakers because they prey on livestock.

All varieties of dogs are endurance runners, and many can reach high speeds—such as the coyote at practically 40 miles per hour (65 km/h). Their prey is frequently hunted down after a chase, especially in the case of the larger strains that hunt in a pack.

The wolf is the most typical member of the family. It can adapt to nearly all living and climatic conditions, and it has disappeared only in places where humans have hunted it. In North America, however, there has been movement in recent decades to reintroduce the wolf into some of its former habitats.

Scarcely less successful are the other canines, including the jackal and the fox, but especially the coyote, the wolf's nearest relative.

Although dogs eat primarily meat, plant food is also part of the regular diet. And contrary to what we would expect from runners and ground-dwellers, there are some canines, such as the gray fox and the korsak (steppe fox) that can even climb trees.

Born to Run

Stubby feet and sprinter's legs, a small waist and a muscular body, a huge nose and a flat nose, an athletic chest and a pigeon breast—domestic dogs come in all sizes and shapes, from the tiny, 2 pound, 8-inch (1,000 g / 20 cm) Chihuahua to the giant, 3-foot tall (1 m) Irish Wolfhound and the Mastino, which at nearly 180 pounds (80 kg) qualifies for the super-heavyweight division.

Endurance Required Above All Else

Despite their versatility, all dogs and breeds hark back to a common "basic model" that in appearance and capabilities reflects the heritage from their wolf ancestors.

Like the wolf, the domestic dog is a carnivore that hunts prey in a pack. Its skeleton is composed of strong, hard bones, but overall, it is somewhat primitive in structure, as is commonly the case with carnivorous mammals.

The dog is a runner, and that is evident in many features of its physique and physiology. As pack hunters, dogs must have endurance, and only for brief moments do they reach the high speeds that are important for most solitary hunting animals. When necessary, the members of the dog pack can, however, also pick up the speed, for example, when they need to cut off the prey's escape route.

An animal that runs a lot and covers long distances needs long, strong legs that facilitate extensive mobility. The dog's thrusting power comes primarily from the muscular hind legs.

Better than Any Marathon Runner

Even breeds that have been bred solely as family dogs still have an astonishing ability to run, usually more than the owner of a Dachshund, Miniature Schnauzer, or Papillon would give their dog credit for.

Sled dogs are especially primordial, and they can hold their own against their wolf progenitors. These dogs, in fact, are not all that different from their ancestors in physical appearance or abilities.

Siberian Huskies can pull a load far greater than their bodyweight for 60 or more miles (100 km) without tiring, and after a short break they are completely fit for action. In the yearly Iditarod dogsled race in Alaska the top teams cover the astonishing distance of 1,100 miles (1,800 km) in less than ten days—far from roads and streets and through ice and snow.

With a height at the withers up to almost 3 feet (95 cm), the Irish Wolfhound is the biggest dog in the world. A Chihuahua doesn't stand much over 5 inches (13 cm).
▽

Greyhounds Are the Sprint Champs

The gaits of dogs are walk, trot, moderate run, and top speed. The trot is the most efficient way to get around, and it gives the dog staying power with comparatively little energy expenditure. Pack hunters such as the Greyhound, Saluki, Borzoi, and other greyhound breeds that hunt primarily by sight, are the exception to the rule. They are small and lightweight, with long legs and a long back. In running, the back bends so much that the hind paws touch the ground in front of the forepaws, much like the champion sprinter leopard.

Over short distances Greyhounds can reach speeds of 36 miles per hour (60 km/h) and more, but they tire quickly. The fact that good legs are in themselves no criterion for good running is proven by a comparison involving

 TIP

Dogs Need Exercise

Have more faith in your dog! Even small dogs develop into brave wanderers that can easily master fairly long distances. At least on the weekends you should treat your dog to regular, prolonged walks, and hopefully not always on the same familiar routes.

Dachshunds, German Shepherd Dogs, Saint Bernards, Boxers, and Greyhounds. The surprising results of the study show that despite its short legs, the Dachshund has the best running style! Its long, flexible spine allows the short-legged creature to achieve nearly the optimal movement in running.

As a runner the dog is a ground animal. Thanks to its muscular hindquarters, jumps pose no problem. Unlike cats, dogs will gladly jump over obstacles. Dogs have a disadvantage with respect to cats only in climbing. They can twist their legs only so far, and can't stick in their claws to serve as climbing aids. The forepaw has five toes, and the hind paw four; all have strong, nonretractable claws. The thumb of the forepaw is atrophied.

On Tiptoes, and with a Big Heart

Dogs have evolved into tiptoe walkers. In this means of locomotion only a small part of the foot touches the ground. The reduced surface contact facilitates higher running speeds and increases the capacity to sprint. The tiptoe running style is found in animals that move quickly; flat-footed walkers such as bears move in a more leisurely fashion. The collarbone, which in other mammals connects the shoulder blade and the breastbone, is totally atrophied in dogs and hoofed animals. For running animals this is a distinct advantage, for it provides cushioning in movement and improves flexibility.

Runners have a large heart. In dogs it constitutes an average of one percent of body weight; in some athletes such as the Greyhound, even 1.3 percent. Under extreme demands its pumping capacity can increase up to five times.

Dogs Prefer Things Cool

Those who run a lot and for a long time also sweat a lot; here, dogs are rather underequipped. Whereas humans sweat all over their body, dogs can get rid of excess heat only through their tongues and the mucous membranes in their mouths when they pant (⊙ HEAT REGULATION, p.265). The few sweat glands they have on the pads of their feet are really of no help. Especially in the hot summer months the risk of heatstroke is much greater for dogs than for humans, and they need cool, shady spots. Therefore, walks should be saved for the early morning and the evening hours, and real athletic activity eliminated. In general, dogs feel better in cool areas than in hot ones.

A Magic Coat for All Types of Weather

Dogs are quite immune to bad weather: With a coarse, water-repellant topcoat and a fine, insulating undercoat, their fur is an ideal all-weather cloak.

The original FUR TYPE (⊙p.264) is found on such dogs as the German Shepherd Dog and the Nordic breeds; other dogs have all possible combinations of short, smooth, long, and rough hair, with and without an undercoat. These coats are, in part, the result of human intervention in the dog-breeding process over many thousands of years. Humans have bred dogs for many specific purposes, and this is often evident in the type of hair that various breeds have developed.

Most dogs shed their fur within four to six weeks in the spring and fall. This can create a mess in the home, so you should be prepared to deal with it.

▶ INFO

Show Your Teeth!

Dogs have a scissor bite with sharp incisors, long canine teeth, powerful fangs, and molars with a cutting ridge. The typical predator bite is perfect for biting off and cutting through flesh. With its flattened back molars a dog can also chew and grind plant food; however, dogs are primarily meat eaters, and their teeth have developed accordingly.

1

Born to run. The Russian Borzoi is a typical pack hunter. Like all greyhounds it relies more on its excellent vision than on its nose while hunting.
▽

The Dog's Amazing Senses

Humans live in a world of images; what we see we take at face value. Dogs rely most on one sense organ that plays only a minor role in our daily lives: the nose.

A dog's nose is a sensitive, high-performance detector that registers countless data with many varied scent receptors. And it can even sniff into the past and analyze scent trails that are days or weeks old.

Always Ahead by a Nose

The fact that the dog is a true nose creature is shown by the size of its nose. The true value of the scent organ is inside, however—in a German Shepherd Dog the area occupied by scent receptors covers 23.25 square inches (150 cm^2); in a Dachshund the area is 11.6 square inches (75 cm^2); and in our case, scarcely a half-inch (3 cm^2). The large surface area in the dog nose is the result of multiple folds in the scent area.

A German Shepherd Dog uses some 220 million scent cells when it sniffs; the Dachshund, 125 million; and our nose has just 8 million at its disposal. The scent information (◐ SENSE OF SMELL, p.273) is processed in the dog's brain by 40 times more cells than in our case.

The nose of a healthy dog is moist. The moistness holds the scent matter and transports it to the scent cells. The moist, mobile nose also makes it possible for a dog to sense storms over long distances.

A Very Personal Scent

Dog owners can very easily confirm that dogs rely mainly on their noses and less on their sight—a dog recognizes its master by the scent on clothing. If the owner stands undressed in front of the dog, the dog may take the person for a stranger.

The Dog's Eye—Better than It's Cracked Up to Be

Dogs were long thought to be color-blind. True, there are only a few cones in the retina, the light-sensitive network, but there are many more rods. In mammal eyes, the sight cells are of the cone type for COLOR PERCEPTION (◐ p.260), and rods are responsible for light and dark perception and for seeing in reduced light. The myth of dogs being color-blind is now disproved, even though our most faithful companion lives in a less colorful world than we do. The human eye is sharper than the dog's eye. If a trusted person remains immobile, the dog will see the person in a focus field from only 2 to 30 feet (7 to 100 m). Dogs have better vision for movement; this is a holdover from their hunting past when they used their vision to keep the fleeing prey in view.

Everything in Full View

With breeds that have a short snout such as the Boxer and the Pug, the field of view is 200 degrees, and Greyhounds bred for good vision can take in nearly 270 degrees. (Humans have a field of view of 100 degrees.) Fields of view overlap each other more with short-nosed dogs than with long-nosed ones, which can see in only a limited area (◐ VISION, p.274). People who fall in love with a puppy's blue eyes mustn't be disappointed if the EYE COLOR (◐ p.263) changes. The eyes of young dogs don't yet have any pigmentation. It is later deposited in the iris, and it gives the eyes their ultimate color.

Nothing Escapes a Dog's Ears

A dog's ears are a theme with many variations. Whether large or small, cocked or floppy, hairless or furry, a dog's ears hear practically everything and perceive tones from 15 Hz to the ultrasound region of 50,000 Hz (◉ SENSE OF HEARING, p.272). In humans, the upper limit is 20,000 Hz, but it declines with age.

Since dogs with erect ears can move the ear muscles that attach to their skull, they can locate the source of sounds better than breeds that have drop ears. Despite their sensitive hearing, dogs don't seem to be bothered too much even by loud noises of over 100 decibels; humans, on the other hand, find them stressful.

Taste and Touch

A dog has 2,000 taste-sensitive papillae on its tongue that tell it what is sweet, sour, salty, or bitter. But usually dogs rely on their noses, and first sniff their food before tasting it.

Smell also determines preference for types of food and for tastes. There are hairs and sensory cells located on the mustache, lips, paws, and nose, which react to stimuli and help with orientation. In contrast to cats, which are active in low light, the sense of touch in dogs is of minor consequence.

A Dog's Sixth Sense

Experts are convinced that dogs can perceive force fields. They can thus be guided by magnetic vibrations and electrical charges in the air, and they live in a three-dimensional wave network.

Humans generate force fields. This individual aura depends on mood and well-being. There is evidence that dogs have highly sensitive antennae that register every change in their owner's aura.

1

◉ WHAT TO DO IF...

... my dog's senses become less acute?

The dog stays in the house more than before, moves more deliberately, and sometimes bumps into furniture or doors when he runs. It often takes him a while to realize that someone is standing next to him or behind him, and he seems almost apathetic at his feeding dish.

Cause: The symptoms are unmistakable—your dog is getting old. In old age the senses slowly decline, and in that regard dogs are no different from us humans. Usually that is evident in the dog's vision. In an older dog visual acuity usually falls off markedly, his surroundings seem unclear and shadowy, and he moves more carefully and more slowly. The sense of hearing also dulls. When he hears someone approach him, he may act startled or even aggressive. A reduced sense of smell can create some feeding problems, since the dog can no longer smell the food, and may hesitate to eat.

Solution: A loss of sense perception is not a disease. The dog will get along without major problems in his familiar surroundings. Avoid rearranging the furniture, so that the dog's familiar paths remain clear, announce your presence when you approach the dog, and give him enough time to finish his meal.

A Dog Can
Change Your Life

People who welcome a dog into the house have to make some compromises, turn their routine upside down, and maybe even do without some favorite habits.

MORE THAN JUST A DOGHOUSE. A dog takes part in our life and becomes a part of it. It submits willingly when it finds a home and security with us.

A firm place in the relationship is just as important as the understanding and the closeness of its master. If the dog's demands go unsatisfied for a long time, there is a crisis brewing in the relationship, or it comes apart. Whether those demands turn into problems and stumbling blocks depends on our ideas about life and the expectations that we pin on our relationship with a house pet.

Howdy, Pardner!

You don't just end up with a dog by accident. There are many reasons to decide to get a dog, but they are almost always backed up by our personal desires, longings, and dreams. You shouldn't be the only one to decide. If we really want a dog as a friend and partner, we have to grant it some rights and look after its needs.

A Dog Needs Responsibilities

In earlier times dogs were mainly work animals and had to serve as watchdogs, herders, and draft animals. These were tiring jobs, but clearly defined responsibilities led to fulfillment of the dogs' nature and pack mentality.

Service and work dogs have long been in the minority, and dogs have turned into family members. They no longer have to work as hard, but the demands on them are scarcely any smaller or more modest. New roles and functions developed out of the close relationship with humans. They sometimes require nearly human behavior and understanding, as all-around leisure time companion, comrade in sports and games, playmate for children, single people, and senior citizens, and assistant therapist or nursemaid. But the dog usually can accomplish even unaccustomed tasks with style. The motivating force behind its cooperativeness and willingness to work is recognition from its master for work performed—the greatest reward for any pack-mentality dog.

A Dog Needs Dependability

Dependability seems to be an old-fashioned word for some people. People who want to live with a dog need to rediscover the term in their daily life. A dog's trust and confidence are based on dependability, and this gives shape and intensity to the animal-human relationship. This entails a dependable routine with fixed times for feeding, going for a walk, playing, and cuddling. It is important for the dog to be acknowledged as a full-fledged member of the family or the single-person relationship. Whenever possible, the dog should be included in the action and not left out of communal life. If it sometimes insists on having its own way, that is a dog's innate way; as a member of the pack it tests the stability of the pecking order, but also expects the boss to show where the limits of the permissible lie. Dogs need attention, kindness, and dialogue, but at the same time, a clear hierarchy with commands and obedience. People who attempt training without authority experience failure, jeopardize the relationship, and are pitiful paper tigers in the eyes of their dogs.

The Relationship Proves Itself in Daily Life

Every dog needs exercise—several times a day, in all weather, including Sundays and holidays. That looks fairly innocuous in print, but it often seems different in practice. Even with small breeds a once-around-the-house doesn't cut it, and going out in cold and messy weather is not for everyone. If going for a walk turns into a burdensome duty that everyone shirks, the dog's attested rights will get left behind sooner or later, and with rather unpleasant consequences. Dogs that aren't fully occupied get on people's nerves and become disobedient, and a lack of exercise endangers fitness and physique.

Dogs are clean animals, but even short-haired breeds drag dust, dirt, and other souvenirs from the walk into the house. And there is usually some splashing around the food bowl. This can be a tough test for cleanliness fanatics—and sometimes the start of a crisis in the relationship.

What You Need to Know About Dogs

Humans and dogs have traveled a long road together. In the process the dog has come closer to us than all other domesticated animals. There are many similarities between the dog world and the human world, and that makes it easier for a dog to integrate and feel comfortable in a family pack.

Adaptability and a desire for recognition help a dog master unaccustomed situations, but it's not a genius at everything. The limits of cooperation become evident when we either intentionally or unknowingly expect it to display human qualities and behavior.

Dog Ownership Takes Time

A dog is a central figure. You can't keep a dog casually or as an afterthought, whether in a family or in a relationship with a single person.

▷ The dog must be cared for. Providing and preparing food takes time; puppies need to be fed several times a day, and adult dogs twice daily. Depending on the breed, coat care can be very demanding. In addition, there are the health checkups and shot appointments at the veterinarian's.

▷ A dog needs exercise. Two to three walks a day are important; they allow the dog to do its business and satisfy its strong impulse to move, and they contribute to physical fitness.

▷ A dog wants to be kept occupied and needs attention. A dog that is not given something to do on a regular basis becomes bored, whines, and often does stupid things. The daily play and cuddling with its human keep its mind fit and alert and strengthens the relationship.

▷ A dog has its own life's rhythm. Tasks take longer with a dog, such as shopping, strolling through town, and vacation trips. On trips in the car the dog needs regular stops, and when you travel you often have to take a circuitous route to dog-friendly hotels and restaurants. If the dog has to stay home alone, you have to arrange for someone to care for and watch over it, and even putting it up in a KENNEL ( p.266) takes time and money.

Typical for Dogs

In the twinkling of an eye a dog wins the heart of its new family. But it also comes with some qualities and quirks that we often have to get used to and come to terms with. Humans, therefore, must be patient with their dogs. Learning to live with each other is a long-term process that both man and dog must go through for a strong relationship to develop. Specifically, humans must be willing to deal in a patient manner with:

Demanding puppies. Lots of attention and regular activity are the basis for a smooth relationship between human and animal.
▽

▷ **Barking.** It's a given that dogs bark but that's really not so self-evident; wolves, the ancestors of domestic dogs, are capable of barking, but they communicate much more commonly by howling.

Barking has become the most important vocalization only with dogs, and it is used especially for communicating with humans. There are some breeds that like to bark more than others, and in general, small dogs are more "talkative" than large ones.

People try to eliminate barking through special therapy and DOG TRAINING COURSES (◐ p.262) but, in general, barking is part of the typical behavior of the species.

▷ **Digging.** Dogs dig in the dirt to hide their bones or dig up treats. Burying is a typical behavior that follows a fixed pattern. A dog demonstrates this whenever it wants to bury real or imaginary bones in the living room.

Dogs even scratch with their hind legs, for example, after doing their business. In so doing, the dog flings dirt onto the spot and leaves a scent message from the sweat glands on the balls of its feet for other dogs to find.

▷ **Rolling.** Dogs and people have very different ideas about what smells good. We find this out when the freshly bathed good-for-nothings roll in some smelly mess. That's an important action for them; after a bath our four-legged friend feels naked without its own scent. The scent gives dogs security and personality, so they perfume themselves when the opportunity arises.

▷ **Marking.** Adult males intentionally deposit urine in specific spots in their territory. This so-called MARKING (◐ p.267) is used to identify their territory and cover over markings by possible rivals. A dog may also mark in its own house, especially if new, strange-smelling furniture is brought in. Female dogs also mark, but rarely.

▷ **Straying.** All breeds that have hunting in their blood tend to STRAY (◐ p.273). Dogs that don't get enough activity and are bored, or that get too little exercise, also frequently take off.

◐ TEST

Are You a Dog Person?

Before you get a dog, check to see if you are ready to live with one and meet its needs.

1

	Yes	No
1. A dog changes your rhythm of life. Are you ready to make compromises?	○	○
2. Are you ready to forego familiar habits?	○	○
3. Are you prepared to cancel your vacation if there is no one at home to take care of the dog?	○	○
4. Can you deal with going for several walks every day, regardless of the weather?	○	○
5. Dogs bring dirt into the house and sometimes smell strong. Is that acceptable to you?	○	○
6. Sick and elderly dogs need a lot of attention and care. Do you have time and energy for that?	○	○
7. Do you have patience and understanding if the dog doesn't want to do what you want it to?	○	○
8. A dog costs money. Can you cope with extra costs in the case of illness or accident?	○	○

Key: Only if you can answer *Yes* without reservation to all eight questions are you a true dog person. A dog will be happy with you.
For every *No* you should carefully consider how important that is to you, and be absolutely certain of what that means for the new partnership.

The drive to run free is particularly strong when love calls. Females in heat and amorous males then take advantage of every chance to slip away.

▷ **Coming into Heat.** Female dogs come into heat and are ready to mate twice a year (❍ COMING INTO HEAT, p.265).

The female becomes restless, drips blood, and searches for a sex partner. This is a nerve-wracking time for dog owners.

The only way to prevent unwanted pregnancy and possible false pregnancies is through NEUTERING (❍ p.268).

▷ **Territorial Behavior.** A dog's hereditary behavior includes protecting its home territory and its inhabitants. The dog takes over the role of defender especially when the leader of the pack is away. Dogs that are overly territorial might cause problems—with the neighbors, the mailmen, joggers, and so on. If your dog has a problem, you should seek help from a qualified professional who can "treat" this problem.

▶ CHECKLIST

Basic Needs

As a dog owner and the "leader of the pack" you accept responsibility for your dog and make a commitment to meet its basic needs. These include the following:

- ○ proper accommodations and setup
- ○ daily exercise
- ○ healthy food
- ○ regular care
- ○ health maintenance and shots
- ○ jobs and tasks to perform
- ○ playing together
- ○ attention and affection

Which Dog Is Right for Me?

There are more than 330 dog breeds officially recognized by the FCI (the Fédération Cynologique Internationale), the umbrella organization of the national breed associations, including BREEDS (❍ p.284) of all sizes and colors, athletic or contemplative, suited for families and particularly fond of children, dogs that take their protecive role seriously, and others that have hunting in their blood (→ Breed sketches starting on p.42).

Every dog owner connects very personal expectations with the ideal dog. If these desires conform to the particular qualities of a breed, there should be nothing in the way of a harmonious relationship. But perhaps you will also fall in love with a saucy mongrel that wins your heart through charm and intelligence.

A Dog for the Whole Family

A family dog needs to get along well with everyone. That's not always an easy job if some family members act rather reserved toward the dog and others practically smother it with affection.

A family dog shouldn't withdraw anxiously in strange surroundings and tuck its tail between its legs in unfamiliar situations; what's needed is a casual jack-of-all-trades that doesn't react negatively to children, ignores chaos and hustle and bustle with equanimity, and for which even a noisy house is still a trusted home.

In many homes there are a number of animals. Often there is another dog or a cat, a rabbit, and a guinea pig. Tolerance is needed within the domestic animal faction, but there can also be some lifelong friendships between dogs or between a dog and a cat (→ Chart, p.41).

A Single Person Needs a Dog More

A dog that lives with a single person usually enjoys privileges that otherwise are granted to a human partner. The dog is the all-purpose buddy, a patient listener and soul mate, a companion in free time, on vacation, and in sports.

Dogs of single owners internalize the qualities of their owners so much that they even reflect a little of their human character. Trust and dedication, and closeness and tenderness characterize dogs in relationships with single people, plus a willingness to stay alone and wait without howling and grumbling, sometimes for hours on end, until the key finally turns in the door (→ Chart, p.51).

A Picker-upper for Senior Citizens

Many elderly people become withdrawn, especially when their partner is no longer around. Often it's just one small step to isolation. A pet brings life back into the house; the person has to be responsible and perform duties and keep a fixed daily rhythm.

As long as the elderly person still gets around well, a dog should have an advantage over a cat, as a dog keeps the person mobile, and incidentally helps him or her make new contacts.

Small dogs place no great demands on the fitness and physical strength of their owners. Most senior citizens prefer quiet, affectionate dogs, but many of them can't be spirited enough to suit older people (→ Chart, p.63).

1 *A full partner in family life: The family dog is truly multi-talented, and a real artist at adaptation. Its motto is* Present always and everywhere.

2 *An all-purpose buddy: A dog that belongs to a single person would walk through fire for its owner and is the ideal partner for sharing free time, sports, and games.*

3 *A heart and soul: A dog frequently brings back closeness and warmth that elderly people who live alone miss so acutely. Many times the animal turns into their most important companion and confidant.*

What to Look for When Getting a Dog

Heart and mind play a role in selecting a dog, but you should never choose a dog based on spontaneous whim.

WHO, WHEN, AND FROM WHERE? These three questions figure in the ultimate decision. Which will it be? A puppy or an adult dog, a male or a female, a purebred or a mutt, one dog or a pair? And where will it come from? From a breeder, a private owner, or an animal shelter?

Stop! A dog won't be happy here; it will be alone more than five hours every day, it will have no fixed reference person, it won't get enough exercise, it will be too large for the house, it will cost too much to keep, and it's not clear if dogs are permitted by the rental contract.

What's It Going to Be?

Your living conditions and your familiarity with dogs determine the choice of a dog (→ Which Dog Is Right for Me? p.24). Taking care of a puppy is more work and takes more time than dealing with a grown dog, and a male dog needs a more experienced hand than an obedient female does.

A Puppy or an Adult Dog?

A puppy is ready to go to a new home at the age of eight to twelve weeks (→ Tip at right; also, Character Test, p.28). By that time it has been wormed and inoculated (→ Vaccination Schedule, p.203), and it may be house-trained. The separation from mother and siblings is a painful experience for the little fellow until it gets used to the strange surroundings and its new family. In the first four to six weeks it will need constant attention and care, including at night. The puppy gets fed with special, nutritious puppy chow, and several times a day, because its tiny stomach can handle only small servings. As soon as possible, you should get the young dog used to the collar and leash and start it on its first short walks.

Male, Female, or Even a Pair?

Newcomers to dog ownership will get along better with a female dog. Females are almost always more obedient and devoted than males, and easier to train. However, in clashes, females are unforgiving; struggles are more dramatic than with males.

A female dog comes into heat two times a year. That's no easy time for her, nor is it for the owner. Especially at the peak, female dogs tend to stray in search of males that are ready to mate. It's also not uncommon to find interested males right by your door.

Brother and sister from the same litter make an ideal pair. They become inseparable.

It's easier for dogs to adjust in pairs, and there are fewer demands placed on the owner, as the dogs are not fixated on only the person. Shyness with strange people and situations also abates more quickly. Naturally, however, the upkeep and expenses are higher for two dogs than for one.

A Mixed Breed Is No Second Choice

You can be just as fortunate with a mixed breed as with a purebred. The only thing is that you know less about what qualities the dog has. The oft-repeated view that mongrels are smarter and more adaptable than purebreds is false.

 TIP

When Can the Puppy Move In?

Eighth week of life: The puppy bonds very quickly with its new family.
Ninth to tenth week: The puppy has already had many experiences, but willingly adapts to the strange customs.
Eleventh to twelfth week: The puppy knows what it wants. In the coming weeks it learns step by step what is allowed and what's forbidden.

The Right Time to Get a Dog

In the first weeks a puppy needs around-the-clock care; without specific planning (factor in the annual vacation), it won't work. But getting adult dogs to adjust is also no easy matter. And think about your travel schedule: in the first six months the new dog shouldn't be left alone for very long.

▶ TEST

The Puppy Character Test

The behavior of the puppy is an indicator of how the grown dog will behave.

	Yes	No
1. When you call it, does it come running to you wagging its tail?	○	○
2. Does it observe the things going on around it?	○	○
3. Does it let you pick it up without resistance?	○	○
4. Does it take part in play with the other puppies?	○	○
5. Does it hold its ground against its littermates?	○	○

Key: Did you answer all questions with *Yes*? Then you should be proud of your choice. Your puppy will turn into a self-assured dog that likes contact and gets along well with people and other dogs.

Where Should My Dog Come From?

For purebred dogs a breeder is the right starting point. You can also buy purebreds and mixed breeds from private parties. Animal shelters give away many more grown dogs than puppies.

A Purebred Dog from a Breeder

If you have decided to get a purebred dog, you should go to a recognized breeder. The breeder should be a member of a breed association that's connected to a national umbrella organization such as the American Kennel Club (AKC) (→p.284 for addresses). The national organizations, which are easy to find on line or in a library, can direct you to the corresponding associations that will lead you to their breeders. Especially with rare breeds, there may be a wait involved until a litter can be given up for adoption. You may even have to travel fairly long distances if there are not many breeders of a particular dog.

What Difference Does a Good Breeder Make?

Anyone who has a clear idea of what the future pet should be like in appearance and temperament should decide on a purebred dog from a breeder. A good breeder lives with and for the dogs and has specialized in one breed, without owning too many animals. All the dogs have a connection to the family and have been raised as briefly as possible in the kennel. The dogs appear friendly and interested in strangers; they are confident and act neither anxious nor aggressive.

The first impression on a visit to a breeder counts: Do the dogs impress you as healthy? Does each one have its own bed and resting spot? Are food dishes and water bowls cleaned regularly? Can the animals play and keep themselves busy? Are the kennels protected from the weather, and is the floor clean? Is there a separate room set aside for pregnant females and for mother dogs with puppies? Is the litter basket or birthing room adequately heated?

Breeding Dogs Takes a Lot of Experience

Breeding dogs takes time and money. Breeders must be knowledgeable about the character and breed-specific qualities of their dogs, and about previous generations. They must know the laws of genetic inheritance (◉ GENETICS, p.264), and must know how specific traits are passed on. They must have contact with other breeders and check carefully which males are appropriate for breeding. Many breed associations even maintain standards of BREEDING SUITABILITY (◉p.260). This makes it easier to find appropriate breeding mates and facilitates planned breeding.

Getting a Dog from a Private Party

Frequently a new dog comes from a circle of friends, acquaintances, or neighbors. Often this involves a litter for which the owner, who is not a breeder, doesn't have room and would like to put into good hands. Usually the dogs are mixed breeds, but they may also be purebreds.

If you know the dog owner and the animals well, there is only a minor risk of getting a bad deal. Things are different, however, when you get a dog through a newspaper ad or an Internet offer. There may be irresponsible dog breeders lurking behind the ads, and their dogs may come from questionable conditions. With such offers get some advice from an expert in breeding or animal welfare. If there is any doubt, steer clear!

A Dog from an Animal Shelter

Animal shelters are collection stations for abandoned, runaway, and ownerless dogs, as well as dogs whose owners can no longer keep them. Generally you find grown animals and, rarely, young dogs or puppies, in an animal shelter. The shelter director and employees know a lot about the character, qualities, and origins of most of their charges. It's very important to have a detailed consultation before deciding on a particular dog.

All shelter dogs are under constant veterinary care, have had their shots, and have been wormed.

A dog is usually released only with a contract, which contains a return clause in case the relationship doesn't go as expected. The purchase price or all-inclusive expenses vary from shelter to shelter and serve mainly to cover the ongoing costs of operations, care, and veterinary bills.

1

All children are proud when they can feed and care for their dog themselves. Of course, the grownups keep an eye on things to be sure the dog gets what it needs.

Getting to Know and Love a Dog

You have passed the "Dog Person Test" (→ p.23), and you know what you expect from a dog and what it expects from you. Everybody is happy about the new family member and has already agreed to play a part in taking care of the dog.

Talking with the Breeder

You have learned some things by reading books, dog magazines, and articles on the Internet, and you have interviewed friends and acquaintances who have experience with dogs. Now it's time for the next step on the road to a happy life with a dog—a visit to a breeder of your chosen breed.

You can get addresses in your area from the local or national dog breed associations (see Addresses, p.284). You can phone to find out how many animals a breeder has on hand and when the next litter is expected.

Frequently, some or all of the puppies are already spoken for by other parties, and you may have to wait until the next litter. The breeder also can't predict what the male-to-female ratio in the new litter will be. If the mother dog gives birth only to female pups, you may have to join the waiting list for your desired male or go to a different breeder.

Before you make a final decision, you should examine two, or better yet, three breeding facilities to find the best breeder for your needs.

The breeder also takes a good look at you as early as the first visit, and may ask about your living conditions, and will especially want to know if you can devote enough time to taking care of a dog. It's a sign of a good breeder to decline the sale if there is any doubt.

Also, with breeds that are less suited to beginners, the breeder will check how much you know about dogs. The breeder may refuse to sell you a dog that is not appropriate for you.

Sniffing Around

Now you have gone to visit a breeder about a pup; first you should gain the trust of the adult purebred dogs. You can study their personalities and behavior in their familiar surroundings; you can determine how the males and females react in various situations when you walk with them.

Take your time, even if your puppy won't be born until the next litter. If the whole family will later help care for the dog, the children must also see if they can control a grown dog, for example, while walking it on a leash.

Remember that children under the age of eight can't take on responsibility for a dog and shouldn't take a dog on a walk without being accompanied by an adult. Indeed, young children should be supervised around dogs at all times to avoid any injuries to the children or dogs.

▶ CHECKLIST

What My Dog Will Cost Me

Average ongoing costs for a medium-size dog. For more detailed information consult the relevant chapters.

- ○ Food: $25–80 per month
- ○ License: $20–50 per year
- ○ Veterinarian: $100–200 per year
- ○ Accessories: $30–200 per year
- ○ Care: $10–15 a day in a kennel, $3–8 per day for a dog-sitter
- ○ Travel and Vacation: approx. $10–15 per day for hotel or vacation home
- ○ Liability insurance: starting at $60 per year

The Puppies Have Arrived

Finally you get the awaited call from the breeder that the mother dog has had her puppies, and all are healthy and active, and you can come look for a dog. Still, a little time goes by, for the mother and the newborns need lots of quiet in the first days.

At around four weeks after the birth the hormonal balance of the mother dog returns to normal. Before then she may act distrustful or even aggressive when disturbed; then the breeder will give the green light for the first visit to the puppies.

Even if everyone is curious and wants to see the dogs, don't descend on the breeder and the dogs with the whole family. The puppies will remain another six to eight weeks with their mother, so there is plenty of time for more visits. These visits are also on the breeder's mind. It's important to the breeder that you get to know your puppy even before you bring it home.

On the first meeting, behave as quietly as possible and observe what goes on in the nursery. It doesn't take long to distinguish the different temperaments and reactions of the lively little puppies (→ Puppy Character Test, p.28).

At six weeks the puppies are active and curious about everything and everyone. Now they can be picked up. The close contact is important so that the young dog notices your scent and imprints on it.

Many buyers follow their feelings and choose particularly inquisitive, bold puppies. It is also fun when a little puppy shows no inhibitions with strangers and nips and bites to its heart's content. But in such cases you should also consider that the rebellious young dogs need very firm training and are hardly the right choice for beginners.

Getting an Adult Dog

A grown dog has a history that has influenced it and determined its behavior. The seller can tell you about the animal's needs and charac-

△
Attention and affection. The separation from mother and littermates and the start in the new relationship are major events in the puppy's life.

teristics, but consultation is no substitution for a thorough acquaintance.

Often you can tell if you are going to get along well as early as the first meeting with the dog. Wait and observe how the dog reacts to you. At first this takes place while the owner is present; with dogs from an animal shelter the guardians initiate the contact. Later you can try out the new partnership on a walk and deepen the trust through feeding and coat care. If certain behaviors absolutely rub you the wrong way you should calmly reconsider the purchase.

Remember, a dog is a long-term commitment, so it's important to find the right dog for you. Otherwise, you could end up in a very unhappy relationship.

Dogs and the Law

The purchase and ownership of a dog are regulated by ordinances and laws. You should be familiar with the most important ones so you can avoid problems and conflicts.

UNDERSTANDING AND TOLERANCE. As a dog owner you have a special responsibility to the dog, but also to your fellow humans. By paying attention to the needs and rights of others you can avoid misunderstandings, disputes, and possible legal consequences from the outset. This applies especially to keeping a dog in a house or apartment and supervising it in public.

Some people are afraid of dogs. Your dog should stay at your side or on a leash wherever it may encounter many people, even when there is no leash law in effect. Dog ownership in rental properties is regulated by rental contracts. Even when the law is on your side, always take the first step toward peaceful coexistence and apply your understanding of others' viewpoints.

Your Rights as a Dog Owner

All citizens have a legal right to the unfettered pursuit of happiness. Legal precedents also leave no doubt that owning a dog is part of that. However, rental agreements may make dog ownership dependent on certain conditions, or even forbid it under specific circumstances.

Dog Ownership in Rental Properties

If the rental agreement contains a prohibition against dog ownership, all tenants are bound by it and have no recourse to laws guaranteeing the unhindered pursuit of happiness. Even if dog ownership is permitted to other renters in the house, a rental contract may exclude dog ownership. In many instances, dog ownership is up to the landlord. The landlord generally consents, however, if the dog neither endangers nor bothers the other tenants. The landlord may refuse to accept fighting dogs and others that are classified as dangerous. As long as the rental agreement doesn't forbid owning an animal, it is possible to own a dog; in any case, there is no law on the books against owning a dog. Nevertheless, it makes sense to get the landlord's permission in order to avoid any possible problems with him or the other residents. Permission to own a dog can later be revoked if the dog— for example, through constant barking— turns into an unreasonable nuisance. The district court almost always has jurisdiction in rental property disputes. Since the amount in dispute usually doesn't exceed $600, an appeal to a higher court is generally not allowed. The ruling of the district court pertains to the specific instance and sets no precedent for other proceedings, even if they are similar in nature.

Dog Ownership in a Condominium

The community members are held to mutual consideration by the good conduct clause of the owners' contract. That also applies to animal ownership. Thus, the condominium owners can take action against the owner of a dog that the residents feel is a nuisance, if their owners' contract provides appropriate steps and if they act as a two-thirds majority. There can also be a general prohibition of dog ownership as the result of a specific clarification of the owners' contract or a subsequent resolution by the owners. The resolution goes into effect if it is passed unanimously or is not contested. Ownership of dangerous dogs can be excluded through a resolution by majority vote.

On the Right Road with a Dog

Towns decide independently where dogs must be kept on a leash, for example, in many city parks and in playgrounds. Ownership of dangerous dogs is subject to conditions, but there generally is a requirement that they be kept muzzled and on a leash. Dog owners are responsible for removing their dogs' droppings from sidewalks and crosswalks. Violations may be punishable by fine. Continual barking and howling, especially before seven in the morning, between one and three o'clock, and after 10:00 P.M., is considered disturbing the peace. In the woods a dog must be

◁

No disturbing the peace. Permission to own a dog in a rental property can be withdrawn if the dog bothers the residents or endangers them. Check with the owner about the rules of conduct ahead of time to avoid a problem later.

1

under the control of its master. If a dog is hunting without supervision, a fish and game officer may be authorized to shoot or impound it.

A Certificate for Dog Handlers

The DOG HANDLERS' CERTIFICATE (◉ p.261) testifies that owners are capable of functioning responsibly with their dogs. The focus in the basic training courses for the test is the owner's general knowledge, plus the dog's obedience and sociability. The test covers both theory and practice.

Earning the Dog Handlers' Certificate is voluntary; some towns give dog owners with a general knowledge certificate reductions in dog registration fees and a partial exemption from liability insurance requirements.

Some breed associations and national dog organizations offer dog handlers' certificates (check the addresses on p.284 for possible leads).

Liability Insurance for Animal Owners

Owners are responsible for damage that their dogs cause (LIABILITY INSURANCE, ◉ p.267). Specific regulations vary from location to location, and you are well advised to check into them.

Dog owners may be responsible for restitution or replacement of damaged property. The financial consequences are even greater if a dog causes harm to people. Depending on the extent of the damage, the owner may be liable for medical and hospital costs, rehabilitation and care, and perhaps even punitive damages, loss of earnings, and paying the expenses of the victim or the surviving dependents.

Since liability may cover the dog owner's entire assets and income, liability insurance for animal owners is strongly recommended. This is not just an obligation, but rather a precondition in the case of fighting dogs.

The insurance provides for replacement up to the specified maximum. For a yearly premium of around $80, personal injury and damage can be covered up to $500,000, and property damage up to around $100,000. Included in the coverage are all persons who help care for the dog or take care of it during your vacation. The insurance covers legal fees and defense against unjustified or excessive claims.

Coverage does not extend to violations on the owner's part, such as ignoring a muzzle law. Usually the protection is limited to one year in the case of foreign residence.

Health Insurance for Dogs

Health insurance for dogs covers illness and accidents, usually including such things as shots, worming, flea and tick treatments, and medical checkups. Expenses for operations may be covered in part or entirely, depending on the policy.

The amount of the premium is based on coverage, size, and age of the dog, deductible, and duration of the coverage. Depending on the insurance carrier, the monthly premiums can fall between $8 and $50.

Leash and Muzzle Requirements for Dangerous Dog Breeds

Generally the Pit Bull, American Staffordshire Terrier, Staffordshire Bull Terrier, Bullmastiff, Bull Terrier, Mastiff, Mastino Napoletano, and mixes involving these breeds are considered to be dangerous. In many places a general MUZZLE REQUIREMENT (→ p.268), leash law, and mandatory identification by electronic chip are in force. Check into further local regulations.

Laws pertaining to fighting dogs commonly contain breed lists and define the danger of a particular dog based on its breed. A police permit may be required for ownership and breeding, and it may be forbidden to breed certain types of dog.

Registering a dangerous dog may cost more than the registration for other dogs. These measures are intended to limit ownership of these dangerous breeds.

Rights and Duties in Buying a Dog

According to the law in many places, dogs are not objects, but the sale and purchase of dogs is subject to similar conditions. The purchaser of a dog has a legitimate claim to a healthy dog. The seller must therefore be responsible for possible flaws, such as a chronic cough or a dental defect. This liability applies regardless of the dog's age.

In the case of clearly established defects, the purchaser has a right to demand compensation. That can involve elimination of the fault, or even replacing the dog. If these possibilities don't exist, the buyer can withdraw from the purchase, reduce the purchase price, or put in for damages. All expenditures incurred, for example, through treatments by a veterinarian, must be figured into the compensation by the seller.

These costs must not be excessive, but they certainly may exceed the value of the dog. The statute of limitations for defects is generally two years. For "used" items this period is reduced to one year. Puppies are considered "new," but older dogs that have already had several owners are classified as "used."

Ownership of a dog carries with it a great deal of responsibility. All dog owners should do their utmost to make sure that their pets do not become nuisances or dangers either to other people or to other people's property. To avoid problems, it is crucial that owners not only inform themselves fully about the health regulations and legal rules that apply to dogs in their areas, but also that they take the appropriate measures to protect themselves if their dogs nevertheless do cause personal injuries or physical damage. A responsible owner, in short, is a good neighbor.

▶ WHAT TO DO IF...

... there's trouble with the neighbors?

A dog that constantly barks or howls is the most common cause for an unfriendly discussion at the garden gate.

Cause: The dog is regularly unsupervised in the yard and barks at passing pedestrians and cars. For the dog this is the most natural thing in the world; it is making it loud and clear who the boss of the territory is. Other dogs often howl without interruption for hours if they have to stay alone in the house.

Solution: Let the dog out into the yard only under supervision. The dog will rarely bark if it sees that its owner has already seen the "intruders." Correct undesirable barking with a harsh *"No!"* Being left alone is a distressing situation for a pack animal such as a dog but it must learn to cope with it (→ p.155). Distractions, games, and items to keep it busy, and even soft background music, may help.

Ten Questions on Purchase, Ownership, and Law

A clean house is very important to me. Can I still own a dog?
You can't avoid making some compromises. Get your dog used to the clean-up procedure after every walk. If it's raining, rub the dog dry vigorously with a towel and leave it in the hall for a while. Feed the dog only in the kitchen or the hallway. Also, it's often harder to vacuum up the hair of short-haired dogs than of long-haired ones from carpets and sofa.

Our Golden Retriever is 15 months old. We have planned our vacation, and the dog will have to stay home for the first time. Should my conscience be bothering me?
Starting when they are young, all dogs should get used to being in strange surroundings and with other people for hours or even days at a time, without their family nearby. Then there are no problems when the owners are away on vacation. Give the dogs to friends or acquaintances who know them and whom they will obey, or else bring the dogs to a kennel. Before making a reservation, check to see if the accommodations meet your expectations.

▷

Lots of exercise. The daily romp is just as important to proper dog care as the right amount of food, attentive care, and conscientious health measures.

A dog-sitter that watches out for the dog only part-time is not the right choice if you're going to be away for a long time.

I can handle the ongoing expenses for a dog. But what if it gets sick or needs an expensive operation?
In thinking about the upkeep a dog requires, many owners think only about the cost of food. That surely is the biggest expense, but it's not the only cost factor (→ Checklist, p.30). Illness, an operation, and even training at a dog school can add considerably to the expense. Regularly set aside a sum (for instance, $50 a month) as a cushion against emergencies.

My work hours change, so it's hard to stick to regular feeding times. Will this be a problem for my dog?
Dogs are more flexible about their mealtimes than cats, which really insist on observance of mealtimes. If you set aside a couple of minutes for petting and cuddling after eating, your dog will take more pleasure in its meals.

Grandma is 82 and likes to take a nap in the afternoon. How can I keep our wild puppy under control during that time?
It's simple: Let the dog take a siesta too. Of course you can't just have that happen on command, but rather, after the little fellow has first played enough games and sports to be tired. Even the wildest puppy needs a certain amount of sleep. And if nothing else works, the dog will have to be banished from the room for a couple of hours.

△
Togetherness makes it easier. Two dogs in the house are an ideal pair. And the friendship lasts for the entire life of the dogs.

I would like to have a dog, but I am quite sensitive to noise. What if it barks a lot?
There's no such thing as a mute dog. Barking is part of the characteristic behavior and serves as a means of communication with the human. In general, larger breeds are more silent than smaller ones (→ The Most Beloved Dog Breeds, p.38). Dog training can help the most vocal animals.

My friends advise against getting a dog from an animal shelter as you never know what they're going to be like. Is this true?
Most dogs in animal shelters are grown dogs that have had quite a varied life. In nearly all cases, the caretakers know the nature and qualities of their charges and they can help you choose an appropriate dog. A thorough consultation in this instance is particularly important. Shelter dogs are given away only with a contract. It contains a return clause just in case life together doesn't turn out as hoped.

Now and then my dog does his business in a field on the edge of town. The residents object to this. Are they justified?
Especially in cities, there are few places where dogs can do their business. And you don't always have the time to drive your pet to the nearest woods. If this field is public property, or the owner has no objection, the residents in adjacent houses have no legal standing. But you should be sure that your dog uses the edge of the field, rather than a path or the adjacent sidewalk.

My dog is on a leash in the city so shouldn't I be able to let him run free in the woods? He has no hunting instinct.
In the woods there is generally no leash requirement. But responsible dog owners still keep their dogs on a leash where game may be present. Even dogs that normally aren't thrilled by the hunt can rarely resist a fresh rabbit or deer track. Dogs are a major nuisance to wild animals, especially in the winter and while they are raising their young. Also, many wild animals may present a danger to dogs. Racoons, for example, can inflict serious wounds. And, in some areas of the United States or Canada, bears, mountain lions, poisonous snakes, and other wild animals can kill dogs that are allowed to run free in wilderness areas.

◁
A romp in the grass. Treat your dog to a chance to play in nature, but it should always be kept under supervision.

I am 71 years old. The house has been quiet and empty since my husband's death. I would love to have a young dog. Do I dare?
For older people living alone a dog can become the focus of life. It is not just a partner, for it also automatically ensures more exercise and fitness, and incidentally helps make new contacts.

The overview on page 63 indicates some of the best breeds for senior citizens.

1

37

The Most Beloved Dog Breeds

Purebred dogs are recognizable by certain typical physical and behavioral features. The following profiles introduce the most beloved breeds and the best dogs for families, single people, and senior citizens.

THE THOUSAND FACES OF THE DOMESTIC DOG. There are a nearly incalculable variety of dog breeds; in size, shape, fur color, and character traits, no breed is quite like another. All modern dog breeds are the result of selective breeding. The phenotype of a dog is the image of what humans have made of it. Dogs have been bred for thousands of years. Previously, usefulness and suitability were the focus of attention, and appearance, size, and color were of secondary importance. Appearance became the most important goal only with the fairly recent advent of purebred breeding.

The Origin of the Breeds

It's no accident that humans and dogs have been running mates and have formed associations since time immemorial. Both lived in societies, both marked off their territory, and both usually hunted in groups. The social behavior of the dog is an inheritance from its forefather, the wolf (→ The History of the Dog, p.13). The wolf's communal life is distinguished by many correlations that have been partially lost in dogs.

Hunting Companion or Baby-sitter?

Dogs have taken over duties in service to humans. In the early days of their domestication, they were principally helpers to the men in hunting and defenders of the property. But perhaps women also kept early dogs in their tents and huts as baby-sitters and protectors of the children. Wolf and dog researcher Erik Zimen doesn't find that improbable, and he calls into question the exclusively masculine viewpoint. Evidence for Zimen's thesis is found even today among certain native populations; among the Turkana tribe in Kenya, dogs watch over infants, and the women of Brazil's Yanomami Indians raise puppies almost like their own children, even nursing them.

The domestication of the dog was a long process; specializing in different tasks and functions required many generations, and the dogs took to their new jobs willingly and on their own initiative. This is the basic difference between domestication and taming; in the latter instance, animals are made obedient against their will so they can be made to perform specific tasks.

Work Animals and Social Lions

Dogs were already essential helpers on the hunt. The greyhounds were the first. These quick and silent harriers would catch the game in open areas where the hunter didn't have enough cover to get close enough to the quarry. In contrast to greyhounds, which hunt by sight, bloodhounds hunt with their nose. They follow a scent trail tirelessly and for hours until the prey is cornered. New hunting methods made it necessary to breed specialized hunting dogs. With firearms came pointers and retrievers, which point out the game or fetch it. For hunting foxes, badgers, and rabbits, people eventually needed small, agile, and fearless dogs that dared to get into the underground dens. This led to the appearance of terriers (from the Latin *terra*, meaning *earth*). Even though most of them haven't crawled into a foxhole for a long time, the terrier breeds have retained the big heart and the leonine courage of their ancestors. Dogs also exhibited their intelligence, versatility, and abilities in many other arenas—as herding dogs and watchdogs, as draft animals and beasts of burden, as military dogs, and as rescue dogs.

Working dogs have long been in the minority, and only a few dogs still have to earn their keep. The great majority of the millions of domestic dogs now live with families or as partners for single people and senior citizens. Dog ownership based on a love of animals is certainly no latter-day discovery—as early as

◁

The German Shepherd Dog is revered the world over as a helper to humans, in the role of Seeing Eye dog, drug searcher, and rescuer of people buried in avalanches, as well as in police work.

39

△
The fuss over the Lassie films didn't do the dog much good but, fortunately, that's in the past. Today, the Collie is a loving and easily trained family dog with a motivation as a watchdog and defender that is characteristic of the breed.

2,000 years ago people were breeding dogs for sheer pleasure. Those were primarily small breeds that provided company and diversion, and served as lapdogs for noble ladies in the court.

Today's Dog Breeds

Starting in England in the nineteenth century there came a change in dog breeding. For centuries usefulness and suitability had been the determinants of breeding partners, so within a single breed there were great differences in size, conformation, and color. But then BREED STANDARDS (→ p.259) were introduced that precisely described appearance. Dogs that didn't meet these standards were no longer permitted to breed.

Breed associations sprang up and presented the new breeds in shows, first in London in 1859. Today there are over 400 breeds worldwide, of which some 330 are recognized. The Fédération Cynologique Internationale (FCI) divides the breeds into ten groups:

▷ **Herding Group (except Swiss Cattle Dogs):** These include such breeds as the German Shepherd Dog, Kuvasz, Komondor, Border Collie, Briard, Collie, and Bouvier des Flandres

▷ **Pinscher and Schnauzer-Molossoid Breeds (Working Dogs):** Bernese Mountain Dog, Saint Bernard, Boxer, Doberman Pinscher, Rottweiler, Mastiff, Schnauzer, Landseer, and Leonberger

▷ **Terriers:** Includes Airedale Terrier, Fox Terrier, Bedlington Terrier, and Yorkshire Terrier

▷ **Dachshunds:** All Dachshunds

▷ **Spitz and Primitive Types:** Includes Siberian Husky, Samoyed, Akita, Basenji, Finnenspitz, Eurasier, Greenland Dog, and all spitzes

▷ **Scenthounds and Related Breeds:** Includes Bloodhound, German Bracke, Rhodesian Ridgeback, Dalmatian, and Berner Niederlaufhund

▷ **Pointing Dogs:** Includes German Wirehair, Small Münsterländer, Weimaraner

▷ **Sporting Dogs:** Includes Golden and Labrador Retriever, English Springer Spaniel, and Cocker Spaniel

▷ **Toy Dogs:** Includes Maltese, Havanese, Pug, Papillon, Chihuahua, Kromforhländer, Pekingese, and Poodle

▷ **Sighthounds:** Includes Afghan Hound, Borzoi, Irish Wolfhound, Whippet, Saluki, and Sloughi

In the United States, there are seven variety groups of recognized breeds: sporting, hound, working, terrier, toy, non-sporting, and herding. There is also a miscellaneous division for breeds attempting to gain official recognition from the American Kennel Club (AKC).

▶ THE BEST DOG BREEDS FOR THE FAMILY

A family dog is practically an all-round genius. It is an obedient and uncomplicated companion on walks around town and on trips, is the best playmate for the children, has fun at sports and games, and brings life and variety into the house.

Breed	Portrait on Page	Partner in Sports and Games	Likes Children	Appropriate for Beginners	Care	Brief Portrait
Basset Hound	→ 43	●	●●	●●	little	A character; sometimes stubborn. Weight problems with inadequate exercise
Beagle	→ 44	●●	●●●	●●	little	Very quietly behaved and tolerant, but has a hunting instinct
Bearded Collie	→ 44	●●●	●●	●●●	a lot	Needs attention and activity
Bernese Mountain Dog	→ 45	●●	●●	●●	a lot	Good watchdog; always wants to be with the whole family; sensitive to summer heat
Bobtail	→ 46	●●	●●●	●●●	a lot	Lively, bright; needs closeness, but also free space
Bouvier des Flandres	→ 47	●●	●●	●●	a lot	Unerring watchdog and defender; needs lots of regular activity
Boxer	→ 48	●●●	●●●	●●	little	Very active; ideal for an athletic family
Cocker Spaniel	→ 52	●●	●●	●●	medium	Ideal companion and family dog; needs a lot of attention and even more exercise
Collie	→ 52	●●	●●	●●	a lot	Extensive coat care and a lot of exercise
Coton de Tulear	→ 53	●●	●●	●●●	little	Easy to train, lovable, and calm
Eurasier	→ 56	●●	●●	●●	medium	Confident, alert; distant with strangers
German Shepherd Dog	→ 57	●●●	●●	●	medium	Strong guarding and defense instinct; firm training and discipline are needed
Golden Retriever	→ 58	●●●	●●●	●●●	medium	Easy to train and always friendly; good with other pets
Hovawart	→ 58	●●	●●	●	medium	Strong defense instinct; not a good dog for beginners
Irish Setter	→ 59	●●	●●	●●	medium	Lots of exercise; not always a good choice for the city
Irish Wolfhound	→ 59	●●	●●	●●	little	Not for city life; gentle and devoted; needs sensitive and firm training
Newfoundland	→ 65	●	●●	●●	medium	Needs lots of room and likes to swim
Pembroke Welsh Corgi	→ 66	●●	●●	●●	little	Often acts independent; needs firm training and tasks
Poodle	→ 68	●●●	●●●	●●●	medium	Standard and miniature: intelligent and very active
Schipperke	→ 70	●●	●●●	●●●	little	Lively, quick learner; alert, but also noisy
Schnauzer	→ 71	●●	●●	●●	medium	Medium Schnauzer: ideal companion, good watchdog; firm training needed
Spitz	→ 74	●●●	●●●	●●	medium	Medium Spitz: very lively and sometimes noisy
West Highland White Terrier	→ 75	●●●	●●	●●●	medium	Confident, charming, good for city living; also ideal for senior citizens

KEY: ● good   ●● very good   ●●● ideal

▶ AFFENPINSCHER

More substance than style: Behind the comical appearance there is a good fellow with lots of courage, vitality, and intelligence.

▷ **Appearance:** 10 to 12 inches (25–30 cm) at the withers. Length of torso is nearly the same as shoulder height. Domed head with prominent forehead. The apelike facial expression gave the little Pinscher its name.

▷ **Coat:** Stiff, short, and thick, the bush beard and brows form a wreath of fur. Black, brown, or gray markings. Easy to care for, it needs only occasional trimming.

▷ **Character:** Brave to daring; a capable and noisy guardian of house and yard; reacts with distrust or anger to strangers. Very lively and closely attached to its owner.

▷ **Health:** A robust dog with no breed-specific problems.

▷ **Life Expectancy:** 15 years.

▷ **Particular Qualities:** Quick intelligence; learns very easily, but can also turn into a little domestic tyrant.

▷ **A Good Choice for:** Apartment dwelling; an especially loving partner for older people.

▷ **Less Suited for:** Families with small children that regard the dog as a toy.

▶ AFGHAN HOUND

A special dog that stands out for its beauty, elegance, and worthy disposition. Needs a lot of exercise.

▷ **Appearance:** Height at withers: males, 25 to 29 inches (64–74 cm); females, 24 to 27.5 inches (60–70 cm). Medium-length body with straight back; a lightweight at 44 to 55 pounds (20–25 kg) (males). Long head, close-lying drop ears, carried high in motion, tail slightly curled at end.

▷ **Coat:** Very long and silky. All colors permissible. Daily coat care.

▷ **Character:** Very independent and freedom loving. Not submissive; it sees itself as a partner to the human. Often seems unapproachable, and yet needs lots of attention. The hunting instinct of this pack hunter remains intact.

▷ **Health:** Robust and rarely sick.

▷ **Life Expectancy:** 12 to 14 years.

▷ **Particular Qualities:** Walks only on a leash because of its passion for hunting; needs a fenced area for running and regular opportunities to run.

▷ **A Good Choice for:** Sighthound connoisseurs, who will be patient and sensitive partners to the Afghan Hound and devote lots of time to it.

▷ **Less Suited for:** People who are merely captivated by the dog's beauty.

▶ AIREDALE TERRIER

Lively, alert, and courageous: the king of the terriers is a true and dependable companion in all situations.

▷ **Appearance:** Height at withers 22 to 24 inches (56–61 cm). An athlete with a strong body and powerful legs. Long, narrow skull, V-shaped button ears that drop toward the front. The tail is carried erect.

▷ **Coat:** Thick, coarse, and wiry with soft undercoat. Light brown background color, dark to black saddle (blanket). The fur needs trimming every two to three months.

▷ **Character:** Alert, fearless, and watchful, intelligent and eager to learn. A dog with the best protective qualities. Also playful and a real pal to the children.

▷ **Health:** Except for eczema, very robust.

▷ **Life Expectancy:** 13 to 15 years.

▷ **Particular Qualities:** Not always easygoing around other dogs and pets. One of the recognized working breeds.

▷ **A Good Choice for:** Owners who have time to train it and keep their dog's head and body fit.

▷ **Less Suited for:** Good-natured people who won't give their lively Airedale Terrier enough exercise and activity.

▶ BASSET HOUND

Always looks a little downcast, but is a lively and happy dog with lots of charm and character.

▷ **Appearance:** Height at withers 13 to 15 inches (33–38 cm). Sturdy dog with elongated body on short, powerful legs. The folds on the forehead are a typical Basset Hound trait. The red rim of the lower eyelid is visible.

▷ **Coat:** Thick, smooth, short hair with black, brown, yellow, and white patches. Easy coat care.

▷ **Character:** Despite its small size, the Basset Hound cuts a worthy figure. Part of that is the leisurely gait. Devoted and good with children. Confident, with lots of character and intelligence.

▷ **Health:** Eye problems, bladder stones.

▷ **Life Expectancy:** 12 to 14 years.

▷ **Particular Qualities:** With too little exercise, tendency to become overweight; gladly ignores commands if its nose is on a trail.

▷ **A Good Choice for:** People who can deal with a strong-willed personality and see the dog more as a partner.

▷ **Less Suited for:** Dog owners who expect unconditional obedience and have a preoccupation with cleanliness.

1

◗ BEAGLE

Used for rabbit hunting as early as the Middle Ages. Lovable and quietly behaved. Its passion for hunting remains intact.

▷ **Appearance:** Height at withers 13 to 16 inches (33–40 cm). Compact, athletic body, straight back. Long ears, thick flagpole tail.
▷ **Coat:** Short, smooth, and waterproof. Colors: especially tricolor with black, brown, or red spots on white, or two-colored. The fur needs little care.
▷ **Character:** Lovable and alert. A Beagle does not shrink from any challenge and remains collected in unfamiliar situations. A friend to children, and a lover of action-packed games. It's not much of a watchdog, since it quickly makes friends with strangers.
▷ **Health:** Susceptible to vertebral disk problems, eye and heart diseases.
▷ **Life Expectancy:** 12 to 14 years.
▷ **Particular Qualities:** Must be kept on a leash while walking in areas where there is wild game. Like other pack dogs, it doesn't like to be left alone.
▷ **A Good Choice for:** People who become infected with the Beagle's good nature, but who can also control its hunting instinct.
▷ **Less Suited for:** Dog owners who want a watchdog and protector.

◗ BEARDED COLLIE

Lovable and robust, with high-maintenance shaggy fur. This happy Scottish sheepdog needs lots of exercise.

▷ **Appearance:** Height at withers 20 to 22 inches (50–56 cm). Long body with straight back. Broad head with fur-covered drop ears. Heavily feathered hanging tail.
▷ **Coat:** Abundant topcoat, soft undercoat. Color variants of black and white, shading of blue-gray to brown. Impressive beard. Fur needs daily brushing.
▷ **Character:** A born family and companion dog; alert, happy, and composed. An ideal pal for children. This herding dog is always looking for something to do. Watchful but not noisy.
▷ **Health:** Susceptible to hip, eye, and skin diseases, but, generally, a healthy breed.
▷ **Life Expectancy:** 12 to 14 years.
▷ **Particular Qualities:** Puppies are late bloomers and need careful training.
▷ **A Good Choice for:** Sensitive dog lovers who can devote plenty of time to their Bearded Collie.
▷ **Less Suited for:** People who can't give the dog enough activity and exercise.

BERNESE MOUNTAIN DOG

The Bernese Mountain Dog is the best known of the mountain dog breeds. Handsome, watchful, and a protective playmate for children.

▷ **Appearance:** Height at withers: males, 25 to 27 1/2 inches (64–70 cm); females, 25 1/2 to 31 1/2 inches (58–66 cm). Powerful, compact body, flat skull, long, bushy tail.
▷ **Coat:** Long, wavy, and shiny. Black with reddish brown blaze and white markings on head, chest, and paws. Needs regular care with brush and comb.
▷ **Character:** Mountain dogs were used for herding cattle and pulling carts. The Bernese still has those instincts and likes all kinds of tasks. A devoted family dog, it fits right in with children. A good watchdog that is reserved with strangers.
▷ **Health:** Susceptible to hip and elbow dislocation.
▷ **Life Expectancy:** Around 10 years.
▷ **Particular Qualities:** Not very athletic or active; suffers in the heat; puts on weight easily if it doesn't get enough exercise.
▷ **A Good Choice for:** Families with children, and ideally a house and yard.
▷ **Less Suited for:** City apartments and as partners for very athletic people.

BICHON FRISE

For centuries the pet of noble ladies, until it sank into oblivion. Now the happy little fellow is on the rise again.

▷ **Appearance:** Height at withers no more than 12 inches (30 cm). A muscular body with a deep chest on short legs. A short muzzle and flat skull covered by thick hair. Long, heavily furred ears; the tail curls just slightly over the back.
▷ **Coat:** Relatively soft and wavy; hairs up to 4 inches (10 cm) long; thick undercoat. Considerable care required.
▷ **Character:** A generally pleasant, happy small dog, devoted and good with children; gets along well with other dogs. Watchful, but not too noisy. Quick to learn and easily trained.
▷ **Health:** Robust, without the illness profiles of other miniature dogs; isolated knee problems and epilepsy.
▷ **Life Expectancy:** 15 to 17 years.
▷ **Particular Qualities:** Appropriate even for small apartments; surprisingly good at heel.
▷ **A Good Choice for:** Dog lovers who dream of a lovable, playful, but also a fundamentally sturdy small dog.
▷ **Less Suited for:** People who can't deal with a lively small dog.

1

BOBTAIL

A dog with long, shaggy fur, the unmistakable Bobtail is inside and out a clever and playful dog and a real work animal.

▷ **Appearance:** Height at withers 22 to 23 inches (56–58 cm). Compact body; the outline of the skull under the full-bodied fur is hard to determine. Often has inherited bobtail.

▷ **Coat:** Straggly and very abundant, with water-repellent undercoat. Gray to blue with or without white markings. Intensive coat care is the only defense against matting.

▷ **Character:** Good natured, devoted, good with children, and playful. The Bobtail has its own mind and needs a sensitive but firm owner who gives it things to do, but at the same time gives it some free space.

▷ **Health:** Hip problems, deafness.

▷ **Life Expectancy:** 13 to 15 years.

▷ **Particular Qualities:** Ambling gait and curiously high-pitched bark. The puppies are born black and white.

▷ **A Good Choice for:** Dog lovers who have time for the demanding fur care, keeping the Bobtail busy, and giving it lots of exercise.

▷ **Less Suited for:** Pure indoor living and for people who spoil their dogs too much.

BORDER COLLIE

Many people consider this the most intelligent dog and the best herding dog. It places high demands on its owners.

▷ **Appearance:** Height at withers 20 to 21 inches (51–53 cm). Broad chest and powerful back; head with obvious stop and short muzzle; medium-sized semierect ears and long tail.

▷ **Coat:** Medium long or short. Water resistant, with soft undercoat. Mostly black and white, but some other color combinations exist. White should never prevail.

▷ **Character:** A bundle of energy with extreme work ethic and pronounced herding qualities. Learns quickly and easily. As long as it is worked on a regular basis, the Border Collie is a well-balanced and obedient family dog.

▷ **Health:** Eye problems, some hip dysplasia.

▷ **Life Expectancy:** 13 to 15 years.

▷ **Particular Qualities:** Border Collies that have too little to do lose some of their character and radiance.

▷ **A Good Choice for:** People who are outdoors a lot, can let the dog work, and give it some herding duties.

▷ **Less Suited for:** Owners with whom the dog would lead a normal dog's life.

● BOSTON TERRIER

This dog is a well-kept secret: it is absolutely friendly, devoted, and good with children, and still good for city life.

▷ **Appearance:** Height at withers 14 to 16 1/2 inches (36–42 cm). Athletic, compact body. Square skull with short muzzle. Large eyes, erect ears, natural stubby tail.
▷ **Coat:** Short, smooth, and shiny. Black with white markings, sometimes with dark stripes. Easy coat care.
▷ **Character:** Lovable and adaptable, merry and playful; gets along well with children. Intelligent, quick to learn, and watchful, but not a barker. An ideal companion dog that gets along well in all situations.
▷ **Health:** Birthing problems and eye inflammations, but generally robust.
▷ **Life Expectancy:** 12 to 15 years.
▷ **Particular Qualities:** This breed came from a cross between Bulldogs and Terriers, but quickly turned into a pure family dog. Sensitive to great heat and cold.
▷ **A Good Choice for:** Even for smaller apartments; moderate need for exercise.
▷ **Less Suited for:** Dog owners who like to be outdoors in all kinds of weather.

● BOUVIER DES FLANDRES

This dog is used to hard work, from guard duty to rescue missions. But it is also a loving and good-natured family dog.

▷ **Appearance:** Height at withers: males, 24 to 27 inches (62–68 cm); females, 23 to 25 1/2 inches (59–65 cm). Athletic, fairly short body on sturdy legs.
▷ **Coat:** Coarse, shaggy fur, large beard on chin and cheeks. Fur colors: black, gray, dun (light brown). Requires regular care and trimming.
▷ **Character:** Confident, courageous, and energetic when appropriate. Strong protective instinct; it lets strangers into the yard or house only with its owner's permission. Very devoted to the family and good with children. Not a barker because of its high stimulus threshold.
▷ **Health:** Slightly susceptible to hip dysplasia.
▷ **Life Expectancy:** 10 to 12 years.
▷ **Particular Qualities:** The former herding and cattle dog (Bouvier) was an acclaimed work dog. Even as a family member it needs things to do on a regular basis.
▷ **A Good Choice for:** Experienced dog people who can train it with firmness and love.
▷ **Less Suited for:** Beginning dog owners who are too pliant.

1

◐ BOXER

A powerful and happy bundle of energy. Would go through fire for its owner; good with children; playful even at an advanced age.

▷ **Appearance:** Height at withers 21 to 25 inches (53–63 cm). Muscular, nearly square body with broad chest. Massive head with a black MASK (◐ p.267) and worry lines on the forehead.

▷ **Coat:** Short and shiny. Fawn colored in all shades or striped with or without white markings. Easy to care for.

▷ **Character:** Lively, fearless, and playful even as an adult. Devoted and watchful; reserved with strangers. Males especially are quick to scrap with other dogs; must be trained and dealt with firmly.

▷ **Health:** Susceptible to tumors, eye, and heart diseases.

▷ **Life Expectancy:** 10 to 11 years.

▷ **Particular Qualities:** One of the recognized service and working dogs.

▷ **A Good Choice for:** Athletic families, for whose children it will be the most patient buddy in the world and an absolutely reliable protector.

▷ **Less Suited for:** Because of its effervescent love of life, not the right partner for people who like peace and quiet.

◐ BRIARD

An ancient French noble herding dog; also serves well as a watchdog, police dog, and companion dog. Attractive and impressive.

▷ **Appearance:** Height at withers 22 to 23 inches (56–58 cm). Muscular, supple, and well-proportioned body. Skull with pronounced stop, long drop ears. Tail ends in a hook.

▷ **Coat:** Slightly wavy, long, and shaggy with thick undercoat. Fur colors: black, light brown, gray, and others; dark colors are preferred. White is not desirable. Requires lots of care.

▷ **Character:** Strong instinct for herding and protecting. Very lively, fearless, and alert; may be easily excitable and stubborn. Loves and protects its family unconditionally.

▷ **Health:** Robust and impervious to the weather, with no breed-specific problems.

▷ **Life Expectancy:** 12 to 14 years.

▷ **Particular Qualities:** The Briard (also known as the Berger de Brie) is the long-haired version of the Beauceron (also Berger de Beauce).

▷ **A Good Choice for:** Dog connoisseurs who can provide the Briard with very firm training, lots of things to do, such as dog sports.

▷ **Less Suited for:** Beginners who are not used to a dog with a strong personality.

CAIRN TERRIER

A terrier that complies with all the specifications: happy, courageous, smart, and always out and about. Longs for adventure and variety.

▷ **Appearance:** Height at withers 11 to 12 inches (3.4–3.65 cm). Compact and agile. Dark, lively eyes, small, erect ears.
▷ **Coat:** Shaggy and harsh, fairly long topcoat and short, soft undercoat. All colors from wheat, cream, and red to gray and even black are permissible.
▷ **Character:** At home in the Scottish Highlands, where it hunted foxes and otters in the scree (Gaelic: *cairn* for stones). An independent and courageous little go-getter that learns very quickly, plays enthusiastically, and is a happy pal to the children.
▷ **Health:** Eye and skin disorders, but generally a robust dog that rarely is sick.
▷ **Life Expectancy:** 12 to 15 years.
▷ **Particular Qualities:** Although not stubborn, its curiosity and independence must be reined in through firm handling.
▷ **A Good Choice for:** Terrier aficionados who can give it lots of attention and activity and keep its adventurous spirit in check.
▷ **Less Suited for:** People who are looking for a little dog with a tender nature.

CAVALIER KING CHARLES SPANIEL

Lovable and obedient small spaniel that is comfortable in the house, but also likes to take long walks.

▷ **Appearance:** Height at withers 10 to 13 1/2 inches (25–34 cm). Powerful but not ungainly body with straight back, flat skull, and short muzzle.
▷ **Coat:** Long and usually slightly wavy. Colors: black and red, ruby red, black and white with red, and brown on white. The coat requires little care because of its silky nature.
▷ **Character:** Lively, alert, sociable, and very good with children. Easy to train and obedient. The King Charles can't deny its hunting heritage. It is robust and athletic, as it appears, and it shouldn't be demoted to being just a couch dog.
▷ **Health:** Mostly healthy; some tendency to eyelid abnormalities and ear infections.
▷ **Life Expectancy:** 11 to 14 years.
▷ **Particular Qualities:** Exceptionally adaptable, problem-free in the house, good on walks.
▷ **A Good Choice for:** Ideal for people who value a devoted, happy dog and will take it on long and frequent walks.
▷ **Less Suited for:** Dog owners who would rather have a lapdog.

◉ CHIHUAHUA

The world's smallest dog is a very special kind of lapdog: fearless, robust, and full of personality.

▷ **Appearance:** Height at withers less than 8 inches (20 cm). Dainty, with straight backline. Typically has large, rounded head and flying ears that stand out far from the head.
▷ **Coat:** Smooth, short, and tight, or long, soft, and straggly with a ruff around the throat. All colors are permissible.
▷ **Character:** Confident and very lively, alert, and quick to learn. Affectionate and lovable, this dog forms a close bond with its human.
▷ **Health:** Water on the brain, problems with teeth, throat, and birthing.
▷ **Life Expectancy:** 14 years and over.
▷ **Particular Qualities:** Named after the city in Mexico with the same name. It reportedly was bred by the Aztecs and Incas, but its real origin is unclear. This dog has little respect for large dogs and is not overly fond of children.
▷ **A Good Choice for:** Fans of lapdogs who will take the little fellow seriously and not pamper it.
▷ **Less Suited for:** People who find its constant presence too demanding.

◉ CHOW CHOW

This dog isn't interested in flattery, or in other people or animals. Strong-willed, proud, and different from the rest.

▷ **Appearance:** Height at withers: males, 19 to 22 inches (48–56 cm); females, 18 to 20 inches (46–51 cm). Very compact and stocky body with broad chest. Broad skull with short, square muzzle, small upright ears. The tail curls over the back.
▷ **Coat:** Very abundant, thick, and full with soft undercoat. Impressive mane. In addition to the long-haired Chow there is also a less common short-haired version. All black, blue, red, cream, and dun. Daily brushing required.
▷ **Character:** Typical one-person dog that doesn't like strangers and avoids children. Likes its freedom, sometimes is stubborn, and is only partly trainable. Strong hunting instinct.
▷ **Health:** Inward turning of eyelids (entropium), skin tumors, eczema, hip dysplasia.
▷ **Life Expectancy:** 12 to 14 years.
▷ **Particular Qualities:** The blue-black tongue and the stilted gait are unmistakable.
▷ **A Good Choice for:** Single people who can accept an independent partner.
▷ **Less Suited for:** Families.

▶ THE BEST DOG BREEDS
FOR SINGLE PEOPLE

A single person's dog wants what its owner wants. It goes along in the car and to public places and is a partner in sports. But it will stay alone at home for a couple of hours without grumbling and enjoy the time spent playing and cuddling together in the evening.

Breed	Picture on Page	Exercise and Activity	Good Companion	Good for for Beginners	Care	Brief Portrait
Afghan Hound	→ 42	●●●	●●	●	a lot	Sees itself as a partner of the human; not very subordinate; needs lots of exercise, preferably hard running
Airedale Terrier	→ 43	●●	●●●	●●	medium	Courageous, watchful, and active
Border Collie	→ 46	●●●	●●●	●●	little	Wide awake, intelligent, quick to learn; strong herding instinct; needs regular activity
Briard	→ 48	●●●	●●	●●	a lot	Watchful and courageous; craves work
Cairn Terrier	→ 49	●●●	●●●	●●	medium	A real go-getter and shrewd customer; curious and independent
Chow Chow	→ 50	●	●●	●	a lot	Independent and strong-willed; a one-person dog
Dachshund	→ 53	●●	●●	●●	medium	Confident and strong-willed, especially the wirehair
Dalmatian	→ 54	●●●	●●●	●●●	little	Great runner; a perfect partner for jogging or trotting beside a bike
Doberman Pinscher	→ 55	●●●	●●	●	little	Strong-willed, fearless; wants and needs to work
Fox Terrier	→ 56	●●●	●●●	●●	medium	Live wire that is afraid of nothing; needs jobs for mind and body
German Mastiff	→ 57	●●	●●	●	medium	Gentle and lovable, needs training by an experienced hand
German Shepherd Dog	→ 57	●●●	●●●	●	medium	Strong watchdog with protective instinct; needs firm training and control
Jack Russell Terrier	→ 60	●●●	●●	●	little	Independent and extremely active; passionate hunter that needs firm handling
Kromfohrlander	→ 60	●●	●●●	●●	medium	Alert and devoted; gets along well even in fairly small homes
Kuvasz	→ 61	●●	●●	●	medium	A strong watchdog and protector; for experts
Picard	→ 67	●●●	●●	●●	little	Watchful, independent; former herding dog
Pinscher	→ 67	●●	●●●	●●●	little	Lively, playful, and lovable
Rottweiler	→ 69	●●	●●	●	little	Impressive power pack and fearless watchdog that needs an experienced owner
Saint Bernard	→ 70	●	●●	●	a lot	Needs lots of room, lots of food, and attention
Schnauzer	→ 71	●●	●●	●●	medium	Giant Schnauzer needs activity
Scottish Terrier	→ 71	●	●●	●●	medium	Strong-willed; an individualist for individualists
Sheltie	→ 72	●●●	●●●	●●●	a lot	Lively; very devoted and sensitive
Siberian Husky	→ 73	●●●	●●	●	little	Independent; loves to run, and not aggressive

EXERCISE AND ACTIVITY: ● little   ●● moderate   ●●● a lot
SUITABILITY: ● good   ●● very good   ●●● ideal

● COCKER SPANIEL

The Cocker Spaniel is by far the most beloved and familiar of the spaniels. Athletic and bright—an ideal companion dog.

▷ **Appearance:** Height at withers 15 to 16 inches (39–41 cm); the American Cocker Spaniel is about 1 inch (3 cm) shorter than other spaniels. Powerful and compact. Handsome head with pronounced stop; ears long and well feathered.

▷ **Coat:** Smooth and silky; less feathered in English Cockers, more with American ones. From all red or black, to black and white, orange and white, and other two- and three-color combinations. Requires ample care including trimming on ears and paws.

▷ **Character:** Devoted, intelligent, a quick learner, with a mind of its own. Needs challenges, lots of attention, and even more exercise.

▷ **Health:** Eye and nerve diseases, eczema, and epilepsy.

▷ **Life Expectancy:** 13 to 16 years.

▷ **Particular Qualities:** Fetching is this dog's great passion. Many Cockers like to stray and have a healthy appetite.

▷ **A Good Choice for:** People who are out with their dog in all kinds of weather.

▷ **Less Suited for:** Owners who have too little time for care and long walks.

● COLLIE

This is a great family dog—provided it gets daily coat care and long walks or a jog next to the bicycle.

▷ **Appearance:** Height at withers: males, 22 to 24 inches (56–61 cm); females, 20 to 22 inches (51–56 cm). Slender body, flat skull, cocked ears, and heavily furred tail.

▷ **Coat:** Long and stiff with thick undercoat. Colors: yellow with white, tricolor, blue merle. The voluminous fur needs a lot of care.

▷ **Character:** Intelligent and alert; often shy. Very devoted to the family; good with children. Needs firm training without harshness. Watchful and somewhat prone to barking.

▷ **Health:** Susceptible to eye problems.

▷ **Life Expectancy:** 11 to 13 years.

▷ **Particular Qualities:** Collies don't like to be left alone. In addition to the long-haired Collie there is also a less common short-haired version. Litters of both Collie types can produce pups with both long and short hair.

▷ **A Good Choice for:** Athletic people who will keep the dog fit with long walks and who have time for the demanding coat care.

▷ **Less Suited for:** People who expect Lassie-like miracles from their dog.

◯ COTON DE TULEAR

This dog comes from Madagascar and is winning over our hearts; it's a small, all-round lovable friend to people.

▷ **Appearance:** Height at withers, 10 to 12 inches (25–28 cm). Compact body on sturdy legs; rounded head.

▷ **Coat:** Wavy, fairly long, and fine in texture. The cottony appearance gave the breed its name. White with yellow or gray spots on the ears. Little care required.

▷ **Character:** Adapts easily to every situation and to its owner's living conditions. Friendly and easily trained, it gets along well with children and other pets. With a naturally calm disposition, it's not much of a barker or a watchdog.

▷ **Health:** Scarcely susceptible to diseases.

▷ **Life Expectancy:** 12 to 15 years.

▷ **Particular Qualities:** In Madagascar this was the lapdog of the nobility. The first Cotons were introduced to France and then to other countries, but the dogs are not yet widespread.

▷ **A Good Choice for:** Equally good for families and single people, and an especially good companion for older people.

▷ **Less Suited for:** People who like imposing and showy dogs.

◯ DACHSHUND

A real character on short legs, the Dachshund has won the hearts of dog lovers with its obstinacy and its charm.

▷ **Appearance:** With Dachshunds it's the chest, not the height at the withers, that is measured: the Dachshund measures 14 to 18 inches (35–45 cm), the Miniature Dachshund 12 to 14 inches (30–35 cm), and the rabbit (toy) Dachshund up to 12 inches (30 cm). Long back and short legs; long head, broad ears; saber tail that tapers.

▷ **Coat:** Three fur types. The shorthair lies flat and is shiny; the longhair is soft and smooth with feathering; the wirehair is wiry and thick with an undercoat, a beard, and bushy eyebrows. Colors: Shorthair and longhair, red and black and brown; wirehair, red, badger, or wild boar-colored.

▷ **Character:** Confident and independent. Dachshunds have strong personalities and minds of their own. Family oriented and good watchdogs.

▷ **Health:** Dachshund paralysis and other spinal diseases; gum problems.

▷ **Life Expectancy:** 12 to 15 years.

▷ **Particular Qualities:** Firm training keeps the Dachshund from trying to be the boss.

▷ **A Good Choice for:** Dog lovers with lots of empathy and self-assertiveness.

▷ **Less Suited for:** Compliant people.

◉ DALMATIAN

Despite its exotic appearance, this is a pleasant, friendly, and lively companion dog that loves to run.

▷ **Appearance:** Height at withers 21 to 24 inches (54–60 cm). Muscular and very fit. Long muzzle, high-set ears, long, scimitar-shaped tail.

▷ **Coat:** Short, smooth, and shiny. White with black or brown spots of about the same size. Spots on the ears and tail are desirable. Puppies are born pure white. Easy to take care of.

▷ **Character:** Adaptable and friendly; easy to train. A long-distance runner with plenty of endurance that once accompanied coaches and horseback riders for long distances.

▷ **Health:** Tendency to allergies and eczema. Overall, the Dalmatian is not susceptible to many diseases.

▷ **Life Expectancy:** 12 to 14 years.

▷ **Particular Qualities:** A Dalmatian is happiest when it goes outdoors frequently and for a long time, and has opportunities to run long distances.

▷ **A Good Choice for:** Families and single people who do a lot of jogging or bike touring.

▷ **Less Suited for:** Unathletic people who don't often go outdoors.

◉ DANDIE DINMONT TERRIER

It looks out innocently on the world with large eyes, but is a pure terrier: confident, courageous, and quick.

▷ **Appearance:** Height at withers 8 to 10 inches (20–25 cm). Long, powerful body on short legs. Large, broad head with dark eyes and long drop ears. The short tail is usually carried high.

▷ **Coat:** Relatively long with hard and soft hairs. Colors: mustard and pepper, with a light tuft. Occasional trimming needed.

▷ **Character:** Even though it is a bit calmer than other terriers, its past as a fox and otter hunter lives on. Its strong will demands firm guidance; it doesn't always get along with other dogs and pets. Very devoted and gentle with its master.

▷ **Health:** Robust; occasional back problems.

▷ **Life Expectancy:** 12 to 13 years.

▷ **Particular Qualities:** This dog gets its name from a terrier breeder in a novel by Sir Walter Scott.

▷ **A Good Choice for:** Single people who can guide the terrier with a firm hand and keep it occupied.

▷ **Less Suited for:** Families with children and very compliant dog lovers.

▶ DOBERMAN PINSCHER

Lively, athletic, and elegant. The Doberman Pinscher is an unbeatable watchdog and a loyal partner to its master.

▷ **Appearance:** Height at withers: males, 26 to 28 inches (68–72 cm); females, 24 to 26 inches (63–68 cm). Medium-sized, slender, and very muscular body; flat, wedge-shaped head with long muzzle.

▷ **Coat:** Flat, smooth, short, and shiny. Fur colors: black, dark brown, and blue with reddish brown markings. Easy to take care of.

▷ **Character:** Alert, quick to react, and fearless. A typical one-person dog that will go through fire for its owner. Sensitive to all physical harshness, however; has a low tolerance for injustices.

▷ **Health:** Some susceptibility to hip dysplasia, and skin and heart problems.

▷ **Life Expectancy:** 11 to 14 years.

▷ **Particular Qualities:** With excessively nervous animals the innate toughness can become a problem. The Doberman Pinscher is one of the most familiar duty and work dogs.

▷ **A Good Choice for:** Dog connoisseurs who have experience with strong-willed dogs and can keep them fit and busy.

▷ **Less Suited for:** People who are not sufficiently assertive, or who are not athletic.

▶ EURASIER

Still a young breed that's related to the Samoyed, Wolfsspitz, and Chow Chow. It has been recognized as a breed by the FCI since 1973.

▷ **Appearance:** Height at withers 19 to 24 inches (48–60 cm). Medium-sized, well-proportioned, and muscular dog with triangular, erect ears and a tail that bends over the back or rolls to the side. Wedge-shaped head with flat forehead.

▷ **Coat:** Medium long, strong, with thick undercoat. Wolf gray, black, black with other markings, red, and pale colors. Regular but modest care required.

▷ **Character:** Self-assured, well-balanced, with high stimulation threshold. Strong bond with the family; watchful and reserved with strangers, but not aggressive. Doesn't bark much, and has a modest hunting instinct.

▷ **Health:** Robust and hardy; no breed-specific problems.

▷ **Life Expectancy:** 12 to 16 years.

▷ **Particular Qualities:** Very quick learner; needs firm, understanding training; craves attention and activity.

▷ **A Good Choice for:** Families. An ideal pal and protector for the children.

▷ **Less Suited for:** People who want a dog just for themselves.

1

⊳ FOX TERRIER

An intelligent and self-assured bundle of energy. An alert watchdog and the best pal for the children.

⊳ **Appearance:** Height at withers up to 15 1/2 inches (39 cm). Short, muscular body with straight back on powerful legs. Long, small head with V-shaped ears that fold to the front.

⊳ **Coat:** Short and thick in the Smooth Fox Terrier; in the Wire, kinky and wiry with soft undercoat. Both terriers are handled as separate breeds. Base color is white, with black and brown (tan) markings.

⊳ **Character:** Fearless, full of personality, and ready for any kind of tussle. The passion for hunting of this former fox hunter remains intact. Watchful, and not always quiet.

⊳ **Health:** Robust; isolated eye problems and deafness.

⊳ **Life Expectancy:** 12 to 14 years.

⊳ **Particular Qualities:** The Wire's fur needs trimming.

⊳ **A Good Choice for:** Experienced, firm dog owners who will train their Fox Terrier in sports and test its intelligence.

⊳ **Less Suited for:** Beginners who will be overwhelmed by the dog's temperament and enterprising nature.

⊳ FRENCH BULLDOG

A pint-sized dog personality. Affectionate, uncomplicated, and good-natured, as well as self-assured and fearless.

⊳ **Appearance:** Height at withers up to 12 inches (30 cm). Similar in physique to the English Bulldog, small specimens of which served as founders at the outset of this breed. Compact, with broad skull and powerful jaws. The erect bat ears are characteristic.

⊳ **Coat:** Soft, short, and shiny. From white over pale colors to black and even brindle.

⊳ **Character:** Lovable, happy, and very devoted, but also with a mind of its own. Playful and good with children; watchful, and reserved with strangers.

⊳ **Health:** Frequent birthing problems because of the large head; occasional slipped disk

⊳ **Life Expectancy:** 10 to 13 years.

⊳ **Particular Qualities:** Needs to be with its human. Fairly modest need for exercise; sensitive to heat; tendency to overweight.

⊳ **A Good Choice for:** People who value close contact with a dog. An alert and affectionate companion for senior citizens.

⊳ **Less Suited for:** Sports, long hikes, and frantic activity.

⊙ GERMAN MASTIFF

This dog used to hunt wild boar and was a status symbol of rich townspeople. Today, the Mastiff is a lovable dog for experienced owners.

▷ **Appearance:** Height at withers: males, at least 31 inches (80 cm); females, at least 28 inches (72 cm). Flat skull, deep chest, small drop ears. The tapering tail reaches down to the ankle.

▷ **Coat:** Very short, smooth, and shiny. Colors: black, blue, brindle, yellow, striped (black-and-white checked Tiger Mastiff).

▷ **Character:** Gentle and calm; clings lovingly to its human; very sociable with children. Watchful and reserved with strangers. No aggressiveness and not a roughhouser.

▷ **Health:** Gastric torsion, eye and skin diseases, isolated cases of deafness.

▷ **Life Expectancy:** 7 to 10 years.

▷ **Particular Qualities:** Mastiffs mustn't be uptight or nervous. These dogs are late bloomers that are full grown only at age two. Loving and patient training is important.

▷ **A Good Choice for:** Experienced owners with a lot of room and the necessary money for upkeep (high food costs).

▷ **Less Suited for:** People who get a dog just for the prestige.

⊙ GERMAN SHEPHERD DOG

An intelligent, multitalented dog with a strong protective instinct. It needs careful training and firm direction.

▷ **Appearance:** Height at withers 21 to 26 inches (55–65 cm). Powerful, long body with sloping back and angled hindquarters. Fairly broad head, erect ears, and a tail that hangs down to the ankles.

▷ **Coat:** Smooth, coarse, and waterproof double coat with a thick undercoat. Black blanket with brown, yellow, or gray markings, or pure black. White is not desirable.

▷ **Character:** Self-confident, watchful, and ready to defend. A real work dog that needs to be kept busy and get lots of exercise. A reliable protector for the children.

▷ **Health:** Hip dysplasia, eye diseases, arthritis.

▷ **Life Expectancy:** 10 to 14 years.

▷ **Particular Qualities:** The most beloved service and working dog in the world. Buy a puppy only from a recognized breeder.

▷ **A Good Choice for:** Experienced dog owners with leadership qualities.

▷ **Less Suited for:** People who don't have the time to train their dogs and to keep them busy every day.

1

◖ GOLDEN RETRIEVER

A family dog par excellence. Its friendly nature has made it one of the most beloved of all dog breeds.

▷ **Appearance:** Height at withers 21 to 24 inches (54–62 cm). A medium-sized, powerful, and elegant dog. Drop ears close to the head; long muzzle with a black nose, dark eyes, and dark eyelids.

▷ **Coat:** Long-haired, smooth or slightly wavy with waterproof undercoat. Light shades ranging from gold to cream. Modest daily care with comb and brush.

▷ **Character:** This is a perfect family dog because of its calm temperament, its friendly nature, even with other pets, and its love of exercise.

▷ **Health:** Thanks to selective breeding, only a few problems with joint and eye diseases.

▷ **Life Expectancy:** 13 to 15 years.

▷ **Particular Qualities:** Loves long walks and swimming and always wants to be with its human.

▷ **A Good Choice for:** Families and single people who like to do a lot of things with their dog.

▷ **Less Suited for:** People who go outdoors only when the weather is good.

◖ HOVAWART

Although its ancestors include farm dogs, it has nothing to do with the farm protectors of the Middle Ages.

▷ **Appearance:** Height at withers 22 to 28 inches (58–70 cm). Powerful, elongated body. Males and females have different physiques and head shapes.

▷ **Coat:** Strong, slightly wavy long hair; because there is almost no undercoat, it lies tight to the body; COLOR TYPES (◑ p.262): blond, black, and black markings with blond to golden markings. Needs daily brushing only while shedding.

▷ **Character:** Strong-willed and solid; a reliable watchdog and protector that acts quickly and fearlessly in an emergency.

▷ **Health:** Thanks to dependable breeding in comparison to other breeds, scarcely any problems with hip dysplasia.

▷ **Life Expectancy:** 11 to 14 years.

▷ **Particular Qualities:** The Hovawart requires knowledgeable handling without harshness. It is one of the most widely recognized breeds of watchdog.

▷ **A Good Choice for:** Experienced owners whose authority will register with this confident dog.

▷ **Less Suited for:** Beginners and people who are too pliant.

IRISH SETTER

IRISH WOLFHOUND

An elegant and athletic dog from the British Isles that mostly has one thing on its mind—running, running, running.

This is the biggest dog in the world, and a real treasure as a gentle and obedient companion and family dog.

▷ **Appearance:** Height at withers 24 to 27 inches (63–68 cm). Slender, athletic body. At a maximum weight of about 55 pounds (25 kg), fairly light in build with respect to size.

▷ **Coat:** Thick, short to medium long, with fringe on chest, belly, and throat. Deep mahogany red with no black; a white spot in the forehead, chest, or toes is permissible.

▷ **Character:** Intelligent, devoted, and alert, but also sensitive. Poorly adjusted, nervous, and obstinate if it doesn't get enough exercise. Good with children.

▷ **Health:** Generally stable health; skeletal (hip dysplasia) and eye problems occur rarely.

▷ **Life Expectancy:** 12 to 14 years.

▷ **Particular Qualities:** The Irish Setter is still a real hunting dog that needs plenty to do and even more exercise.

▷ **A Good Choice for:** Active owners who are on the move with the dog at least two hours every day, preferably on a bicycle.

▷ **Less Suited for:** People who lack the time or the will to spend a lot of time with a dog.

▷ **Appearance:** Height at withers: males, at least 31 inches (79 cm); females, 28 inches (71 cm). Impressive conformation, which looks elegant and harmonious despite its size. Long body with dark eyes and small ears.

▷ **Coat:** Wiry and coarse. Recognized colors: red, black, gray, brindle, white, and tan. Daily brushing suffices for care.

▷ **Character:** Easily trained, obedient, calm, and good with children. Needs strong bond with the family; unsuited to life in a kennel. Although it's not a watchdog, its size alone is enough to scare people away.

▷ **Health:** Gastric torsion, heart disease, skeletal and joint problems.

▷ **Life Expectancy:** 8 to 10 years.

▷ **Particular Qualities:** Needs firm, conscientious guidance. Has no tolerance for harshness.

▷ **A Good Choice for:** A house with a fenced yard and owners who can afford to keep and feed it.

▷ **Less Suited for:** City houses and people who want to make an impression with a large dog.

JACK RUSSELL TERRIER

A genuine terrier: full of energy and ambition; a daredevil and bold character. No dog for a stay-at-home.

▷ **Appearance:** Height at withers 10 to 12 inches (25–30 cm), 13 to 14 inches (33–35 cm) for the larger Parson Jack Russell Terrier. Supple body with a straight back. Flat skull, triangular and forward-tipped button ears, tail carried high.

▷ **Coat:** Smooth and shiny shorthair or hard, coarse hair. Predominantly white with brown or black markings or combinations of the two.

▷ **Character:** This former fox and rat hunter is a passionate hunter. A Jack Russell is independent, fearless, and full of get-up-and-go. Lovable in a family and a great playmate for the children.

▷ **Health:** Hardly any susceptibility to disease; eye disease to a small degree.

▷ **Life Expectancy:** 12 to 14 years.

▷ **Particular Qualities:** Hard to control only when it catches the scent of wild game.

▷ **A Good Choice for:** People who are very active themselves and who can deal with an energy-charged dog.

▷ **Less Suited for:** New dog owners who lack assertiveness.

KROMFOHRLANDER

Devoted, quick to learn, and physically fit; just right for families and single people who always have their dog close by.

▷ **Appearance:** Height at withers 15 to 20 inches (38–46 cm). An elegant body with somewhat elongated back. Skull with no clear stop at the forehead; rounded ears; long tail that hangs down.

▷ **Coat:** Smooth or wirehair, thick, with undercoat. Pure white with brown spots of different shades. The hair structure of the Kromfohrlander is very resistant to dirt.

▷ **Character:** Lively and lovable, and easy to train because of its intelligence and willingness to learn. Playful into old age; watchful, reserved with strangers. No hunting instinct.

▷ **Health:** No breed-specific diseases; occasional knee problems.

▷ **Life Expectancy:** 15 years and longer.

▷ **Particular Qualities:** This dog is descended from the Fox Terrier and the Griffon. In the Siegerland, the homeland of the breed, *Krohm fohr* means *crooked furrow*.

▷ **A Good Choice for:** People who can take care of an active, devoted dog. Also a good choice for fairly small homes.

▷ **Less Suited for:** Dog owners who don't have much time for their four-legged friends.

KUVASZ

The image of a dog: powerful, strong, inspiring respect. This incorruptible watchdog belongs in experienced hands.

▷ **Appearance:** Height at withers 27 to 30 inches (70–76 cm). Rather cream-colored body; head with a small stop and V-shaped drop ears. The full tail is carried low.

▷ **Coat:** Relatively long, coarse, and wavy; the fur forms a collar around the throat. Colors: white or a suggestion of ivory.

▷ **Character:** Above all, a protector and watchdog, and nothing escapes its attention. As a former herd protector, it defends its family courageously and without reservation. Distrustful of strangers. Its strong personality makes ownership and training a bit difficult.

▷ **Health:** Hip dysplasia, as with many large, heavy breeds.

▷ **Life Expectancy:** 10 to 12 years.

▷ **Particular Qualities:** The breed name hits the nail on the head: Kuvasz (pronounced *Kuvass*) means *protector* in Turkish.

▷ **A Good Choice for:** Experts with authority and leadership qualities who can provide the Kuvasz a solid place in the pecking order.

▷ **Less Suited for:** Inexperienced owners who simply want a strong, handsome dog.

LEONBERGER

An imposing, and confident giant. It needs lots of room and loves to swim.

▷ **Appearance:** Height at withers 30 to 32 inches (76–80 cm). Well-proportioned, large, muscular body with moderately broad head. The heavily haired tail is carried low.

▷ **Coat:** Medium long, thick, and fairly soft; also waterproof. Mane on throat and chest. Yellowish gold to reddish brown ("lion colors") with a dark mask. Needs moderate care.

▷ **Character:** Good natured, easygoing, and calm. An outstanding watchdog and an attentive protector, especially with children. Devoted and loving, but reserved with strangers. Rarely barks, and doesn't care to romp.

▷ **Health:** Hip dysplasia, heart disease, knee problems.

▷ **Life Expectancy:** Up to 10 years.

▷ **Particular Qualities:** This breed can be traced back to the Saint Bernard, Newfoundland, Landseer, and Pyrenees Mountain Dog.

▷ **A Good Choice for:** Families with children and a large house and yard.

▷ **Less Suited for:** City dwellers and single people who don't have a lot of time to take care of a dog.

◗ LHASA APSO

This dog guarded the temples and monasteries in Tibet and was considered a harbinger of good luck. The Lhasa Apso is a happy family dog.

▷ **Appearance:** Height at withers about 10 inches (25 cm). Long body with straight back. Flat skull that nearly disappears beneath the abundant fur. Thickly haired ears; the likewise heavily haired tail is carried over the back.

▷ **Coat:** Rough, long topcoat with moderate undercoat. All colors from white, sandy, and brown to smoke and black are permissible. Very extensive daily care required.

▷ **Character:** The Lhasa Apso is a confident dog with a mind of its own. Watchful, friendly, and fond of the family, but also tries to impose its will. Almost always distant with strangers.

▷ **Health:** Eye and kidney problems.

▷ **Life Expectancy:** 12 to 14 years.

▷ **Particular Qualities:** Remarkably impervious to the weather and good on its feet. Draws back if it is used as a toy by small children.

▷ **A Good Choice for:** Families, single people, and seniors who can give the dog lots of attention and devote themselves to the intensive coat care.

▷ **Less Suited for:** People who are looking for a lapdog to spoil.

◗ LITTLE LION DOG

An affectionate and vital little fellow that nearly sank into oblivion and is still rare today—unjustly so.

▷ **Appearance:** Height at withers 12.5 inches (32 cm). Slender, light body with straight back. Broad head with large, dark eyes. The tail is carried over the back.

▷ **Coat:** Long, soft, and wavy. Except for brown, all colors are allowed, either a single color or spotted. The breed name is due to the way it's trimmed; the hindquarters look like a lion's.

▷ **Character:** Intelligent and quick to learn. Loving and lively, including with children, its playfulness is remarkable. Watchful but not very noisy.

▷ **Health:** Not particularly susceptible to disease; occasional teeth problems.

▷ **Life Expectancy:** 12 to 14 years.

▷ **Particular Qualities:** Feels at home, even in small apartments, as long as it can participate in regular, lengthy walks.

▷ **A Good Choice for:** Beginners who desire an obedient and affectionate companion; city dwellers, families, and senior citizens.

▷ **Less Suited for:** People who don't know what to do with a lively little dog.

THE BEST DOG BREEDS FOR SENIOR CITIZENS

Most older people would like to have a devoted and obedient small dog that doesn't require too much exercise. But for some seniors the four-legged partner can't be active and independent enough. This chart will show you dog breeds for every requirement.

Breed	Portrait on Page	Exercise and Activity	OK for Small Houses	OK for Beginners	Care	Overview
Affenpinscher	→ 42	●	●●●	●●	little	Very lively and lovable, but also a fearless and not always quiet watchdog
Bichon Frise	→ 45	●	●●●	●●●	a lot	Happy, peace loving, and easy to train
Boston Terrier	→ 47	●●	●●●	●●●	little	Intelligent, quick to learn, and adaptable
Cavalier King Charles Spaniel	→ 49	●●	●●●	●●●	medium	Lovable and usually good natured; does well on long walks
Chihuahua	→ 50	●	●●●	●●	little	Lively; no respect for large animals
Dachshund	→ 53	●●	●●		medium	Strong personality and a healthy measure of strong will; needs firm handling
Dandie Dinmont Terrier	→ 54	●●●		●	medium	Strong willed and robust; needs lots of activity; not suited to compliant people
French Bulldog	→ 56	●	●●●	●●●	little	Alert, playful, and affectionate, but with a mind of its own
Lhasa Apso	→ 62	●●	●●●	●●	a lot	Alert and friendly; waterproof and good on its feet; knows just what it wants
Little Lion Dog	→ 62	●●	●●●	●●●	medium	Obedient, adaptable, and a real treasure
Maltese	→ 64	●	●●●	●●●	a lot	Very lively and quick to learn; needs closeness
Miniature Pinscher	→ 64	●●	●●●	●●●	little	Lovable, lively, and quick to learn
Papillon	→ 65	●●	●●●	●●●	medium	Playful and alert; sometimes noisy
Pekingese	→ 66	●	●●●	●	a lot	Exceptionally confident and strong willed; usually fixated exclusively on its owner
Poodle	→ 68	●●●	●●	●●	medium	Miniature Poodle: intelligent, happy, and always active
Pug	→ 69	●	●●●	●●	little	Intelligent and crafty, but goes its own way
Schnauzer	→ 71	●●	●●	●●	medium	Miniature Schnauzer: brave, lively, and robust; watchful and not always quiet
Sealyham Terrier	→ 72	●●	●●		medium	Self-assured and crafty; needs a firm hand
Shih Tzu	→ 73	●	●●●	●●●	a lot	Charming, devoted, and loving
Spitz	→ 74	●●	●●	●●	medium	Small and Dwarf Spitz: cute and quick to learn; watchful and often noisy; close bond with human
West Highland White Terrier	→ 75	●●●	●●	●●●	medium	A small dog with a large personality; clever, confident, and fresh
Yorkshire Terrier	→ 75	●●	●●●	●●	a lot	Totally fearless, watchful, and fond of barking

EXERCISE AND ACTIVITY: ● little   ●● moderate   ●●● a lot
SUITABILITY: ● good   ●● very good   ●●● ideal

⬗ MALTESE

A clever little dog whose devoted and lovable personality has fascinated people for many centuries.

▷ **Appearance:** Height at withers 8 to 10 inches (20–25 cm). Short, compact body. Medium-size head with evident stop, oval eyes, and long, fur-covered ears. The long, hairy tail rolls over the back.
▷ **Coat:** Long, very thick, silky hair. White, but a discreet ivory color is also permissible. Considerable daily care required.
▷ **Character:** Lively, intelligent, and quick to learn; always wants to be with its owner. Watchful, distrustful of strangers, but not a barker like other small dogs.
▷ **Health:** Eye and teeth problems; deafness.
▷ **Life Expectancy:** 11 to 13 years.
▷ **Particular Qualities:** Needs only a little exercise; prefers to stay indoors when it's cold, snowy, or rainy.
▷ **A Good Choice for:** People who appreciate an alert companion that will stay by their side. An ideal dog for senior citizens.
▷ **Less Suited for:** People who spend a lot of time outdoors and want to engage in sports with their dog.

⬗ MINIATURE PINSCHER

Physically this is a miniature, but by nature it is a hearty fellow and takes no backseat to the Pinscher, its large cousin.

▷ **Appearance:** Height at withers 10 to 12 inches (25–30 cm). Well-proportioned, light-weight body on solid, slender legs. Elongated head with well-chiseled facial features, large eyes, and ears that tip forward.
▷ **Coat:** Short, smooth, and tight. Red and brown tones predominate; all brown to stag red, two-colored in black with red or brown markings.
▷ **Character:** Lively and always in a mood for play; very devoted and quick to learn. A good watchdog and defender that will even tackle larger dogs. Not necessarily silent.
▷ **Health:** Robust, as it appears. Occasional bladder stone; heart problems.
▷ **Life Expectancy:** Commonly more than 14 years.
▷ **Particular Qualities:** The red version used to be called the Deer Pinscher.
▷ **A Good Choice for:** Small and very small apartments. Thanks to its devotion and curiosity, this dog is easy to train even for beginners.
▷ **Less Suited for:** Inhabitants of apartments where sound carries easily, as its fondness for barking could lead to conflicts with the neighbors.

▶ NEWFOUNDLAND

A slightly clumsy bear, a levelheaded disposition, lots of heart and charm, plus a real passion for the water.

▷ **Appearance:** Height at withers 25 to 28 inches (65–70 cm). Powerful body with a broad chest and strong back. Massive head with small eyes and ears. The powerful tail extends down to the ankle.

▷ **Coat:** Thick, long, and flat. The oily undercoat is waterproof. Black, brown, and black and white. The coat must be brushed vigorously at least once a week.

▷ **Character:** Very sociable and calm. Forms a close bond with its family; watches over and protects the children with special attention. Neither nippy nor fierce; rarely barks, but in a tight situation will threaten by growling.

▷ **Health:** Hip dysplasia, knee and heart disorders.

▷ **Life Expectancy:** 10 to 11 years.

▷ **Particular Qualities:** An enthusiastic swimmer, this dog is also used for water rescue.

▷ **A Good Choice for:** Families with children and lots of room in and around the house. There should be a brook or a river within walking distance.

▷ **Less Suited for:** City people and condominium dwellers or homeowners with no yard.

▶ PAPILLON

The little butterfly dog is a lively and lovable companion dog with an exceptional history.

▷ **Appearance:** Height at withers 8 to 11 1/2 (20–29 cm). Long body with straight back. Head with small muzzle and dark brown eyes. Large, erect ears that resemble a butterfly's wings (Papillon = butterfly in French). The closely related Phalène (= moth) has drop ears.

▷ **Coat:** Abundant, silky hair with no undercoat; thick ruff on the throat; feathered hindquarters and ears. White with markings in various colors. Regular coat care required.

▷ **Character:** Playful and intelligent; watchful and very devoted. With insufficient training can also turn into a barker.

▷ **Health:** Dislocated kneecap.

▷ **Life Expectancy:** 13 to 16 years.

▷ **Particular Qualities:** An old breed from Holland and France that has been kept in the homes of many nobles over the centuries.

▷ **A Good Choice for:** Even small apartments, but it still needs regular exercise.

▷ **Less Suited for:** Dog owners who will spoil the Papillon and degrade it by turning it into a lapdog.

1

● PEKINGESE

An exotic conformation with a very unique personality. Strong-willed, often irascible, but also devoted and loyal.

▷ **Appearance:** Height at withers up to 10 inches (25 cm). Powerful, short body. Broad head with pushed-in muzzle and large nostrils. Widely separated eyes and long, hair-covered ears. The tail, which rolls over the back, is likewise heavily haired.
▷ **Coat:** Thick, very long, and straight with thick undercoat and impressive mane. All colors except albino are permissible. The coat requires daily care.
▷ **Character:** This dog's characteristic confidence doesn't correspond to its size. Mostly friendly and sociable, but also irascible. Bestows its affection as it sees fit; training is frequently unsuccessful. Very watchful.
▷ **Health:** Birthing problems, shortness of breath, bladder stones, water on the brain.
▷ **Life Expectancy:** 12 to 14 years.
▷ **Particular Qualities:** Frequently acts jealous, so this is a one-person dog.
▷ **A Good Choice for:** Individualists who can cope with an extroverted pasha.
▷ **Less Suited for:** People who appreciate obedient and well-adjusted dogs.

● PEMBROKE WELSH CORGI

An intelligent and quick charmer on short legs. Long ago this little sheep guardian moved up the ladder to become a family dog.

▷ **Appearance:** Height at withers 10 to 13 inches (25–33 cm). Long body with foxlike head and large, erect ears. Pembrokes sometimes are born with a short tail.
▷ **Coat:** Smooth, medium long, and relatively coarse with soft undercoat. Except for white all colors are permissible; red, sand, and pale yellow are most common.
▷ **Character:** Lively and sociable. As a former herding dog it is accustomed to making decisions independently. A reliable watchdog and protector that also knows how to use its teeth. Needs firm training and control and regular activity.
▷ **Health:** Robust; with inadequate exercise, it easily gains weight.
▷ **Life Expectancy:** 12 to 14 years.
▷ **Particular Qualities:** Closely related to the Cardigan Welsh Corgi. For centuries both have herded animals in Wales. Corgis are Queen Elizabeth's favorite dog.
▷ **A Good Choice for:** People who can give their dogs things to do and plenty of exercise.
▷ **Less Suited for:** Beginners and compliant dog lovers.

▶ PICARD

Shaggy fur, an angular body, and powerful legs; you can tell by looking that it doesn't shy away from work. This is a dog for all purposes.

▷ **Appearance:** Height at withers: males, 23 to 26 inches (60–65 cm); females, 21 to 23 inches (55–60 cm). Very solid and supple body. Balanced head shape, dark eyes, and large, upright ears with rounded tips

▷ **Coat:** Coarse and shaggy, medium long, and not curly. Reddish gray, blue-gray, gray, and gray with black. Easy to care for and weatherproof.

▷ **Character:** Ancient noble French herding dog with an intact will to work. Very alert, nimble, and courageous. Grasps situations instantly and acts independently. Watchful but not nippy. Devoted to its master and a patient friend to children.

▷ **Health:** No breed-specific problems.

▷ **Life Expectancy:** 12 to 14 years.

▷ **Particular Qualities:** The Picard (also known as the Berger de Picardie) is calm in the house, but needs a lot of exercise.

▷ **A Good Choice for:** Active dog fans who can regularly challenge its physical and mental abilities, preferably in dog sports.

▷ **Less Suited for:** Owners who provide no variety and adventure for their dogs.

▶ PINSCHER

Maybe this dog's name is a barrier. The Pinscher is not common and is underestimated, for it is practically the perfect companion dog.

▷ **Appearance:** Height at withers 16 to 19 inches (40–48 cm). Elegant, muscular, and angular body. Elongated head, and ears that stand up straight or tip to the front.

▷ **Coat:** Short and shiny. All one color from black to russet and tan with red or brown MARKINGS (◑ p.258). Little care required. Its rough-haired counterpart is the Schnauzer.

▷ **Character:** Lively, brave, and playful. Watchful, but not a barker. Learns very quickly and is easily trained.

▷ **Health:** Hardy, with no breed-specific diseases.

▷ **Life Expectancy:** 13 to 15 years.

▷ **Particular Qualities:** Calm and unobtrusive in the house, but it still should have a chance to be involved in sports and is best suited for Agility and competitive dog sports.

▷ **A Good Choice for:** An ideal and devoted dog even for beginners as long as it gets plenty of attention and keeps busy.

▷ **Less Suited for:** People who want a dog to impress others.

1

▷ PON

A real dog right to the core: confident, watchful, robust, and with lots of personality and a love of exercise.

▷ **Appearance:** Height at withers: males, 18 to 20 inches (45–50 cm); females, 16 1/2 to 18 1/2 inches (42–47 cm). Compact, powerful body that is scarcely visible under the abundant fur. Fairly broad, large head with long, heart-shaped ears.

▷ **Coat:** Thick, long, and shaggy. All colors are permissible. Regular combing and brushing prevents matting.

▷ **Character:** As a former herding dog, an incorruptible watchdog. Lively, quick to learn, playful, and good with children.

▷ **Health:** Robust; rare susceptibility to eye problems and hip dysplasia.

▷ **Life Expectancy:** 12 to 14 years.

▷ **Particular Qualities:** Polish herding dogs were the basis for the PON breed (Polski Owczarek Nizinny). In its homeland it is still used as a herder and watchdog.

▷ **A Good Choice for:** Dog owners with leadership qualities, who can give the PON clear duties and engage it in sports.

▷ **Less Suited for:** Inactive people and those who are not sufficiently firm in training.

▷ POODLE

Poodles are true picker-uppers whose happiness is contagious. Favorites are the Standard Poodle (in photo) and Miniature Poodle.

▷ **Appearance:** Height at withers: Standard Poodle, 18 to 23 inches (45–58 cm); Miniature Poodle, 11 to 14 inches (28–35 cm); Toy Poodle, 10 inches (25 cm). Square body, short back, small head, drop ears, and high-set tail.

▷ **Coat:** Woolly, thick, and curly. The hair grows continuously and must be clipped. All one color in black, white, gray, brown, silver, and apricot. Poodles don't shed.

▷ **Character:** Intelligent and easy to train. Happy dogs that gladly take part in children's games.

▷ **Health:** Eye and skin diseases, epilepsy, bladder stones; some problems with the Toy because of breeding for small size.

▷ **Life Expectancy:** Miniature Poodle, 14 to 17 years; Standard Poodle, 10 to 14 years; Toy Poodle, 10 to 12 years.

▷ **Particular Qualities:** Poodles are descendents of water dogs and are among the oldest of dog breeds.

▷ **A Good Choice for:** Families, single people, and senior citizens (Miniature Poodle); also appropriate for city life.

▷ **Less Suited for:** Dog owners for whom obedience is the main consideration.

▶ PUG

People either fall under this dog's spell or don't care for it. An ancient noble dog from the Far East, it is very quick to learn and devoted.

▷ **Appearance:** Height at withers 10 to 12 inches (25–30 cm). Compact body with a broad chest. Large head with a wrinkled brow, a stubby muzzle, and a black mask. Small drop ears, and a rolled tail that is carried to one side over the back.

▷ **Coat:** Short and soft in silver, apricot, fawn, and black. Black mask and ears; dorsal stripe. Limited coat care required.

▷ **Character:** Very devoted and affectionate; loves its family above all else. Intelligent and easily trained, but sometimes stubborn.

▷ **Health:** Birthing and eye problems, jaw deformities; generally robust, however.

▷ **Life Expectancy:** Up to 15 years.

▷ **Particular Qualities:** Gets along well with nearly all other housepets. Has a tendency to become overweight and to snore.

▷ **A Good Choice for:** Individualists to whom a dog's personality is more important than appearance and convention.

▷ **Less Suited for:** Athletic personalities and people who desire a perfectly average dog.

▶ ROTTWEILER

Bursting with strength, fearless, unspoiled; the Rottweiler is a wonderful work dog that belongs in the hands of experienced dog owners.

▷ **Appearance:** Height at withers: males, 24 to 27 inches (61–68 cm); females, 22 to 25 inches (56–63 cm). Muscular, very stocky body with deep, broad chest. Broad skull with a pronounced stop; small, high-set ears; and powerful tail.

▷ **Coat:** Coarse and short, close lying topcoat. Fur color always exclusively black with reddish brown markings (black and tan).

▷ **Character:** Solid and self-confident, sometimes domineering. A fearless watchdog that takes its job seriously. A loyal and devoted family dog.

▷ **Health:** Mostly robust; hip dysplasia only in a small percentage of dogs.

▷ **Life Expectancy:** 10 to 12 years.

▷ **Particular Qualities:** Formerly used for driving cattle, later as a police dog, at the borders, and in the military.

▷ **A Good Choice for:** Experienced, firm dog owners with whom the Rottweiler has close family contact and can be kept busy.

▷ **Less Suited for:** Beginners and people who are not accustomed to the strong personality of a large dog.

◗ SAINT BERNARD

This giant among dogs leans toward quiet contemplation. Devoted to its family and a patient friend to children.

▷ **Appearance:** Height at withers: males, 27 1/2 to 35 1/2 inches (70–90 cm); females, 25 1/2 to 31 1/2 inches (65–80 cm). Weight up to 176 pounds (80 kg). Massive body with broad chest, powerful head with small, dark brown eyes, and ears that lie close to the head. Long tail.
▷ **Coat:** Short- and long-haired type. Short and thick or medium long and slightly wavy. Fur colors: white with red or red with white markings. The long-haired variety needs regular care with a coarse comb and brush.
▷ **Character:** Easygoing and steady. Needs to be with people; a reliable friend to children. Strong defense instinct.
▷ **Health:** Susceptible to hip dysplasia, gastric torsion, and skin and eye diseases.
▷ **Life Expectancy:** 6 to 10 years.
▷ **Particular Qualities:** Needs firm training and early bonding with people. Not to be kept in a kennel.
▷ **A Good Choice for:** People who have room and understanding for a large dog and can afford it (it eats lots of food).
▷ **Less Suited for:** Beginners.

◗ SCHIPPERKE

Formerly the Ship Spitz was found on practically every canal barge. This is a lively and clever, but not always silent, watchdog.

▷ **Appearance:** Height at withers 9 to 13 inches (22–33 cm). Short, compact body with a pointed, foxlike head. Small, erect ears, usually with natural stumpy tail.
▷ **Coat:** Short and hard with abundant ruff at throat and thick undercoat. Absolutely waterproof. Only color: black with no markings.
▷ **Character:** Intelligent, very quick to learn, and an avowed friend to children. As in the past, the watch instinct of this former ship dog remains intact. A Schipperke is not a quiet dog, it loudly reports everything it sees. Distrustful of strangers.
▷ **Health:** Generally healthy.
▷ **Life Expectancy:** Lives to be very old; 16 years and older is not unusual.
▷ **Particular Qualities:** In Flemish, *scheperke* means *small sheepdog*. The breed resembles the Spitz more, however.
▷ **A Good Choice for:** People who value a dainty, lively, and devoted dog.
▷ **Less Suited for:** People with sensitive ears who would be bothered by frequent barking.

SCHNAUZER

Whether Giant, Medium (photo), or Miniature Schnauzer, in every size this dog is confident, fearless, and robust.

▷ **Appearance:** Height at withers: Medium Schnauzer, 18 to 20 inches (45–50 cm); Giant Schnauzer, 25 to 28 inches (65–70 cm); Miniature Schnauzer, 12 to 13 inches (30–35 cm). Powerful, squarely built, stocky body.
▷ **Coat:** Coarse and thick; typical Schnauzer head with pronounced beard and bushy eyebrows. Colors: black, salt and pepper; also silver and black and white in the Miniature. Occasional trimming; otherwise brushing is sufficient.
▷ **Character:** Brave, watchful, but also with a mind of its own. Lively, good with children, and playful into old age. Medium Schnauzers like to tussle; Miniatures can be quite noisy.
▷ **Health:** Heart and eye diseases in the Medium Schnauzer; HD in the Giant; eye diseases and epilepsy in the Miniature.
▷ **Life Expectancy:** Medium and Miniature, up to 15 years; Giant Schnauzer, 12 years.
▷ **Particular Qualities:** Firm training and regular activity are necessary.
▷ **A Good Choice for:** Owners with good dog sense and leadership qualities. The Miniature is ideal for senior citizens.
▷ **Less Suited for:** Unassertive people.

SCOTTISH TERRIER

A big-dog personality on short legs; very confident and always somewhat on its own wavelength.

▷ **Appearance:** Height at withers 10 to 11 inches (25–28 cm). Stocky with a straight back. Small head with long muzzle, eyes hidden under bushy eyebrows; erect pointed ears. The tail is carried high.
▷ **Coat:** Wiry, thick, and waterproof with soft undercoat. The coarse beard emphasizes the long muzzle. Black is the most common color; wheat and brindle are also permissible. The Scottie's fur needs regular trimming.
▷ **Character:** An individual through and through; independent and strong willed; keeps its distance from strangers. Receptive to and sociable with its reference person; pronounced protective instinct.
▷ **Health:** Eczema, occasional epilepsy.
▷ **Life Expectancy:** Up to 16 years.
▷ **Particular Qualities:** Even with firm training this dog doesn't entirely abandon its idiosyncrasies.
▷ **A Good Choice for:** People who can accept the terrier's obstinacy.
▷ **Less Suited for:** Dog lovers who dream of having an uncomplicated partner.

1

● SEALYHAM TERRIER

Compact, powerful, robust, confident, the Sealyham knows what it wants and needs an owner who will tell it what's allowed.

▷ **Appearance:** Height at withers up to 12 inches (31 cm). Powerful body on short, stocky legs. Distinguished from the Scottish Terrier especially by its drop ears.
▷ **Coat:** Hard, simple topcoat that lies close to the body. Soft, thick undercoat. Pure white or white with yellow and brown or gray and black markings on head and ears. Needs regular trimming.
▷ **Character:** Even today, this dog is slightly influenced by its past history as a fox and badger hunter. It is courageous, confident, often independent, but also clever and playful. A perfect alarm system, mistrustful of strangers; sometimes too rough for children.
▷ **Health:** Skin and ear diseases; inborn deafness.
▷ **Life Expectancy:** Up to 14 years.
▷ **Particular Qualities:** A big voice that one would not expect from a small terrier.
▷ **A Good Choice for:** Dog owners who can stand up to a self-assured dog.
▷ **Less Suited for:** Compliant personalities and people who prefer things to be more steady.

● SHELTIE

This dog always had to work and still wants to: lots of exercise, sport, and jobs make a Sheltie happy.

▷ **Appearance:** Height at withers 14 to 15 inches (33–37 cm). Elegant and noble-appearing body with long, wedge-shaped head; small cocked ears and slanted eyes. The long, thickly haired tail comes down to the ankle.
▷ **Coat:** Thick, coarse, and long with soft undercoat; impressive mane and ruff. Colors: sand, blue-merle, tricolor (black, white, brown), black, black with white. The fur needs regular care.
▷ **Character:** Intelligent, lively, and confident, but also very sensitive. Very loving and devoted to its family; distant with strangers. A good but loud watchdog.
▷ **Health:** Epilepsy, heart problems; deafness in blue-merle (blue dappling).
▷ **Life Expectancy:** Up to 15 years.
▷ **Particular Qualities:** Looks like a small Collie, but it has its own personality.
▷ **A Good Choice for:** A wonderful family dog that needs lots of activity and exercise.
▷ **Less Suited for:** Unathletic people and people who lack sensitivity.

▶ SHIH TZU

This confident and lively dwarf from China captivates us with its charm and lovable personality.

▷ **Appearance:** Height at withers approx. 11 inches (27 cm). Long body with straight back. Broad head with short snout and dark eyes. Drop ears scarcely visible under the long hair; the tail rolls over the back.

▷ **Coat:** Thick, tight, and very long with short undercoat. All colors permissible; white markings on the forehead and the tip of the tail are desirable. Extensive daily care required.

▷ **Character:** Full of life and playfulness; also exceptionally devoted and loving. Needs only moderate exercise; sensitive to excessive heat.

▷ **Health:** Ear and eye problems; breathing difficulties; dislocated kneecap.

▷ **Life Expectancy:** 10 to 12 years.

▷ **Particular Qualities:** Was one of the Lion dogs in the monasteries and palaces of China. Related to the Lhasa-Apso (p.62).

▷ **A Good Choice for:** Single people and senior citizens who can devote themselves to the daily coat care of a small indoor dog.

▷ **Less Suited for:** Active sports enthusiasts who like to be outdoors.

▶ SIBERIAN HUSKY

The best-known sled dog feels at home only in the ice and snow when it's going flat out as part of a team.

▷ **Appearance:** Height at withers: males, 21 to 24 inches (53–60 cm); females, 20 to 22 inches (51–56 cm). Muscular and slender with straight back. Wolflike head with pronounced stop, brown or blue eyes and triangular, erect ears.

▷ **Coat:** Medium long, woolly topcoat over soft undercoat. All colors are acceptable, most commonly gray and black and white.

▷ **Character:** Adaptable and free of aggression. Quick to understand, but not always obedient. Likes it best outdoors and in the cold. Has a great love of exercise.

▷ **Health:** Scarcely susceptible to illness; slight tendency to hip dysplasia.

▷ **Life Expectancy:** 10 to 12 years.

▷ **Particular Qualities:** Keeps its independence even among the family. It needs to be kept under control while running because of its hunting instinct.

▷ **A Good Choice for:** Specialists who can challenge the Husky regularly with running or pulling a sled or training wagon.

▷ **Less Suited for:** Unathletic people.

◯ SPITZ

The Spitz is considered the oldest form of housedog. It is bred in five sizes; all Spitzes are great watchdogs.

▷ **Appearance:** Height at withers: Wolf Spitz, 17 to 22 inches (45–55 cm); Standard Spitz, 16 to 19 inches (42–48 cm); Medium Spitz, 12 to 15 inches (30–38 cm); Small Spitz, 9 to 11 inches (23–29 cm); Miniature Spitz, 7 to 9 inches (18–22 cm). Short back, foxlike head, small, pointed ears; bushy tail curved over the back.
▷ **Coat:** Thick, fluffy topcoat. Wolf gray and cloudy gray in the Wolf Spitz; black, white, brown in the Standard and Mediums; also orange and wolf colors in the Smalls; cream and spotted colors are allowed in the Dwarfs.
▷ **Character:** Quick to learn; alert, and devoted to the family; mistrustful of strangers. Very watchful, and not silent.
▷ **Health:** Very robust breed.
▷ **Life Expectancy:** 12 to 15 years.
▷ **Particular Qualities:** Often tolerates no other housepets; the little Spitzes bark a lot.
▷ **A Good Choice for:** Large Spitzes are ideal companion dogs and watchdogs; the small ones are also fine as city dogs.
▷ **Less Suited for:** People who are sensitive to noise and owners of other house pets.

◯ TIBETAN TERRIER

A lively and lovable family dog with great athletic ambitions and a beautiful, abundant coat.

▷ **Appearance:** Height at withers 14 to 16 inches (35–41 cm). Powerful, angular body. The not especially broad head and V-shaped ears are almost completely covered in long hair. Medium long but heavily haired tail that curls over the back.
▷ **Coat:** Long, abundant topcoat with straight or slightly wavy hair; thick undercoat. The hair on the head falls over the eyes. Except for chocolate, all fur colors are acceptable; black and gold predominate.
▷ **Character:** Intelligent and receptive. A good watchdog that mistrusts strangers. Sticks with its family and doesn't hesitate to defend it when necessary. Active and fond of running.
▷ **Health:** Rare hip dysplasia.
▷ **Life Expectancy:** 14 and older.
▷ **Particular Qualities:** Despite its name, the Tibetan Terrier is not a terrier.
▷ **A Good Choice for:** Athletic people who value a devoted companion dog.
▷ **Less Suited for:** People who don't have enough time and leisure to devote themselves to a dog.

WEST HIGHLAND WHITE TERRIER

A small dog with a big personality. Charming, confident, always in good spirits and ready for any kind of fun.

▷ **Appearance:** Height at withers 11 inches (28 cm). Compact, powerful body, short head with pronounced stop, dark brown eyes, and small, pointed ears. The tail is carried straight.
▷ **Coat:** Coarse, wiry topcoat over short, soft undercoat. Pure white is the only acceptable color. Regular trimming and removal of dead hairs required.
▷ **Character:** A dog with lots of character. Full of confidence, but also lovable and happy. Watchful, full of endurance, and a good buddy to the children.
▷ **Health:** Allergies; jaw problems; liver problems.
▷ **Life Expectancy:** 13 to 15 years.
▷ **Particular Qualities:** Sometimes stubborn; also refuses to be intimated by much larger dogs.
▷ **A Good Choice for:** People who can give lots of attention to a lively and omnipresent companion.
▷ **Less Suited for:** Stay-at-homes who are looking for a lapdog.

YORKSHIRE TERRIER

From a rat hunter to a dog show champion. A dog through and through in which even today a fearless terrier heart beats.

▷ **Appearance:** Height at withers 7 to 9 inches (18–23 cm). Compact body with straight back, small head with dark brown eyes, and small, V-shaped, erect ears.
▷ **Coat:** Long silky hair with no undercoat. Dark steel blue, light tan on the chest, head, and legs. Constant care is the only way to prevent matting. The hair is put into rollers before dog shows.
▷ **Character:** The former rat hunter in the Yorkshire coal mines knows no fear and has no fear even of large dogs. Devoted, playful, and good with children. Watchful with a tendency to bark.
▷ **Health:** Spinal paralysis; eye diseases; knee problems.
▷ **Life Expectancy:** 12 to 14 years.
▷ **Particular Qualities:** Early socialization through contact with other dogs is important.
▷ **A Good Choice for:** City and apartment dwellers and people who can deal with the stubbornness of a Yorkshire Terrier.
▷ **Less Suited for:** As a fashion accessory, a Yorkshire Terrier is in the wrong place.

Offspring and Breeding

Granting your dog the joys of motherhood or taking on the breeding of pedigreed dogs —
a stimulating and beautiful challenge, but also a strenuous one.

WITH LOVE AND PASSION. It takes time, energy, and experience, and even more patience and understanding; raising dogs is no mere pastime or weekend hobby. Follow-through and lots of personal commitment are required, whether you have your dog bred just once or want to raise pedigreed dogs. And nobody who takes the responsibility seriously strikes it rich.

To begin with, there is the matter of choos-

ing a partner: female and male, who's a good match for whom? The parents' appearance and character help determine the personalities the pups will develop. In raising recognized pedigreed animals, specific demands and breeding standards must be adhered to. That's the only way to clear the way to dog shows and championships, and for top dogs, maybe even best of show.

Choice of Partner and Mating

Veterinarians and breeders will gladly supply you with appropriate contacts and valuable tips as you search for a suitable male dog for your female. Gather information about the specific traits of the breed's females and males, and ask your veterinarian about any breed-specific health problems, especially hereditary diseases. The female must be healthy and have had all her shots, and should be wormed about a week before mating. If she meets the breed standards, and you want to raise the offspring and show them at dog shows, breeding conditions and requirements must be met (◉ RAISING PUREBRED DOGS, p.83).

Responsibility for the Offspring

First, consider the puppies, then the mating. Is this backwards? Not at all: Before you have your bitch bred, you have to have a clear idea about what will become of the puppies. For reasons of space most of them won't remain with you. Find out from experienced dog owners and breeders if there is a demand for the puppies and at what price they should be offered. You should not have to worry once people indicate an interest in buying the puppies. Here's what absolutely must be avoided: You fail to locate trustworthy takers, and in your desperation you sell the puppies into dubious hands at bargain prices. An unenviable fate often awaits such animals; they get shunted back and forth and often get passed from one owner to the next.

When Is a Bitch Ready to Have Pups?

When a bitch first comes into heat she is not fully grown. With small and medium-sized breeds, that usually happens in the seventh or eighth month of life; with large breeds, which nearly always are late bloomers, between the tenth and twelfth month. A male dog takes until at least the tenth month to be fully grown. A bitch should not be bred until after coming into heat for the first time. Depending on the breed, her body and organs need up to one more year to mature. Up to the age of 15 or 18 months many breeds often show by their immature behavior that they are not yet done with puberty (→ p.137). A young bitch that is bred too early usually gives birth to only a few puppies, not all of which are viable. That also disturbs the development of the mother and overburdens her with raising the puppies.

 TIP

Etiquette for Dogs in Heat

When they're in heat, even well-behaved female dogs may become disobedient. A dog in heat should be kept on a leash while on a walk to keep her from running away. Avoid areas where you know there are male dogs. At home, make sure the doors and windows are closed properly.

The Scent of Love

A bitch remains in heat for about three weeks. During this time the dog displays typical changes in behavior—she becomes increasingly agitated, sheds first blood and then flesh-colored secretions, frequently marks, and either develops a ravenous appetite or practically stops eating. But the most reliable indicator of her being in heat is the male dogs that come from all around.

They are lured by scents given off by the dog in heat. Free-running dogs perceive the love scent even over long distances, and often cover many miles to present themselves for the rendezvous at the lady's home. However, a bitch is ready for love only in what's referred to as the peak of the rut, which lasts around five to ten days. At that time, the female is also active and wants to get out of the house to look for males.

Experience Counts in Mating

The eleventh to the thirteenth day of heat is usually a good time for mating. At least one of the partners should have some experience; an inexperienced male and an inexperienced bitch make one another nervous. The bitch chases the male away, or the animals hurt each other when they lock on. But even experienced dogs need time to sniff each other in peace. Many male dogs have just enough confidence in their own territory to get involved with a dominant female. That's why the female is usually brought to the male. If she accepts him, she moves her tail to the side, and the male mounts her for about a minute. Even after the mating the two can't separate; they continue to "hang on." The male dismounts and turn his hindquarter to the bitch. Since his penis is swollen, it takes him 10 to 40 minutes to get loose. Under no circumstances should the partners be separated; both would suffer severe injury. That's why the female is generally held firmly in place while mating, for inexperienced and impatient animals sometimes try to separate from the male prematurely.

Pregnancy Symptoms

Sometimes the offspring arrive totally unexpectedly, at least for the dog owner, if the female dog does not change either in physical

The food dish is one place where the mother's example is not right for the young dog; for healthy development it needs special puppy chow.
▽

appearance or in behavior until the birth of the pups. That's an exceptional case, but in the first four or five weeks after mating, many female dogs don't exhibit signs that they are expecting. An ultrasound examination can put an end to the uncertainty; this is recommended especially with females that are pregnant for the first time. Many times the veterinarian can tell from the ultrasound how many puppies will be born, and that should be taken into account in feeding the expectant mother. The dog's PREGNANCY (◐ p.270) usually lasts 63 days, but the puppies may be born up to a week sooner or later. Normally the teats enlarge slightly in the fifth to the sixth week of pregnancy and become pink; they enlarge visibly starting with the eighth week. Now the belly increases in size, and, depending on the dog's disposition, she may take things a little easier. In the days before giving birth her need for rest and sleep increases noticeably.

The stimulating world beyond the birthing bed. Starting in the fourth week of life this Jack Russell puppy can no longer be confined to the bed. It develops its physical abilities and makes its first social contacts in playing with its littermates.

Caring for the Expectant Mother

The last weeks before the arrival of the puppies are stressful—for both dog and owner. As early as the fifth week of pregnancy the feeding program should be changed subtly. Because the mother has to provide for the unborn pups, she needs at least a third more food than usual—and 50 percent more in the last phase before birth. You can't go wrong with a high-quality commercial food for pregnant dogs that contains nutrition and additives specially formulated for the particular needs of pregnancy. The feeding times are changed from once or twice daily to several smaller meals. Regular exercise is important, even in the days before giving birth, but the future mother should be spared from very long hikes, strenuous sports activities, and wild games. Many pregnant dogs are especially affectionate at this time and thankful for any kind of attention.

A Comfortable Birthing Place

The precise birthing day can't be planned on with certainty, thus the preparations should be in place two weeks before the calculated delivery date—especially the location. If you take care of that too late, the dog will look for a spot on her own, and that doesn't always agree with the owner's ideas. In addition, last-minute offerings are often declined. The birthing bed must be quiet, protected, and warm. The dimensions depend on the size of the dog, but it must be able to stretch out inside. At 15 to 20 inches (40–50 cm) the sidewalls are sufficiently high to keep the puppies from getting out prematurely. Inside you can install a rod or some bars about a hand's breadth from the sidewalls to keep the little ones from getting squeezed against the wall in case the mother lies down clumsily. Newborn pups get cold easily; an infrared lamp set up over the bed will provide additional heat if needed.

A Normal Birth

Around 24 hours before giving birth, the dog will take in no more food. She becomes increasingly restless and wanders back and forth; her breathing becomes quicker and shallower; she pants and trembles and keeps

△

Puppy love. Puppies need constant nearness and lots of attention in order to develop a natural and trusting relationship with a human.

licking her vagina, from which there is a mucous discharge that is sometimes mixed with blood. Depending on the number of babies, the birthing can stretch out over six or more hours, and the pains that precede the arrival of the first pups last the longest—commonly several hours. But there can also be a delay of several hours between individual deliveries. Many puppies are born with an amniotic sac around their body. Simultaneously or shortly thereafter, comes the afterbirth (placenta), to which the umbilical cord is attached. The mother shakes the sheath until it rips, removes the rest of the membrane with her tongue, especially around the puppy's nose and mouth, and uses her tongue to lick the little creature dry. The mother bites through the umbilical cord with her premolars, and eats the amniotic sack and almost always the placenta. We mustn't interfere with this, for the placenta contains hormones that stimulate milk production and flow.

Hints for Helping with the Birth

Not every mother bites off the newborns' umbilical cord. So you should have available some string and clean (sterilized) scissors on hand for tying and cutting the umbilical cord, plus some towels for wiping off the puppies. If the mother doesn't do anything, you have to work quickly. Remove the amniotic sac with your fingers so that the youngsters can get some air; then tie the umbilical cord right at the puppies' belly and cut it farther along. Then carefully rub the little ones dry with a hand towel and place them at their mother's teats.

After the birth the mother and the puppies need lots of quiet. The mother doesn't eat at this point, but she absolutely must have fresh water available. It may even be possible to offer her some weak tea. If she leaves the birthing bed to do her business, that's your chance to change the sheets and the newspaper liner.

If Things Don't Go According to Plan

The following symptoms are signs that the delivery is not proceeding normally. You can't help the mother on your own, so let your veterinarian know right away. The phone numbers of the veterinarian and the nearest animal hospital should be ready even before birthing begins.

▷ There is a delay of more than two hours between individual deliveries

▷ The mother dog is totally exhausted or is in obvious pain

▷ The discharge doesn't appear normal, is very abundant, or contains an especially large amount of bright red blood.

Many breeds such as the Pekingese and Miniature Pinscher often experience birthing complications (◯ BIRTHING PROBLEMS, p.259). In these cases the veterinarian should be on call.

If the offspring need delivery by cesarian section, the veterinarian will need help. Larger veterinary practices and animal hospitals are set up for such operations.

Mother's Milk and Lots of Sleep

Puppies come into the world unprepared; they are blind and deaf. Still they manage to find the mother's dairy bar, and even though the little legs are still weak, they stimulate milk flow in the teats (◯ KNEADING, p.267).

▷ WHAT TO DO IF...

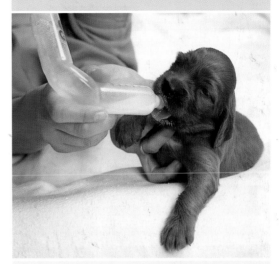

... the mother rejects the puppies

The mother dog doesn't let the puppies nurse or doesn't take care of them.

Cause: Many first-time mothers don't know where to begin with their young ones. Also, frequent disturbances at the birthing bed can make a mother dog so nervous that she will reject the puppies. If her teats are inflamed or painful, she won't let the newborns suckle.

Solution: Reduce all disturbances, especially with nervous mothers. Let your veterinarian know if the mother's teats are red or swollen. The veterinarian can also help by looking for another female dog that can act as a wet nurse. If no such foster mother is available, the newborns must be raised by hand. This is very labor-intensive; it requires feeding with replacement milk from a bottle every two (no more than three) hours, stimulating bowel movements by massaging the anogenital region, and providing plenty of heat.

The only noise the helpless youngsters make is a weak peeping, just the right signal to bring mom at a trot whenever someone is hungry, cold, or stranded in the corner of the birthing bed.

The first days of a newborn's life are filled with eating and sleeping. But things change entirely in the second week of life: Eyes and ears open up, and a world of scents waits to be discovered. The littermates make their first contacts with one another, licking and sniffing each other. And just a few days later the most courageous ones conduct expeditions into the unknown on their still wobbly legs.

Curious About Life

The young dogs' physical and mental development progresses at an astonishing speed. Starting with the fourth week their movements become more coordinated; their senses are now fully developed, and the puppies are interested in everything in their surroundings.

This curiosity is the catalyst for activity, and the receptiveness in this SOCIALIZATION PHASE (Ⓞ p.273) is greater than in any other period of life. The experiences that a puppy has at this stage stay with it for the rest of its life.

A young dog builds a trusting relationship with a human only if the person spends a lot of time with it between the fourth and twelfth weeks of life. If the puppy is confronted early with strange sounds and smells, it later deals more easily with unknown situations and develops into a well-adjusted, confident dog.

Puppies that are neglected or that grow up without close human contact during the socialization phase remain shy and rather unsociable.

Weaning and Separation

A mother dog suckles her puppies for four to six weeks. For her this is a particularly exhausting time, during which she needs nearly three times as much food as usual—high quality, protein-rich nutrients enriched with vitamins and minerals.

After about six weeks the puppies' milk teeth have formed, and the pups can be weaned and gradually shifted over to puppy food. The mother will take care of weaning her young ones herself, and denies them access to the milk source with increasing frequency.

In the days before the changeover, the puppies investigate their surroundings more actively and purposefully and learn to respect the demands of social living by playing with their littermates. At the same time they learn to stick up for themselves, react individually to their reference person, and show themselves to be ready for the first steps in training.

In the eighth or ninth week of life—no later than the twelfth—the young dogs leave the kiddy room and their littermates. Now they want to know where their place is in the pack.

Undesired Pregnancy

In following the call of love, bitches in heat will take every opportunity to run off. And male dogs ready for love are always at hand. The only reliable protection against undesired reproduction is spaying (p.214)—the correct decision if the female dog is not intended for breeding. The puppies in one litter can also be from any one of several fathers if the mother was mounted by more than one male.

Dog owners who decide against spaying, either because they intend to breed or for some other reason, can nevertheless prevent unwanted pregnancies by watching their bitches closely during times when they are in heat. These bitches should not be allowed to have any contact with male dogs at such times, and they should be kept in a secure area from which they cannot escape. Undesired pregnancies result in unwanted puppies, many of whom end up in shelters, with no prospect of ever ending up in a good home. Responsible dog owners should do their best not to contribute to this major problem in the animal world.

1

Raising Purebreds

Dogs have been bred for thousands of years. The main purpose was always performance and suitability for specific tasks. Physique, coat color and structure, and temperament were of interest only if they improved the usefulness of the dogs. That changed with the start of breeding purebred dogs.

The Standard Defines the Breed

Dog breeding, as we understand it today, has a comparatively short history. The first breed associations were formed in the second half of the nineteenth century in England. Breeders developed binding breed standards in which the characteristics of their dogs were prescribed. Breeding among animals from any specific breed was, and continues to be, permitted. For mating, a male and a female are chosen so that their physical traits and temperament complement one another and the puppies approach the breed standard as closely as possible. In mating between closely related animals (○ INBREEDING, p.266) there are obvious hereditary faults and genetic tendencies in the line (○ HEREDITARY DISEASES, for example; p.265). The most important goal of breeding is to encourage and solidify the desirable qualities and traits of a breed. In addition to a dog's physical features, nowadays character traits and health play an increasingly important role in raising purebreds. Beauty alone doesn't make a dog show winner; the dog must also be a champion in nature and free of health problems. DOCKING (○ p.261) ears and tail is prohibited.

The Duties of Breed Associations

People who wish to raise a recognized breed have to be a member of the appropriate breed association. The local or regional breed associations, in turn, are affiliated with the national ones, such as the American Kennel Club and the Canadian Kennel Club (→ Addresses, p.284).

There are scores of breed associations distributed through the country, and together they have many thousands of members. There are also hundreds of recognized breeds, such as the German Shepherd Dog, that produce many thousands of puppies every year, as well as rarer breeds such as the Spinone Italiano and the Xoloitzcuintle. The Fédération Internationale Cynologique (FCI), which has its headquarters in Belgium, is the worldwide umbrella organization for dog breed associations. The FCI is responsible for international breed recognition, as in the case of the White

Small dogs with large ears. The only thing this Papillon puppy lacks is the breed-typical feathering on its butterfly ears.
▽

Swiss Shepherd Dog. The application form must indicate eight bloodlines and include, among other things, detailed information about the dog's appearance, derivation, and health.

If the breed is recognized, the FCI records the internationally valid name of the dog and the breed standard—in the case of the White Swiss Shepherd Dog, Standard number 347. The breed standard is usually controlled by the country of origin, which obviously is Switzerland for number 347.

Breeders Need a Breeding Permit

Every breeder who owns more than three female dogs capable of reproducing, or who produces more than three litters per year, is required by law to have a permit. A breeding permit is issued when the candidate demonstrates the requisite knowledge and provides the proper accommodations, food, and care.

A breeder's dogs have a right to at least two hours of exercise per day and regular care. With eleven or more dogs, an additional competent person must be hired.

The highest duty is to breed only with healthy animals. By using a method for EVALUATING BREEDING SUITABILITY (◐ p.260), today's breeders and breed associations have a way to control the risk of hereditary problems in breeding animals.

Dog Shows

There are many expositions at which dogs are shown and evaluated by judges according to the appropriate breed standards. Here are the most important kinds:

▷ **General Breed Show:** Dogs of all breeds can take part and earn eligibility for national titles.

▷ **Specific Breed Show:** An exposition for only one breed or for several breeds, all of which are overseen by one association. The awards include Club Winner, and Eligibility for the National Beauty Championship (CAC or Certificat au Championnat).

▷ **International Breed Shows:** Dogs of all breeds are eligible to participate. Title: International Beauty Championship (CACIB: Certificat d'aptitude au championnat international de beauté).

▷ **National, European, and World Championship Shows:** The winner's titles are awarded by associations that are allied with the national association.

A Personal ID for Purebred Dogs

When you buy a purebred dog you also get its registration papers. The PEDIGREE (◐ p.270) is important proof of the dog's ancestry even if you don't intend to breed dogs yourself—for example, if the dog is to be shown at an event, if it has to pass a test for work, and of course in case of resale.

The pedigreee is a birth certificate and proof of belonging to a breed. The dog's breed and name, including the kennel name (◐ KENNEL NAME, p.267), sex, date of birth, and perhaps other characteristics are indicated on the form. It also contains the previous generations with their registration numbers and markings.

The registration number is used for entry into the registry book and removal by the overseer. The breeder is responsible for providing the data in the profile. The breeder and the association's bookkeeper confirm the entries with their signatures. Today there are several breed associations for nearly every breed. Be sure that the pedigree has been signed by an association affiliated with the national organization.

Prospective owners who intend to get involved in the world of purebred dogs should familiarize themselves with all of the rules and regulations in this world. An excellent place to acquire basic information is a local breed association or club. Members of these associations or clubs are knowledgeable in all aspects of purebred dogs, and many would be willing to provide advice and assistance to owners new to the world of purebreds.

Origin and Meaning

A dog has a scent memory and equates scents with information that it has "stored up." To keep the scent cells from becoming dulled through continuous stimulation, the air flows through the nose in spurts. As a dog inhales it can change between right and left sides of the nose and form a three-dimensional scent perception of its surroundings.

Your dog recognizes you by the scent of your clothing. A puppy will get used to you quicker if you at first don't change jacket or pants, and dispense with deodorant and perfume.

Housepets have a smaller brain than their wild relatives. This is also true of dogs. But the dog is not dumber than the wolf, it has adapted to life with humans and strengthened abilities that are advantageous to the partnership, such as barking and the "dog smile," which dogs have developed in the course of domestication.

It's part of a dog's pack mentality to adapt to its master's way of life; every owner thus assumes responsibility for keeping the protégé in an appropriate manner and caring for it.

Analysis of genetic material in the mitochondria has shown that the dog is a descendant of the wolf. Mitochondria are cell components that are passed on with the mother's egg cell. Jackals and coyotes, on the other hand, are not direct ancestors of dogs. The genetic difference between coyote and wolf is much greater than that between wolf and dog.

Wolves and dogs even resemble one another in behavior; they are adaptable and social, have a territory, and hunt.

Dogs are relatively insensitive to pain. Most pain sensors are located in the face and the stomach area; there are few in the neck and the back. Here too the fur provides some protection.

◁

Above all, dogs react to movements. A dog frequently will react to a command given as a hand signal even at a distance of more than 305 feet (1,000 m). The dog's eye scarcely perceives immobile objects, however.

A stern reprimand makes a greater impression on your dog than hitting it does. And that's not the only reason that corporal punishment is no way to train a dog.

The dog's eye reacts primarily to movement (❍ MOTION PERCEPTION, p.268); it scarcely perceives stationary objects or overlooks them altogether. A dog will frequently lose sight of its owner if the person remains motionless, even at a distance of only 90 feet (27.5 m).

Dogs have a sharp eye for humans' body language, and they also register moods.

Ten Questions About Offspring and Breeding

My Scottish Terrier is the perfect picture of a dog. I would like to show it at dog shows. How does that work?
The easiest thing is to join a breed association; there you will find out about everything that is important at a breed show and how to get the dog ready for it. Your Terrier's registration number and all the necessary registration data are part of its pedigree papers. First observe a show without your dog and note the things that will be required of your dog and how the judges do their job. Of course your dog must be healthy, it must be able to stand calmly, and must not disturb the peace with noise or hectic activity. Breeders and dog show pros will gladly give you some hints and tell you what class your dog can enter.

What do I have to watch out for in feeding my pregnant dog?
You can continue to feed normally up to the fourth week of pregnancy, but the food must be rich in vitamins and minerals. Thereafter, the amount of food is increased by 30 to 50 percent, but the main thing is the quality of the food. In the last week of pregnancy the food amounts are decreased slightly to facilitate delivery.

There are often female dogs in heat in our neighborhood. At such times we can hardly keep the brakes on our male dog. Should we have him neutered?
Neutering is common in male dogs: a neutered male doesn't try to run off when it catches scent of a female in heat. In addition, sexual behavior is held in check and aggressive behavior and combativeness with other male dogs is reduced. Neutering sometimes leads to changes in behavior. Although these are rarely serious, you should consult with your veterinarian about the pluses and minus of this operation.

I am completely captivated by the charm and the beauty of the Afghan Hound. Will such a dog be short-changed if I don't give it chance to race like a Greyhound?
No matter what, your dog will need lots of exercise. But consider too that the Afghan Hound is a harrier; sometimes all it takes to trigger its hunting instinct is a scent of the autumn leaves on the wind, and away it goes. At that point, audio signals are of no use. Thus, an Afghan Hound must almost never be let off the leash. Also, its pronounced urge for independence makes it a dog for experienced owners. You must never lose sight of the time-consuming, demanding care of the silky coat.

We live in a large house in the country. We have enough room for an Irish Wolfhound, but is it the right playmate for the children?
The Irish Wolfhound is correctly referred to as a gentle giant. Despite its imposing size it is

Born to live in the country. Irish Wolfhounds are calm, lovable friends to humans. This largest of all dogs needs lots of room in the house and a spacious, fenced-in yard.

Child's play. They romp and hunt one another, they tease and cuddle. Puppies try out the proper behavior by playing together.

exceptionally sociable, calm, and obedient. Of course you shouldn't let the children take such a large dog for a walk alone.

Vroni, our female Dachshund, will soon give birth to her first litter. How much danger of complications is there?

Except for a few breeds with unfavorable anatomy (such as Yorkshire Terriers and Bulldogs), dogs almost always give birth without problems, even in the case of a first-time mother. There are, however, major differences in how long birthing takes.

How old should a female dog be before having puppies?

Depending on the breed, a female dog first comes into heat between the ages of six and eleven months. She is not fully grown at that time; large dogs in particular often need a full year until their body is mature. Before that time birthing would impose a serious strain. Many breed associations have set a minimum age of 18 months for eligibility to breed.

What is the significance of the Breeding Suitability Evaluation for raising dogs?

The Breeding Suitability Evaluation became possible with the introduction of computer-assisted record keeping for breeding. A great number of data for a specific trait (such as, hip dysplasia) are evaluated to identify possible risks from a breeding pair. In addition to the individual constitutions of the breeding animals, their genetic history is considered (→ The Standard Defines the Breed, p.83).

All of this information is crucial to maintaining the overall quality of the breed. Lax breeding practices, after all, can quickly result in the decline of the breed.

I don't want my dog to come into heat anymore. Which is better: neutering or sterilization?

With sterilization, only the Fallopian tubes are severed, and the ovaries are still capable of functioning, thus a sterilized dog can come into heat just as before. That is prevented by neutering. With this operation both ovaries and part of the uterus are removed. To spare your dog from the stimulation of coming into heat, neutering is the right choice. Often the veterinarian will wait until the dog has come into heat at least once.

Every dog has a right to daily exercise outdoors; living entirely indoors is inappropriate.

Experienced dog owners have told me that puppies generally are born in the early morning. Is that true?

The dogs certainly don't have a timetable in mind. But in fact, many dogs prefer to give birth in the middle of the night, and the birthing lasts at least until the following morning. Why bitches prefer to give birth in the middle of the night, and precisely how they arrange to do so, have yet to be adequately explained by science.

What Dogs Need

A person who buys a dog makes a choice for an intensive and eventful life. A dog is always present—even a tiny Chihuahua will remind us of our duties. The cornerstone for a happy partnership is laid in the first days and weeks. Patience, understanding, and a readiness to compromise play an essential role in becoming familiar with and adjusted to one another. But we also need the right equipment and appropriate accessories to make the dog feel at home with us.

2

The New Home

It takes patience and understanding for the dog to accept its new family and for strangers to turn into friends—and the accessories must be right for the dog to feel at home.

THINK FOR A MOMENT LIKE A DOG! Is this a peculiar demand? On the contrary, it makes perfect sense. Three things count most for the social creature that a dog is: a firm place in the group, recognition by the leader of the pack, and comfortable surroundings that give it security and strength.

For a dog that is a new arrival in the family, this means it wants to fit in, always be there, and never be excluded. It wants clear commands on what's permitted and what's forbidden. And it wants its own living space that meets its needs and where it feels comfortable. A dog's demands for shelter and equipment are not excessive. A person should provide the basic things required for the dog's living conditions even before the dog arrives. No more is needed at the beginning; that way there is room for later wishes and needs.

Appropriate Living Conditions

Dogs are the oldest and best friends that humans have. What many may dismiss as mawkishness in people who have devoted a lot of care and thought to dogs is well founded. Humans and dogs resemble one another in many of their social and behavioral structures: Both need society, and they wither if they live alone; both communicate with a highly developed vocal and body language; they possess a territory or home area, exhibit pronounced curiosity and investigative behavior, and defend their property and their territory.

All of this constitutes a stable basis for division of labor, cooperation, and partnership. The fact that things have developed even further is due to the dog's reliability and unconditional devotion—plus the many thousands of years that the dog has spent proving it.

Is There a Gene for Compromising?

Cooperating, helping, fitting in, and subordinating: both the human social structure and the dog's pack mentality are based on a spirit of togetherness and a readiness to compromise and put aside personal wishes when necessary. The desire for integration and recognition by the group is so great in dogs that they really don't need much convincing to make compromises, and they do so willingly. Perhaps this very special sense of community is even rooted in heredity; if so, it's at least as strong in dogs as it is in humans.

A Dog's Comfort and Living Space

A dog's sense organs are amazingly sharp (→ p.18). Dogs live in a world of scents and sounds that is closed to visual humans. In our homes and the living areas we have put together, shapes, structures, and colors predominate; in other words, optical signals that don't mean much to dogs. This environment becomes even more uninteresting for a dog if

we turn it into an area devoid of scents through endless cleaning and scrubbing where there is no reading material for a fine dog nose. If a dog had its way, this is what its most comfortable living space would look like:

▷ **Trusted Scents.** Strange scents or SCENT MARKING (◐ p.272) by rivals are a cause for alarm in a dog's nose; however, the dog's own scent or that of trusted people produces a sense of security. The sweater left by the owner or the old socks feel more like home than the most beautiful, luxurious bed.

▷ **Marking.** Dogs MARK (◐ p.267) their territory and leave a scented business card by depositing urine in strategic locations. Males generally mark more frequently than females. A dog will continue to mark its territory as long as strange scents (such as from other dogs) need covering up.

▷ **Cleanliness.** A dog's own scent and scent marking are important, but so is cleanliness. This is no contradiction to a dog; it takes great pains to keep its toilet area as far as possible from the feeding place.

▷ **Feeling.** Physical contact and petting are vitally important for a dog's mental well-being—for puppies in a birthing bed as well as for a 14-year old veteran. Cushions, blankets, and places to cuddle are all essential items in every room for a dog.

◁

Feeling comfortable at home. A dog needs the closeness of the family, but also its own private area into which it can withdraw without being disturbed.

▷ **Caves.** Seeing without being seen. Pregnant dogs among the wild ancestors of the house-dog often retreated into caves to give birth and raise their offspring in safety. Small breeds, in particular, and terriers ("earth dogs") have retained this preference for caves and hiding places. A dog bed and basket are just what they need.

▷ **Digging.** No pet dog needs to think about its daily food. However, the instinct to set aside provisions for hard times is deeply rooted. Every dog takes advantage of an appropriate opportunity to bury leftover food and bones—sometimes even imaginary ones—in the middle of the living room. Then it rubs its nose over the floor to cover up the food. If the dog can lay an old sheet or towel over its hiding place, the digging process is easier.

▷ **Undisturbed Eating.** Many dogs have an allergic reaction to disturbances during their mealtimes. And like their wolf ancestors, they don't like to be watched when they eat.

▷ **Slightly Cool.** Dogs prefer things a little cooler. The temperature in the dog's room should be a little lower than in the rest of the house. Dogs that aren't fortunate enough to have their own living area are happy to retire to a cool corridor.

▷ **Rest Area.** Dogs are active animals; their preferred gait is a quick trot. Anyone who expends lots of energy needs lots of rest to recharge the batteries. A dog has no hankering for a sleeping place right on the main thoroughfare through the room.

▷ **Lookout.** Chairs and couches are preferred resting places. You get a better view of everything that's going on in the area from an elevated resting spot, and it feels secure.

People Are Part of a Dog's Happiness

Here's what a dog needs for an appropriate life: a home territory where it can feel comfortable, the proper accessories, balanced nutrition, exercise and activity, and fitness challenges for mind and body.

But above all, what it needs for happiness is its human. The most comfortable living conditions and the best food won't make a dog happy if it is often left alone or excluded from family life and its people's activities.

Close contact with people is especially important for a puppy in the socialization phase before the twelfth week of life. Anyone who comes up short in that requirement will later fit into society with difficulty or not at all.

But even adult dogs become mentally crippled if they don't get attention and affection. That's a recipe for misunderstandings and problems.

Your Dog Knows What It's Allowed to Do

A dog has a likeable disposition, and it tests what works and what doesn't. That begins in puppyhood, when it intentionally ignores the master's commands. If the owner of the young puppy lets it go at that, the clever partner has already won. The dog wants to know its boundaries, and the main task is to make them clear.

The Business About the Bedroom

How much freedom should you give your dog? Opinions differ on where to spend the night. In the bedroom or not?

A dog pack is never broken up. Your dog won't understand why it has to sleep in the hall, but it will get used to it.

What it doesn't like is shifting winds—an open door today, and outside tomorrow. That creates frustration and problems. In the bedroom it's the presence of the trusted person that counts more than cuddling; your dog really doesn't want to get into the bed anyway, because it's much too warm. The carpet next to the door is perfectly adequate. That's also a good compromise that both you and your dog can live with happily.

The Right Equipment

Whether in a two-room apartment in the middle of a city or a house with a yard in the country—in either place the dog has a right to certain basic equipment that it needs for daily life. It must already be present and in the right places when the dog moves in. You should wait to get supplementary accessories until the dog has become acclimated and you know its special needs and preferences.

Food and Water Dishes

People eat at the table, and a dog eats from a dish. The daily food ration and treats are given only in the feeding bowls. Feeding by hand is used mostly for rewards during training and in certain exceptional cases, such as hand-raising a puppy or in the case of illness. You must never let your dog eat from the table; that applies especially to puppies and young dogs. If there are several dogs in the house, of course each one has its own food dishes.

The dog must always have fresh water available. The best bowl is a heavy one made of glazed ceramic or high-grade steel. Steel is also the right material for the food dish, as it's easy to keep clean. Leftover food is rinsed away with hot water after every meal, but you should avoid using detergent.

By nature, dogs are gobblers that usually gulp down their food quickly without concern for cleanliness and etiquette. A dog won't tip over a heavy food dish with a broad base so easily, and the chunks of food won't land beside the bowl. Set the dishes on a surface that's easy to clean (such as tiles). A rubber mat keeps the bowls from sliding, at least if the bowls have rubber feet or a rubber rim. Breeds that have drop ears should have a special bowl that tapers toward the top and keeps the ears from hanging in the food. So that large and long-legged dogs don't have to bend down too far, their dishes are placed on a

small pedestal. The perfect setup is a holder for the water and food dishes that adjusts for height and can be adapted to the size of the dog. It works for puppies and can grow along with them.

Sleeping and Resting Places

The sleeping place has special significance for the dog and is also the official confirmation of its belonging to the family and its right to be in the house. Naturally, your dog mustn't share its spot with anyone, and it should be disturbed only when absolutely necessary. If several dogs live in the house, each one has its private area, regardless of whether or not they are all friends and even take some siestas together.

 TIP

The Indoor Doghouse

This doesn't have to be made of wood or have a weatherproof roof. But an indoor doghouse is just what your dog dreams about—a real home of its own in which it feels secure and where everyone else has to stay outside. A removable roof makes cleaning a snap.

Dogs like to sleep curled up, and therefore don't need much floor space for lying down. Still, their sleeping place has to be big enough so they can stretch our full length. Stretching and flexibility exercises are important for dogs as well as for people when getting up; they are important for comfort and they loosen up the spinal column and other body parts. The sleeping place for a Mastiff is necessarily very large; a Dachshund's is more

HOME SWEET HOME—BASICS FOR THE DOG HOME

Every dog that lives with us under one roof has a right to a private area into which it can always retreat. The basic equipment for a dog home guarantees the proper living conditions and care, and can be expanded to meet the needs of individual dogs. You can find a broad array of appropriate products in pet shops and on the Internet.

A PLACE FOR SLEEPING AND RESTING

Description	A soft, cushioned surface or cubby hole with removable, washable cushion and cover
Product	Wicker basket, dog bed, or mattress
Recommendation	Choose according to dog's size; baskets are best for smaller dogs

FOOD AND WATER DISHES

Description	Secure, heavy, and easy to rinse dry
Product	Made from high-quality steel, ceramic, or heavy plastic
Recommendation	Rubber rim prevents sliding; special bowl for dogs with drop ears

COLLAR AND LEASH

Description	Collar that fits the dog properly, neither too tight nor too loose; leash with a secure attachment with a strong clip
Product	preferably made of leather or nylon; retractable leash for more length
Recommendation	Reflective leash and collar offer greater safety in low-light conditions.

ACCESSORIES

Description	Brush, comb, and knobby glove for coat care
Product	Carding comb for brushing short hair; curry comb for long-haired dogs; rubber glove or brush for cleaning the fur
Recommendation	Special accessories for trimming terriers and schnauzers

TOYS

Description	Safe and bite resistant, for play and activities
Product	Mostly balls, pull ropes, Frisbees, fetching sticks
Recommendation	Careful with small balls; danger of swallowing

DOG HEALTH CARE

Description	Bandages and medicines designed for dogs
Product	From pet shop: dog drug kit or first aid kit
Recommendation	Replenish after use; watch for expiration dates

modest. Small dogs like closed-in baskets or sleeping boxes.

The dog doesn't care if it has a box, basket, mattress, or dog bed. The cushion must insulate the dog from the cold floor, especially on tiles and cement floors. All blankets, cushions, and covers must be removable and washable. Special dog blankets are more practical than wool blankets. A vacuum cleaner serves well for regular cleaning.

Where Should the Dog's Bed Be Located?

A quiet, draft-free corner with visual contact with the family is just right for your dog's sleeping place. Many animals change between day and night beds—in the kitchen or living room during the day, and in the hall or in front of the bedroom door at night. Of course it would be nicer in the bedroom, but that's usually off limits, so the alarm is posted at the strategically best place. But a watchdog that keeps reporting loudly on every movement in the stairwell during the night will not endear itself to the other people in the house. If your dog is allowed into the bedroom, a wicker basket isn't the best choice; it creaks audibly every time the sleeping dog turns over.

Puppies Live Simply

Buy an expensive dog basket or a real cushy dog bed when once your dog has reached its final size. A puppy doesn't need a luxury bed; a well-padded sleeping box works just fine. You should also remember that young dogs gnaw and chew at will so a dog bed or a box made of wood or plastic is quickly broken into pieces.

A Collar That Fits

The choice of collar depends on the size of the dog, its strength, and its temperament, and perhaps on the shape of its body. And naturally it must be fit for daily use and match the breed and the character of the wearer.

▷ **Leather, Nylon, or Fabric.** A leather collar will hold even the strongest dog in place;

△

In top shape: With the right accessories coat care is much quicker and easier, and fun for both dog and human.

nylon and fabric collars, on the other hand, are particularly easy to clean. A leather collar is not the best choice for dogs that like to swim, as it quickly becomes brittle and breakable. The best choice for such dogs is a nylon collar. The usual dog collar has a buckle and can be adjusted to the size of the dog's neck. That's not always so easy; if you tighten the collar too much, the dog can't get enough air; if it's too loose the dog can get hung up on branches and bushes, or even pull the collar off over its head by pulling backward. Breeds such as the Bulldog and Mastiff, which are characterized by a big head, pose no problems of this nature.

▷ **Head Halter.** A halter for a dog works like a horse halter; a strap passes across the muzzle that exerts an unpleasant but painless pressure on the nose if the dog pulls impetuously on the leash. This is a good way to keep large, strong male dogs under control. The halter

△

Just what it wants. Some dogs like their wicker basket; some prefer a cushy dog bed or an inflatable puppy cushion (photo). In any case the bed must be large enough for the dog to stretch out properly.

▷ **Chest Harness.** A chest harness is a good choice for breeds that have a very tough neck, or like the Chow Chow, which have problems with a normal collar because of the volume of their fur. Chest harnesses are not a good choice for dogs that pull hard. Harnesses that sled dogs use for racing or that Bernese Mountain Dogs use for pulling their milk wagons are special cases.

You should buy a collar that matches the breed and disposition of your dog only after it has reached full size. With puppies and growing dogs you can get by with simple accessories. The dog should wear a registration tag and a tag with the name, address, and phone number of its owner.

Safety on the Leash Is Important

The leash is the dog owner's long arm. It controls the dog's movements and restricts its movement in places where it is not allowed to go. Modern leashes made of leather, metal, or nylon show no signs of wear even after yearlong use. Large, strong dogs need a thick leash of strong leather or a chain leash. Nylon sheds dirt better than leather and can also be washed. A spring clip assures a secure connection between leash and collar. Make sure that the clip doesn't open too easily or unexpectedly; that can't happen with models that have an additional safety catch. A retractable leash provides more exercise for dogs that frequently or always are on a leash. It provides from about 12 to 20 feet (4–8 m) of leash length. It has a stop button, and it rewinds automatically. The fairly large and cumbersome case for the coil is a disadvantage. It takes longer to hold a dog back with a retractable leash than with a normal one, so it is not as useful for quickly changing situations in a city. Retractable leashes are available in various sizes and models.

A dog should always wear its collar, and the leash should always go along on every walk, even with very obedient animals. The dog should be kept on the leash in areas where

was developed by the English animal behavior researcher Dr. Roger Mugford under the name of Halti. Today it is available in stores.

▷ **Spike Collar.** Spike collars and highlanders (leather chokers with spikes on the inside) are for professionals and should be used only in exceptional cases and for limited times with dogs that are difficult to train. Many dog trainers refuse to use these training aids. The same is true for electronic collars that dispense an electric shock as punishment.

▷ **Gentle Dog.** This is a collar with two straps that pass under the dog's shoulders. Every tug tightens the straps and causes chafing. This is unsuited to general use.

there are wild animals, around children's playgrounds, and in public places and parks, depending on local regulations. Some places require that fighting dogs always be kept on a leash (◐ LEASH LAWS, p.34).

Brush, Comb, and Currycomb

Proper coat care is a pleasure for the dog (→ starting on p.192), which enjoys it like petting. For short- and smooth-haired breeds, brushes with natural bristles (or, as an alternatively, a bristle glove) and soft rubber brushes (or rubber gloves) are basic equipment. With long-haired dogs, depending on coat structure, combs with coarse and fine teeth, a wire brush with rounded edges, and a currycomb for removing tangles in case you can't free them by hand. Some breeds, such as terriers (→ Breed Portraits, p.42 on) need to be trimmed (◐ TRIMMING, p.274) or shorn. Look over the shoulder of the professionals in a dog-grooming salon to learn the technique and steps to follow. If you want to do it yourself you will need some special accessories. A dog stylist will gladly advise you.

Sturdy, Bite-proof Toys

Puppies develop normally only when they are allowed to play. But play and activity are important for adult dogs, too, to keep them fit in body and mind (→ p.228 on). Dog toys come in all imaginable styles, sizes, shapes, and materials. Favorite classics include rubber balls, squeak toys, tossing rings, and fetching sticks. A good toy has no sharp edges, doesn't splinter, is not toxic, and is durable and bite-proof. With squeak toys made of soft plastic, which don't stand up to teeth for very long, the squeaker can hurt the dog. Balls must be large enough so that they can't be swallowed. Chew bones and rawhide both keep a dog busy for a long time and are good for the teeth; puppies aren't the only dogs that like them.

Practical Tips for Every Day

▷ **Cleaning Cloths and Towels.** Your dog wants to go outside in all kinds of weather. A walk in the rain, ice, and snow leaves its mark on the fur. Keep a couple of cleaning cloths and towels especially for the dog. In the warmest weather the garden hose will serve well, but spray only the legs and belly.

▷ **Cleaning Station.** Before the dog goes back into the house after a walk, it is cleaned off outdoors. An even better option is a sheltered location in the basement or the hallway that can be easily cleaned (tiles, cement, rubber mats).

▷ **Warm-up Area.** A dog that has just had a bath or been drenched by rain is still damp even after vigorous toweling. To keep it from catching cold, it needs a place to warm up and dry off that is free of draft and preferably near a heat source in the cold weather.

▷ **Nonslip Mat.** A dog doesn't belong in the bathtub often, but sometimes it's appropriate, for example, when it has rolled in some filth or its fur is covered with tar. A dog's paws find no foothold on a slippery tub surface, and that makes the unpleasant procedure even less agreeable to the dog. A nonslip mat lets the dog stand securely.

◁

Everything under control. Security comes first with a collar and leash. They both must be of strong material, especially for large, powerful dogs. A sturdy spring clip, preferably with an additional safety catch, assures a solid connection.

▷ **Everything in the Right Place.** Everything that your dog needs—care accessories, first-aid kit, Vaseline, flea powder, tick tweezers, towels, another leash, and a second collar—should be kept in one place. A small chest or a box is best; that way no one has to hunt for very long to find what's needed. As the items are used up they should be replaced or refilled. Also include a note card with the veterinarian's address and phone number, just in case.

Does Your House Match the Dog's Personality?

Dogs place specific demands on their accommodations and care. The dog's home must contain everything that a dog needs for daily living (→ Comfort and Living Space, p.91). Depending on bloodlines and breed, dogs exhibit clear differences in temperament, behavior, and activity. It usually doesn't take much expense to address the dog's individual type and personality, and provide for its particular needs.

▷ **Giants and Dwarfs.** The dog's size is an important criterion for its living conditions, but it's not the only one. Other important considerations include liveliness, need for exercise, and playfulness.

▷ **Pussyfooters and Activists.** In addition to dogs with a fairly steady disposition (Scottish Terrier, Irish Wolfhound, Chow Chow, Basset Hounds), there are normally active types (Dachshund, Kromfohrlander, Schnauzer, and German Mastiff) and hyperactive devils (Boxer, Border Collie, and many terriers such as the Yorkshire, Jack Russell Terrier, and Fox Terrier).

A worthy and reserved Basset Hound feels fine even in a fairly small house as long as it can sometimes withdraw to a quiet corner. A Jack Russell Terrier, on the other hand, is a demanding houseguest and insists on regular entertainment. Only if the house or apartment is roomy enough is it possible to keep such activists, no matter how you love them, off your back and busy in another room.

▷ **Woods Runners and Couch Canines.** Breeds that need lots of exercise (Afghan Hound, Siberian Husky, Dalmatian, Collie) are generally unsuited for average-size apartments). They should at least have a house with a yard. But that's not entirely true—a Dalmatian needs to be active preferably for several hours every day to satisfy its hereditary love of running. As long as this dog and other long-distance and woods runners get their daily ration of exercise, they are reserved, affectionate, and nearly invisible in the house. Couch canines, even lively ones such as Chihuahuas,

Mischievous bunch. The three curious Papillon puppies see no problem at all in turning the whole house topsy-turvy.
▽

Malteses, French Bulldogs, and Pugs, are more likely to whine and become nervous, simply because, for lack of opportunity, they are rarely as tired as an Afghan Hound after two hours of intense training.

▷ **Watchdogs and Social Lions.** Many dogs have a very strong watchdog and protective instinct. To avoid unpleasant encounters, visitors shouldn't come unannounced into a house that is guarded by a Briard, Hovawart, Doberman Pinscher, or Rottweiler.

Noisy watchdogs such as Miniature Schnauzers, Affenpinschers, or Miniature Pinschers that bark at everyone they see through a window or hear in the stairwell often disturb the neighborly peace in houses where there are lots of residents.

There is no problem with the calm breeds that greet even strangers (Golden Retrievers, Cocker Spaniels, Cavalier King Charles Spaniels, and Beagles).

▷ **Players and Men of Honor.** A Boxer lives to play and will play for its whole life. You should make plenty of room for play and activity for this and other playful dogs such as the Little Lion Dog, Tibetan Spaniel, Boston Terrier, Bobtail, and West Highland White Terrier, especially when there are children in the house to romp with.

Dogs that are more reserved by nature and take life more seriously (Kuvasz, Rottweiler, Chow Chow, Dandie Dinmont Terrier, and Pekingese) are less demanding in this regard.

▷ **Cool Characters and Hot Hounds.** Most dogs feel better in cool temperatures rather than warm, both inside and outside. Room temperatures over 70°F (21°C) are not a great climate for them. Especially breeds with thick fur (Bernese Mountain Dog, Newfoundland, PON) need a cool resting spot in the house.

But dogs still have to be protected from the cold of the floor. Tiles are not an appropriate place for a dog to lie on. That doesn't apply to fresh air fanatics and outdoors freaks such as the Hovawart, Siberian Husky, and Saint Bernard; they are happy to stay outdoors even

in ice and snow. A securely fenced-in piece of yard is just right for them.

But even among the breeds with thin coats there are few dogs that are cold by nature. Even Miniature Pinschers and freshly trimmed Bedlington Terriers cope well with the cold as long as they are active. Boston Terriers, Chihuahuas, and the Xoloitzcuintle—the Mexican Hairless—like things warmer.

Homework for Job Seekers

A dog that in an earlier life was active as a watchdog or a sheepherder still is on the look-

▶ **TEST**

How Much Freedom Does Your Dog Have in the House?

A dog moves into the house. Your living space and life's rhythm change—you decide how much.

	Yes	No
1. Can the dog go anywhere it wants to in the house?	○	○
2. Can it climb up on the sofa to cuddle with you?	○	○
3. Is it allowed into your bedroom if it becomes sick?	○	○
4. Is it always present, even when guests are in the house?	○	○
5. Is it allowed to visit you at your desk from time to time?	○	○
6. Is it OK if it has to go out during the night?	○	○

Key: Six *Yeses* is great. You have a big heart for your dog. It knows that and shows you its gratefulness and devotion. For every *No* answer, think about how important it really is to you.

2

out for employment when it lives as a family dog.

A Hovawart, Fox Terrier, Bouvier des Flandres, Spitz, Pinscher, or Shepherd takes pleasure in any kind of little job and service, from fetching the newspaper to watching over the master's old sweater.

And you can kill several birds with one stone. That task is perfect fitness training for mind and body; the dog is proud to do it and be praised for a job well done, and the owner is not continually annoyed by an unchallenged or a totally bored animal.

The tasks make sense especially if the dog has to stay alone in the house. If we give the dog some object to guard, it usually doesn't have time to get any dumb ideas into its head (→ Games to Combat Boredom, p.234).

How Puppies Want to Live

A puppy comes to live at your house at the age of 10 to 12 weeks (→ p.105). Here are some important elements that will help the little fellow feel at home in the strange, new world:

▷ **Sleeping Place.** Puppies don't need luxury beds and expensive wicker baskets; a cardboard carton and a wooden box work fine. The bed has to be soft and warm, as young dogs need more warmth than adult dogs.

A good choice is a small "cave," such as a closed moving box with an opening cut into the side. The puppy will feel especially secure inside the cave.

The sleeping place should be in a quiet, draft-free corner where the dog can lie undisturbed, but can also watch everything that's going on around it.

The newcomer feels especially abandoned during the night. For the first few nights you can put the sleeping box next to your bed to reassure the dog if it whines or howls. As soon as it has gotten over the initial excitement, it can be moved back outside the bedroom.

▷ **Potty Place.** After every meal or whenever the dog searches for a place to do its business,

it should be brought to the door. At night you can put down newspapers or install a cat's litter box. This is just an aid at the beginning.

If the dog attracts attention during the night, you should go to the door with it as soon as possible to help it become housetrained quickly.

▷ **Food and Water Dishes.** Food and water are provided only in the dishes. From the first day on, the dishes have a fixed place in the house, preferably in the kitchen.

A puppy's food and water must be kept clean; therefore, if your kitchen is the scene of a lot of activity, check frequently to see that the puppy's food and water bowls don't become soiled. It's best to keep them in a part of the kitchen that's away from the normal traffic pattern in the room. Also, make sure that insects don't get into the food and water bowls.

Puppies can become ill very easily, so food and water cleanliness should be a major consideration in the household.

▷ **Child-proofing.** Young dogs are curious and want to discover the world. Block off staircases, patio doors, terraces, and balconies with protective gates so that the puppy doesn't go astray or get hurt.

Another reason for "child-proofing" your house when you bring a puppy into it is that a puppy can cause injury (unintentionally) or damage (intentionally). A puppy, of course, can't be nearly as destructive as an adult dog, but that certainly doesn't mean that it can't cause any problems. A puppy can nip a person or could cause a nasty fall by getting underfoot. And a puppy's curiosity can result in a lot of property being ruined: documents or items being chewed up beyond salvage, furniture scratched or banged up, houseplants overturned, and so on.

▷

An adventure playground. Puppies like to run an discover the world. Child barriers in the house prote it from major and minor injurie

Equipment and Accessories

With the right equipment and appropriate accessories, your life and the dog's become better and easier. Products such as the following are available in pet shops and over the Internet (→ Addresses, p.285).

Sleeping

▷ Oval dog basket made from peeled, varnished wicker, 24 × 18 inches to 43 × 34 inches (60 × 46 to 110 × 85 cm)
▷ Synthetic bed with insulated cushions, hygienic, and easy to clean, in assorted sizes up to 39 × 28 inches (100 × 70 cm)
▷ High-quality dog bed with a sleeping blanket, size 24 × 39 inches and 31 × 47 inches (60 × 100 cm and 80 × 120 cm)
▷ A cozy bed with a soft inner lining and a wide rim, sizes 24 and 31 inches (60 and 80 cm)
▷ Dog blanket, washable at up to 200°F (95°C), in sizes from 20 × 28 inches to 39 × 55 inches (50 × 70 to 100 × 140 cm)
▷ An easy-to-care-for insulated blanket with a special nonslip coating, in various sizes from 20 × 15 inches to 39 × 59 inches (50 × 38 to 100 × 150 cm)
▷ A fur bed with a plush lining, in sizes up to 39 inches (100 cm)

Eating

▷ High-quality steel bowl with a rubber ring, heavy construction, nonskid; the rubber ring can be removed for washing; 1/2- to 3-quart capacity (0.45–2.8 l)
▷ Feeding station: Metal stands adjustable for height with two high-quality steel dishes, available in heights of 16, 20, and 24 inches (40, 50, and 60 cm)
▷ Dish for long-eared dogs: a nonskid steel bowl with a rubber ring for breeds with drop ears
▷ Plastic mat of rugged quality with rubber feet, in various colors
▷ Transparent nonskid underlay for dog bowls, 17 × 21 inches (42 × 54.5 cm).
▷ Leak-proof water dish for use at home and on the move, 2-quart (1.8 l) capacity

Walking

▷ Nylon lead line, strong and adjustable, in various colors; length, 78 inches (200 cm), width, 1/2- to 1 inch (1-2 cm)
▷ Multifunction leash; length 83 inches (210 cm), in widths from 1/2- to 1 inch
▷ Double-clip leash for walking two dogs on one leash, with a clip ring for all leashes; size 1 × 30 inches (2 × 75 cm)
▷ Reflective leash: adjustable nylon leash with reflective stripes, 1 inch wide, 78 inches long (2 × 200 cm)
▷ Agility leash in red or black, 59 inches long and 1/2 inch wide (150 × 1 cm)
▷ Retractable leash: automatic roll-up leash up to 15 feet (5 m) long. Small for dogs up to 24 pounds (11 kg), large for dogs up to 88 pounds (40 kg)
▷ Flexi-leash: a strong roll-up leash in three colors for large dogs up to 110 pounds (50 kg)
▷ Leather lead line made of strong, supple belt leather, hand-stitched in cognac or black colors, 78 inches (200 cm) long
▷ Leather collar: standard collar made from full-grain leather lined with soft leather for different-size necks
▷ Appenzeller: a classic collar with cow designs in black or beige
▷ Safety reflective collar in two widths and four lengths, yellow
▷ Master Control: No-pull halter, force-free training aid in various sizes; doesn't block the dog's snout
▷ Trekking harness made of strong nylon, in several colors, several sizes for chest measurement of 12 to 37 inches (30–95 cm)
▷ Blinking collar with light diode for greater safety in the dark
▷ Nylon muzzle, smooth and adjustable
▷ Plastic address tag, durable and waterproof; belongs on every collar
▷ Spring attachment for bicycles; used with all dogs and leashes

The Dog Arrives

Set aside at least a whole day for picking up your dog and make an appointment with the breeder or seller for early morning. If you have to travel a long distance, it's a good idea to spend the night in the area. In any case you should plan the return trip so that you arrive home during the day. Then the dog will have at least a little time to explore the new dwelling before spending its first night.

Have You Thought of Everything?

Before the pick-up date check to see if everything has been talked over and made ready:

▷ The breeder, seller, or personnel at the animal shelter have confirmed the pick-up time.

▷ The dog is healthy. You need to be informed of any unforeseen developments, such as the dog suddenly coming down with diarrhea.

▷ Your veterinarian is on standby.

▷ The dog bed and food and water dishes are in their proper places, and a collar and leash are on hand. The puppy's room is at least room temperature.

▷ You have seen to it that at least on the first day other house pets are kept far away from the new family member.

▷ You have put off visits by friends and guests to a later time.

▷ The car is ready for the drive with the dog, and your companion knows how to handle a dog.

▷ You know the shortest or quickest route and know where you can take a break if the trip is a long one. You have reserved a room if it's necessary to spend the night.

A Small Dog on a Long Journey

Usually a puppy from a breeder is the first four-legged creature in the dog lover's life. The separation from the world of its childhood is a deeply painful experience for the young dog. Here's how to make the separation from the mother, littermates, and the familiar family of the breeder a little easier:

Play with the puppy until it becomes tired so that it sleeps through the separation and maybe even part of the journey. Before leaving, give it only half its usual food. The breeder may give you some puppy food that you can offer during the trip, but only little bits. Usually, the excitement affects the puppy's tummy and it won't want to eat anything. A favorite toy or the blanket with the smell of home will give the pup a little security. Your helper can take care of the pup in the backseat, talk to it, pet it, and hold it in his or her lap. Remember that at this age dogs are not leak-proof. A sheet of plastic under the travel blanket makes a good moisture barrier. If you have to travel any distance, even the unfamiliar motion of the car can have an effect on the puppy's stomach. A little water and a paper towel will eliminate the small accident. Take a break after no more than two hours—earlier if you need to and the weather is hot. The puppy must be allowed to drink and have a little food. Roll the windows down; the fresh air is good for the dog. During the drive the windows should remain closed and the fan should be kept on low to reduce drafts. Air conditioning is ideal for the summer.

Picking Up an Adult Dog

You have visited the dog numerous times before picking it up; you have fed it, and have taken it for walks. Maybe it has already taken you into its heart. Now take the dog for a walk or play ball with it to tire it out some; that will make the departure more manageable. The dog shouldn't be fed before then or during the trip, but of course it can be given water at every stop.

Dogs are excellent observers and they register the smallest changes in our behavior. Your new friend will quickly catch on that things

2

1 Curiosity wins out. Young dogs are interested in everything and everybody. Simple training exercises will teach them what's permitted and what's forbidden.

2 My bowl, your bowl, every dog has its own bowl right from the start. If they covet one another's food, feed them in separate rooms.

3 Puppy bed. Of course the puppy has its own resting place. You can wait until it's grown before getting the top of the line, though.

are now a little different than previously. Still, the separation should go fairly casually; big departure scenes would only make the dog suspicious.

Your car has to be prepared for the trip. All rules for safe driving with a dog apply here, and especially because you don't know how the dog will react. With a puppy you should be accompanied by a second person. The best arrangement is a station wagon or van with a dog compartment in the rear separated from the passenger area by a net or a grate. In a standard sedan the dog goes into the backseat. The dog needs to be held on a leash. A special seat belt gives the dog some mobility but also reliably protects the passengers and the dog from injury in case of abrupt braking or an accident. The passenger seat and the floor space in front of it are inappropriate places for the dog. On stops, clip the leash onto the dog before opening the car door.

Alternatives to Picking Up the Dog Yourself

If you don't have a car, or if you don't think that it's appropriate for driving the dog home, ask the seller to deliver the dog. The advantages are that the seller knows what to do when transporting a dog by car, and a grown dog usually feels at ease in a car. This is a possibility even with animal shelters. It doesn't cost anything to ask, but delivery may be an extra expense.

It's not very practical to bring a puppy home by train as the dog would have to stay in a travel cage for the whole trip. The train might work for an older dog, as long as it is accustomed to riding on a train and obeys voice commands.

Forget the Red Carpet Treatment

The trip was strenuous. The puppy is confused and anxious; it feels lonely and abandoned. The grown dog, depending on its temperament, appears restless or nervous, and even withdrawn. Both now have a need for a little time off to collect their strength and get used to the new surroundings. Despite the understandable enthusiasm and curiosity, you should do without a welcoming committee. The strange voices and faces would make the dog feel even less secure.

A Little Food and Lots of Sleep

On the day it moves in the puppy should have a room set aside where it won't be disturbed. The room contains the puppy's bed and food and water dishes. The little dog will feel especially secure in a sleeping "cave" that's hard to see into from the outside. Of course the favorite toy and the familiar blanket move in with the dog. Bring the dog outside to do its business before it takes a nap after drinking some water or eating. From that time on the dog is taken out after every meal. To play it safe in emergency situations, spread out some newspapers near the sleeping area.

 TIP

Ticktock Therapy

This trick is not new, but it works: Put a ticking alarm clock under the blanket in the puppy's bed. The regular ticking has a visibly calming effect on the little fellow. Fortunately, you can still get a traditional alarm clock even in these days of digital timepieces.

An Inspection Tour of the New Territory

In contrast to a puppy, an adult dog won't simply lie down to sleep in the unfamiliar environment. It will want to try it out more, inspect the whole house, and register attentively every sound in the house or the street. It will calm down more quickly if you take it on a tour of the premises. Show it every room

and give it time to sniff around. That won't work, however, if there is already another dog in the house. A male dog will mark to cover up the scent of its colleague. To find out what to do in such instances, turn to page 118. If there is a yard with the house, inspect that too. Then you can finally feed the dog, and human and dog can take a first short walk to loosen up their legs after the trip. Your dog will want to stick its nose into everything and find out all about the local dog scene. As a corollary it will also search for a couple of appropriate places to do its business. The dog must be kept on a leash at this point.

The First Night

▷ **Puppies.** You shouldn't leave the little dog alone during the first night. It should be allowed to sleep next to your bed. A padded basket is its sleeping place (but a cardboard box also works) with sides high enough to keep it from clambering out. Place the basket or box in a place where you can soothe the dog and pet it from bed if it whines in the night (→ Tip, left).

You won't sleep through the night very often in the first days. A puppy can't hold its business until morning. As soon as it becomes restless, you should bring it outdoors, even if it sometimes turns out to be a false alarm. That way the little one quickly understands that it has to announce its needs, and then it won't take long for it to become house-trained.

If you want your bedroom to be off-limits right from the start, you have to put the puppy where it will feel as secure as possible during the night and can let loose if it has to. The best places are the kitchen or the bathroom. The accessories for the night include the dog's bed or pad, the water dish, and the newspapers for the dog's business. Basket, box, or sleeping area have to be set up so that the dog can climb out without outside help. A cat's litter box may take the place of newspapers. You will get over the fact that many puppies consider themselves to be moles and spread the litter all over the room. And if the puppy also does its business on the bathroom floor, it's not the end of the world, as that's an easy surface to clean up. Of course, during the first couple of nights you should keep an ear open in case something is going on inside the bathroom. You needn't jump out of bed every time you hear a peep; otherwise the little fellow will figure out how to keep you on a short leash.

▷ **Adult Dog.** A lot depends on how it is used to spending the night. Dogs are creatures of habit: If the previous owner has given you the dog's bed or cushion, you're halfway there. The favorite ball and familiar blanket are also helpful. Still, in the first nights your new friend may wander around in the room. Fresh water should be available, and since the dog was outside before going to bed, it shouldn't have to do its business during the night. Things aren't so easy when it comes to doing without old privileges such as sleeping in the bed. The only help here may be special behavior therapy (→ p.162 on).

Operation "Safe House"

After the first long night your dog will want to get to know its new home better. Here's how to be sure that neither the dog nor the furnishings come to any harm:

▷ A puppy can be allowed to roam free in the house only under supervision. Gnawing is part of a puppy's stock in trade; books, newspapers, shoes, exposed electric cords, and all foods must be kept out of reach.

▷ A curious puppy likes to try out its teeth on green plants. That not only looks unattractive, but it can also be very dangerous, as many plants are poisonous (→ Poisonous Plants, p.270).

▷ Medicines and all the chemical products such as cleaners, paint removers, furniture polish, and insecticides have to be kept under lock and key (→ Poisonous Substances, p.270).

▷ Small objects may be swallowed quickly.

The dog's life may be endangered by plastic lids, bottle caps, rubber rings, Ping-Pong balls, and pointed or unwieldy objects such as thumbtacks, staples, bolts, and nails.

▷ Gates and grates can be used to secure stairs, steps, landings, terrace- and balcony doors.

▷ Large dogs with a long, powerful tail can knock glasses, vases, table lamps, and other breakable objects from shelves, cabinets, and tables.

▷ Birdcages, terrariums, aquariums, and small animal cages must be out of reach. This also applies to a cat's food dish and litter box.

The Yard Is Part of the Territory

At first the dog is allowed to be free in the yard only under supervision. The yard should be fenced, and the door must be lockable. That will keep your dog from getting out and other dogs from getting in. If the puppy hasn't yet had all its shots (→ Shot Schedule, p.203), it should not be allowed into contact with strange dogs. Be sure that the yard is free of manure and pesticides. Remove poisonous plants (→ Poisoning, p.217), or make sure that the dog can't chew them (by using sprays or wire mesh).

The Ground Rules for Getting Acquainted

The dog will find it difficult to cope with the many new stimuli and experiences. That's especially true of puppies, but also for grown dogs. It continually meets new people, people with unfamiliar faces, strange voices, and strange smells. To keep from confusing the dog completely, everyone should observe the following basic rules of acquaintanceship:

▷ **Establishing contact:** The dog must be awake; in no case should you disturb it while it's sleeping.

▷ **Take time:** The dog needs it to imprint the scent, voice, face, and movements of its new acquaintance. Hold out your hand for it to sniff.

▷ **Remain calm:** Speak softly to the dog and

avoid animated gestures. This applies especially to children.

▷ **Respect:** Don't pet the dog if it acts shy or withdrawn.

▷ **Show Your Size:** A grown dog must look up to you. Don't sit down, and don't kneel before it.

The New Daily Schedule

A dog fits into our life's rhythm and habits quite well because it is a pack animal. Still, the new family member is sure to change our daily schedule. This is particularly true during puppyhood when the young dog will upset lots of scheduling, especially in the first six weeks. Somebody always needs to be near it to watch over it, take care of it, and keep it occupied. Everybody in the family should play the role of puppy-sitter; single working people should count on taking a fairly lengthy vacation to be with the dog. Theoretically it should be possible to get an experienced dog-sitter to come to the house. However, that makes no sense, since this precise phase in the puppy's life, the so-called hierarchical phase between the thirteenth and sixteenth week of life, is when the pecking order within the pack is established. That's when it's determined if the young dog will recognize the authority of its new owner.

Even the small breeds prove that dogs are runners. A dog has to go out for a walk at least three times a day: once briefly in the morning to do its business, a longer walk at midday (or in the evening hours if it's very hot out), and in the evening, depending on the desire and the mood of the dog and master, and on the weather. There's another trip outdoors for relief before heading to bed.

⊙ WHAT TO DO IF...

... the puppy doesn't want to fit in?

Even after seven weeks the puppy nips everybody in the calves, gets on the family's nerves with its constant begging, and often howls through half the night.

Cause: Regrettably, such puppies are fairly common. What they need is firm training from the very beginning. First-time dog owners, in particular, let a young rowdy get away with nearly everything "because he just wants to play." This is more than just play for the puppy; it is testing to see what is permitted and what isn't, and where its place is in the pack.

Solution: If you don't deal with problem behavior when it begins, you will later have to contend with a dog that takes liberties that make life together difficult or even impossible. Stop undesirable behavior right from the first day. Punishment will have no effect. Here's the best way: Steer the dog in a different direction and encourage desirable behavior. The calf-biter is given its favorite toy or a chew bone every time it attacks; the beggar gets fed only in its dish, and before the family takes their meals; the nighttime spirit gets an old sweater in its basket that still has the master's scent, and the master doesn't jump up every time the dog starts to whimper. Improvement can also come from puppy school, where the untrained blockhead can quickly learn some manners.

△
Traveling together: The anxiety over strangers is only half as great when there are two of them. The puppies still have to learn that the leash is not a toy.

Breeds that really love to run (see Breed Portraits starting on p.42) count on daily walks of two hours and more. Feeding, coat care, and playtime require further time investment. For a dog with an average need for exercise and a coat that's not too demanding, figure on about three to four hours per day.

Feeding According to Plan

A small dog has a small stomach. Before the twelfth week of life a puppy's daily ration is divided into four feedings; after that, up to the seventh month of life, into three feedings; and thereafter, into two. Drinking water must always be available. Young dogs are sensitive to a change of food. At least in the first few weeks, stick with the brand and mix of foods used by the breeder. An adult dog can be fed once or twice a day, depending on what it is used to. Its type of food should likewise not be changed from one day to the next.

Everything That's Important at This Time

▷ **Coat Care.** It's especially important for long-haired breeds to get used to the grooming procedure early on. The dog must remain still for brushing and combing, especially if it's on a platform or a table.
▷ **Health Check.** The daily inspection of eyes, ears, teeth, paws, fur, and skin is the best health measure. This has to become second nature even for puppies.
▷ **House-training.** A puppy should be successfully house-trained after about four

weeks. After every meal, bring it outdoors and praise it after it does its business. Newspapers in the corner and a kitty litter box are only emergency measures. If a dog digs too long in kitty litter, it will later prefer to do its business in soft ground, such as in your flowerbed. Lack of cleanliness in an older dog is a sign of protest (→ p.166).

▷ **Leash Test.** Get the puppy used to the collar in the earliest days. Once it accepts the collar, you can begin leash training, at first in the house. Make sure that the dog doesn't bite the leash or try to play with it.

▷ **Going for a Walk.** Set aside specific times right from the start, and let the dog occasionally sniff around in the unfamiliar surroundings. The puppy should get to know other dogs only when it has had all its shots.

▷ **Staying Alone.** A dog should be able to stay alone for a limited time, without grumbling and howling. As long as the puppy is trained early to stay alone, it will pose no problems for its whole life (→ p.155).

▷ **Off-limits.** You also have to be able to say *No*. Remain firm if you don't want the dog on the sofa or in the bed.

▷ **Playing and Keeping Busy.** The playtime with the human is the highlight of the day for both young and old dogs. The human is the only one who sets the rules for play. When things get too wild it's time to stop.

▷ **Riding in a Car.** Your dog should like to go for rides. Before taking the dog for its first ride, sit with it in the parked car so that it accepts the car as part of its home territory.

▷ **Appointment with the Veterinarian.** As soon as possible after the dog moves in, introduce it to the veterinarian for a checkup; puppies may still need some shots.

▷ **The Hotline to the Breeder.** After you buy your dog, the breeder is still available for advice and support. Don't hesitate to call the breeder if you have any problems or need tips on how to deal with the dog on a daily basis.

▷ **Puppy School.** It's particularly easy for a puppy to learn how to behave by playing with other dogs of about the same age. Sign it up early for puppy school (→ p.160). At the start of the course the dog should not be older than eighteen weeks, and should have all of its shots.

Dog Registration

In most towns dog ownership has to be reported to the authorities within a month. Registration is commonly good for a year. Shots have to be up to date, and the owner pays a fee and is given a tag for the dog's collar. It's generally cheaper to register neutered animals.

 TIP

A Predictable Schedule for Canine Happiness

Even when it's not always easy to do so, stick to regular times for feeding, going for walks, and playing with your dog. Dogs are creatures of habit, and they quickly get the daily schedule into their heads. That makes the anticipation particularly keen, and at other times, the dog won't annoy the owner.

Even if you don't have to register your dog, notifying the local authorities of its existence is always a smart idea. If your dog ever gets loose and is picked up by the area's "dog catcher," it will end up in a shelter. If the local authorities have a means of identifying it, you'll be able to recover your dog in a short time. On the other hand, if the authorities have no means of identifying your dog, the chances that you'll ever see it again are much slimmer. You'll have to conduct the search on your own, calling around to local shelters, putting up posters, asking friends and neighbors to keep their eyes open, and so forth. Because your dog is a valued member of your family, it's definitely worth whatever time and expense it takes to register it with the local authorities.

Children and Dogs

A lifelong partnership: Anyone who has gone through thick and thin with a dog as a child will always retain the memory of that friend's closeness and faithfulness. Other images may fade, but never the one of your youth's companion. Dogs give children strength and confidence and teach them to take on responsibility. Dogs make children happy.

Why Children Need Dogs

Laughing and crying when you feel like it, dealing with things on a visceral level, and allowing closeness—these are not natural behaviors in the adult world, where the head controls communication. But that's the way children act, and they show their feelings unexpectedly. That's how they automatically connect with a dog.

Dogs have a feeling for moods that's as sensitive as a seismograph. A dog participates in them, shares joy and enthusiasm, consoles in times of sadness and dejection. It gives us strength in anger and fear and keeps the deepest secrets and listens patiently if we ever have to unburden our souls.

Children and dogs form a devoted partnership, from which even friends and parents are often excluded. Dogs are quick to establish contact and help introverted and timid children out of their isolation. Of course, dogs are wonderful playmates and the best remedy for rainy, boring days, and especially, they automatically welcome children into their care.

Children have to take care of their four-legged comrade, and gradually they take on increasing responsibility. The proof doesn't need to be drawn out any further: people who share childhood with a dog generally develop a social consciousness as an adult and get involved more frequently in social matters than other people do.

Is There an Ideal Dog for Children?

Most dogs can tolerate a major screw loose and find inappropriate behavior in children a good deal less offensive than they do in adults. Still, even the most patient dog is no plaything that can be pushed back and forth and set into a corner. A good dog for children is identified by an active and happy nature, a high threshold of tolerance, a heightened receptiveness to communication, and intelligence. However, it also makes it very clear what it expects from the partner, and when limits have been exceeded.

Not every dog is appropriate for children. Depending on character and disposition, individual breeds come with different requirements. But a dog's origins and individual experiences also play a defining role; a dog that has grown up with children and experienced love and affection from them will imprint these experiences for life, even if it's from a breed that is not considered particularly fold of children.

The Best Dogs for Children

Smaller breeds generally are more strong-willed and troublesome with children than larger breeds are. But there are exceptions here, too. Here are the breeds that are considered particularly friendly with children (→ Breed Portraits starting on page 42):

▷ **Beagle.** Loves the whole world; is always happy and ready to play

▷ **Bearded Collie.** Composed; a true buddy for all of life's situations

▷ **Bernese Mountain Dog.** A good-natured and reliable companion and defender

▷ **Bobtail.** Lively, smart, and playful; the first to take part in every adventure

▷ **Boxer.** It loves wild play; the right partner for older children

▷ **Eurasier.** With this dog children are safe and secure

▷ **Golden Retriever.** A real pal that would go through fire for its friends

▷ **Newfoundland.** A patient listener; a lovable soul mate, and a reliable defender

▷ **Poodle.** The best partner for sport and play; it knows everything and everyone

▷ **Westie.** A Westie takes part in everything. Lively, self assured, and always on the ball

Less Appropriate Breeds for Children

These dogs prefer to keep their distance from children. They find them too loud, frantic, and stressful.

▷ **Chihuahua.** Loveable and lively, but would rather be alone with its owner

▷ **Chow Chow.** A loner for whom not much except the owner counts for much in the world

▷ **Lhasa Apso.** It has no desire to become a toy. It may accept older children

▷ **Pekingese.** Has its own mind and often reacts quite jealously

Assuming Responsibility

Children are spontaneous: whatever interested them yesterday is not so important today, for there are lots of new and exciting things to discover.

That also carries over into duties. A child may be pleased as punch to take over feeding the dog, and keep up the difficult task reliably for almost a week. But sooner or later, a soccer game with friends or a get-together at the swimming pool gets in the way. And the food dish remains empty...

At around the age of ten a child's personality is sufficiently established so that we can hand over the care of a house pet. Still, it's a good idea to make children familiar with the demands and requirements of a dog as early as possible.

Things work great when the children can help their parents or older siblings with the care, and develop a sense of responsibility for the four-legged friend. Here's the bottom line: The dog must never get short-changed.

△

The start of a wonderful new friendship. All children like dogs, and almost all dogs like children. However, children should take over caring for a dog on their own no sooner than age ten.

How to Treat a Good Friend

Here are the most important rules of behavior that children should observe around dogs:

▷ Never disturb a dog when it's eating or sleeping.

▷ Don't pull the tail or fur; don't touch the eyes, or hit the dog in the face. A dog's nose is particularly sensitive.

▷ Always approach a dog from the front to avoid frightening it. Even a peaceful animal may snap as a defense reflex.

▷ Avoid frantic movements and loud, shrill tones.

▷ Small children should not pick up a dog. There is a serious risk of injury if the dog is not held properly, twists around, and thrashes. It can also be injured if it falls.

▷ Above all, avoid running, or running away, in the presence of strange dogs. Even dogs without a strong hunting instinct will pursue under such circumstances.

▷ Approach and hold or pet strange dogs only in the presence of adults, and never without permission.

▷ Never kneel, lie, or sit down in front of a dog. Smaller people are not taken seriously by a dog.

Things Parents Need to Watch Out For

A dog is a great pal and playmate. Sometimes children forget that it must be treated differently from their human friends. Problems and misunderstandings can be avoided if parents make the boundaries between humans and animals clear right from infancy.

▷ Dogs don't get kisses. Explain to your children why a dog mustn't be allowed to lick them on the face.

▷ Wash hands after playing with the dog, and especially before a meal.

▷ Little children like to sample things from the dog's dish. They must learn that the dog's food dish is just as taboo as their dish is for the dog.

▷ Never take food, chew bones, or a favorite toy away from a dog.

▷ Don't take the dog on a walk without adult accompaniment. Even obedient dogs get into situations on a walk where a child could no longer control them. This is especially true of two or more dogs.

There are Rules Even for Play

Dogs are ideal playmates (→ Chapter 5, p.228)—always on the spot, athletic, and full of enthusiasm. The following rules will make sure there are no injuries and keep the play from becoming too serious:

▷ Playtime only for dogs with basic obedience training, and that also obey children's commands (such as *Off!*)

▷ No disputes over the ball or Frisbee. Never try to take anything away from the dog. Here's a better idea: Get it interested in some other thing, then the dog will usually drop whatever it has.

▷ No fighting or tussling. In the excitement of a physical scrap, many dogs forget that it's only a game.

▷ If there are several dogs involved, an adult should supervise the play.

▷ Good play areas include the yard and fenced fields. Playing in streets and on railroad tracks, in parking lots, at the edge of the woods, and in the woods is dangerous.

▷ Keep a safe distance when swimming together in a brook or pond (watch out for rules against dogs' swimming!); it's easy to get hurt by the dog's claws as it paddles.

▷ Don't tax puppies and old dogs with strenuous play. Short, restrained play with frequent breaks is better.

▷ Schedule games and sports in the mornings and evenings during the hot months.

▷ The game is over when the four-legged player loses interest. The children are responsible for picking up the toys.

▷
Two that belong together: The Briard is a devoted friend to children and a constantly watchful defender. But children should never be left alone with a large dog without adult supervision.

Other Things You Need to Know

▷ **Health Risks from the Dog?** Some infectious diseases can be transmitted from dogs to people, and vice-versa. Children often have closer contact with the dog than grown-ups do, but even for them, the health risk is minimal if the dog gets its shots regularly and is wormed, and general hygienic measures are observed (washing hands, not letting the dog lap a person, etc.)

▷ **Dogs and Babies.** If you are expecting a baby, your dog should be examined by your veterinarian for possible pathogens. Shots and regular worming are essential.

A dog regards an infant as a new pack member and feels responsible for defending the baby.

In the early days and months the dog will need lots of attention so it doesn't feel pushed aside and react to the baby with jealousy. At first the dog should be allowed into the baby's room only under supervision.

△

Health risks from dogs? If your four-legged friend gets its regular shots and is wormed, and the basic rules for hygiene are observed, there's no need to fear infection.

▷ **Dogs as Therapists.** There often arises an especially strong bond between physically or mentally handicapped children and dogs. Dogs react very sensitively to people with disabilities; their cheerful nature, their closeness, and their empathy cheer children up and raise their sense of self-esteem.

▷ **Saying Good-bye.** When the old playmate ages and dies, the parents should explain to the children what happened to the dog and what death means. And they should allow them to say good-bye to their friend. Even for small children the pain and sadness over the beloved dog are a major experience.

Dogs and Other House Pets

A dog comes into the house. It has to adjust to the strange surroundings, become acquainted with new people, and often deal with other dogs or animals.

In many families the dog is not the first housepet. Small children usually start their love for animals with small friends such as guinea pigs, hamsters, or parakeets, and of course cats, those stubborn contenders for the hearts of children. The new house guests almost always get things sorted out quickly, and they often become fast friends—as long as the rules for getting used to living together are observed.

Free Rein for Puppies

Young dogs enjoy special privileges among their adult counterparts. Cats often react stubbornly and unpredictably to the clumsy new family member.

▷ **Puppies and Grown Dogs.** At eight or ten weeks of age the world is in order. There are thousands of exciting things to discover, and restraints are strange to the puppy; it boldly marches up even to the biggest male and invites it to play. Grown dogs put up with a lot more from puppies than from older dogs, endure it graciously when the troublemaker climbs up on it, and usually turn away when it becomes too annoying. Extremely pampered animals (often small dogs), dogs with behavior problems, and breeds that fixate on just one reference person are less easygoing.

▷ **Puppies and Cats.** For adult cats a puppy in the territory is a scandal. The intruder is kept at bay with arched back and spitting. In protest, many cats renounce house-training and manners.

Cats that stay indoors all the time react more than cats that are allowed outdoors. At first the latter may not come home for a couple of days. Female cats are much more unforgiving than males. It takes patience and sensitivity to calm the waves (→ Tips for Acclimatizing, p.119)

▷ **Puppies and Other House Pets.** Unexpected animal friendships are not entirely rare, but you should still keep the puppy away from dwarf bunnies, hamsters, mice, and similar animals. Even if the dog merely wants to play, its awkward behavior is dangerous for the small animals. The birdcage must remain out of the puppy's reach, and the aquarium covered.

Baby Animals Always Understand Each Other

No trace of animosity—puppies and kittens that grow up together get along fine with one another. Even possible language problems don't dampen the enthusiasm. The love often lasts a whole lifetime.

With puppies two females are one heart and one soul even after their early days, and the same applies to brother and sister. When males discover their masculinity, they test to see who has the stuff that bosses are made of. Once that's settled, they usually get along fine.

 TIP

Hunters Under Control

Dog breeds with a strong hunting instinct (such as the Irish Setter, Rhodesian Ridgeback, Jack Russell Terrier, Podenco Ibicenco) should be allowed with other house pets only under supervision. Even with skillful training their hereditary hunting and harrying instinct remains intact.

Demands and Documented Rights

▷ **Male and Male.** When a young male dog moves into a house where there is an older dog, it usually gives in right from the outset. The territorial boss has all the advantages on its side—a good foundation for peaceful coexistence or even friendship. An assertive young rowdy who thinks he's a new champion may also challenge the older dog, especially if he is already has lost his edge to old age. There are marked differences in the sociability of male dogs, depending on breed (→ p.120).

▷ **Male and Female.** Male dogs like to see themselves as cavaliers. If a female moves in with a male, she often willingly accepts him as the boss, and after initial standoffishness he will protect and defend her as the apple of his eye. On the other hand, if the female has the advantage of being the first, it's like the weather forecast: One simply doesn't know. A lot depends on the character, confidence, and backing by the family. If jealousy becomes a factor the antagonists may dig in their heels.

▷ **A New One for the Pack.** If two or more dogs already live under one roof, a newcomer rarely rebels. The masters of the house make it clear where its place is—right at the bottom, at first. If there is any change in the scene later on, it's no big deal. The dogs work that out among themselves.

▷ **Dog and Cat.** Cats become jealous over their home territory and rebel vehemently against intruders—both dogs and other cats. Things get particularly delicate when they believe the relationship with their favorite person is threatened.

A young cat that comes into a house with dogs causes fewer problems. If their protection instinct is awakened, many dogs take loving care of the little creature, except for breeds with a strong hunting instinct.

▷ **Small House Pets.** Small mammals such as hamsters and guinea pigs, birds, turtles, and terrarium animals must remain out of a dog's reach.

2

△
Motherly instinct. There can be no discussion of a hereditary animosity between cats and dogs but many cats even take puppies under their wing.

Tips for Acclimatizing

Whether someone moves in with you or is already there: Harmonious living is founded on understanding and loving attention. Here are some tips that will make adjustment easier:

▷ **Private Sphere.** Whether large or small, young or adult, every animal has a need for its own sleeping place and its own food dish. In the case of cats this also applies to litter boxes.

▷ **Toys.** The favorite ball belongs exclusively to the dog, and the fuzzy mouse to the cat. If this is not respected, there can be trouble.

▷ **Retreat.** Even good friends sometimes want to be alone. The house should be large enough so that a creature can get out of the way if it wishes. Cats commonly choose elevated resting places.

▷ **Siesta.** Older dogs and cats need lots of rest. They become disagreeable if a hyperactive puppy gets on their nerves.

No Chance for Jealousy

Jealousies are often the cause of enmity and conflict among house pets. Whether dog or cat, each one wants to be the family's favorite. If an animal sees its throne wobbling, it becomes contrary, rebellious, or even aggressive.

Such conflicts can be avoided. Make sure that petting and treats are doled out evenly. Many dogs become restless when a cat hops into the mistress's lap. Be prudent and do your cuddling out of sight in the next room.

Affection and attention are called for when a puppy comes into a house where there is an older animal—less for the youngster, and more for the older dog or cat. You don't have to watch out so much for the puppy; it will arrange to get signs of affection by itself.

If you spend a lot of time on the coat of a long-haired dog, its animal colleagues may misunderstand that as unjustified extra attention. Also explain to your children how to avoid scenes of jealousy.

Social Workers vs. Loners

Many dog breeds come naturally to sociability, but others pose problems in getting along with other dogs and other house pets. Here are some peace-loving, sociable breeds:

▷ **Golden Retriever:** Friendly with other dogs and other house pets
▷ **Australian Shepherd:** Sociable and patient; problem-free for humans and animals
▷ **Basset:** Confident, sometimes stubborn, but with a peaceable disposition regarding other animals
▷ **Beagle:** Lovable with other dogs, but also with a very strong hunting instinct
▷ **Cavalier King Charles Spaniel:** Playful and devoted; usually gets along fine with all other dog breeds
▷ **English Foxhound:** Lively and lovable; never aggressive to other dogs

Here are some breeds that are not as well suited to living with other animals:

▷ **Bull Terrier:** Very friendly toward its family, but males in particular are very critical of other dogs
▷ **Chihuahua:** Confident and lively; has no inclination to socialize with other animals
▷ **Dandie Dinmont Terrier:** A problem with other dogs and with cats
▷ **Doberman Pinscher:** Hereditary ferociousness and pronounced defense impulse, needs authority and control
▷ **Fox Terrier:** A passionate hunter that can't get along with cats
▷ **Spitz:** Intelligent and watchful, but somewhat problematic with other dogs

Further Things to Consider

▷ **No playing in sickbay:** Sick or weak animals need rest, such as after an operation. Playful young dogs and cats have no understanding of that. They need to be kept out of the sick room.
▷ **When a dog is left alone:** A dog has to be able to be left alone in the house. If it gets used to that early, there rarely are any problems (→ Staying Alone, p.154).

Two dogs will pass the time better together until your return. But they also cook up some dumb ideas in pairs. Limit their sphere of action in the house, put endangered objects out of reach, and keep dogs occupied with toys or guarding duties (→ Games to Combat Boredom, p.234).
▷ **When the partner is no longer there:** The friendship between dogs or a dog and a cat often lasts a lifetime. But at some point one of the partners will no longer be there. Often that's when the owner first realizes how much the animals needed each other.

Love and attention will help the remaining animal make it through the first difficult weeks. Bach Flowers (→ p.220) can also be a help. It's important to help the remaining pet adjust to the new situation.

Research and Application

Ownership and Partnership

A house with a yard is considered the *ne plus ultra* of dog ownership. But that's not correct. The dog quickly becomes bored with the yard; it knows every corner, and everything smells the same.

A dog with a yard is often worse off than one that has none, for its owner sometimes sends it out and cheats the dog out of a good walk. Only a walk offers the stimulating experiences and exercises that keep body and mind fit.

A dog is good not only for little children, but also for adolescents. In a study, 200 youngsters who had dogs and 200 who didn't have dogs were surveyed; 81 percent of the dog owners felt more emotionally stable because of the dog, and in 69 percent the dog averted self-doubt and depression.

Dogs give young people confidence and security and help them avoid risky behavior. People who grow up with dogs are never bored and run a much reduced risk of slipping into criminal associations.

City dogs are no less fortunate than their colleagues in the country. More important factors for the dog are the closeness of its human, regular exercise, and activities together.

City dogs that often accompany their owners, make acquaintances, and find themselves in unfamiliar situations have a more fulfilling and happier life than country dogs that trot along the same roads every day.

The American doctor Alan Beck has ascertained that a dog can increase a person's life expectancy by 10 to 15 percent.

Dogs improve our quality of life; they provide affection and tenderness, their spontaneity and love of life cheer us up and keep us physically and mentally young.

A dog can't always go everywhere with us. For a pack animal, being left alone is an unpleasant and stressful situation. A social partnership with another dog makes it a lot easier.

◁

My friend the dog. A dog is not only the best playmate in the world for a child, but also a patient listener, a dependable protector, and an understanding soul mate. And a keeper of the deepest childhood secrets.

Two dogs are better than one. For many social behavior patterns another dog is the only good candidate. A male and a female are the ideal combination. The inner relationship with the human is in no way diminished by it.

Dogs are an elixir of life for senior citizens. In a Swedish study 63 percent of the older dog owners reported that they enter conversations quickly about their dog; for 57 percent of them, the dog was even a way to make new acquaintances.

A dog brings life into a house and makes us provide care and regular exercise. The initial uncertainty about being able to take care of it usually vanishes quickly, and older persons make the happy discovery that they are still needed.

2

Ten Questions About Ownership and Acclimatizing

Our Jack Russell Terrier has a great bed of his own but he prefers to sleep on an armchair. How come?

There are several reasons for this. The location of the dog's bed is especially important—no draft, as little frantic activity as possible in the vicinity, and yet contact with the family. The area has to be large enough so that the dog can stretch out, but not so large that the dog feels insecure. The dog finds the armchair interesting because it offers a good, elevated vantage point and smells like its owner. So you might change the location of the dog's sleeping pad and simultaneously insist that the dog stay off the armchair.

Friends of ours kept their puppy in a large playpen for the first few weeks. Is that a good idea?

A playpen is not the worst choice. A puppy feels secure inside it and has everything it needs—a sleeping place, water dish, and toys. Young dogs are very active during the brief play sessions, and in between there are long rest breaks in which they must remain undisturbed. That works out better in a playpen than anywhere else. Of course the puppy should also get adequate exercise in the house. The puppy should never be put into the playpen as a punishment for bad behavior.

I am single and live in a fairly small two-bedroom apartment. Could I own a dog?

Dogs are very adaptable, but of course there are limits. Nobody is going to do tests to find out if a Leonberger feels comfortable in 430 square feet (40 m^2). In addition to size, the dog's nature plays an important role; hyperactive, lively dogs need more room, and you have to be able to get out of their way when they get on your nerves. The best choices for small apartments are small, affectionate breeds with an even disposition. Examples include the Cavalier King Charles Spaniel and French Bulldog. Remember: Regular outings provide the necessary exercise.

We have three children and a steady stream of friends and guests. Is that too much for a puppy to handle?

It's no problem if every visitor doesn't immediately pounce on the dog with enthusiasm. Meeting new people and situations is important for the puppy's socialization. It simply must not be disturbed while it is resting.

We live on the second floor. How soon can a young dog climb stairs?

A soon as the dog can move in a coordinated manner and is large enough so that it doesn't have to take each step at a jump, it can handle the stairs alone. Breeds with a longer spine, such as Dachshunds, whether puppies or adults, have problems with stairs. The only choice is the elevator or the owner's arms.

Time for a little play? Not just puppies, but also adult and even old dogs still love to play. The Boxer is one of the breeds that are most passionate about playing.

Right out of the dictionary of dog language. Dogs invite play by crouching down with the front part of their body and raising their hindquarters.

2

My father owns a Mastiff, but can no longer take care of it. Will our children get along all right with the big dog?

Mastiffs from good bloodlines are very sociable and good-natured dogs, and usually obedient. They get along well with children so there shouldn't be any problems. An adult must go along on walks, though, for children can't hold back such a big, powerful dog.

I'm going to have a baby in five weeks. Our female Dachshund is very sweet, but I am having second thoughts about a risk of infection. Should the dog stay with friends for a couple of weeks?

There's no reason for concern. Just observe these points: The dog must have all its shots and be wormed regularly. For safety the veterinarian can examine your dog once again before the baby's arrival.

I really like a Bobtail that's in the animal shelter. However, it has already had several owners. Should I risk it?

This is no easy decision. Get some information about the dog's past from the people who work in the animal shelter. And spend lots of time getting to know it as you take it for walks. Bobtails are fun and charming, but also confident and somewhat stubborn. They defi-

nitely need a strong owner. You also shouldn't overlook the fact that taking care of their fur is almost a fulltime job.

My German Shepherd Dog continually pulls on the leash when we go for a walk. Friends have recommended that I use a head halter. Will that help?

A dog's halter is constructed like a horse's halter, and it exerts pressure on the snout. The more the dog pulls, the greater the pressure. The effect is like the muzzle-bite that a superior in the wolf or dog pack uses to reprimand a subordinate. At the same time the head is pulled to one side, so the dog has automatic eye contact with the owner and thus responds more promptly to commands. Your dog should be used to the halter after about two weeks. The Halti head halter is marketed in pet shops under the name MasterControl.

The perfect observer. Dogs know what we expect from them from even the tiniest details of our posture.

My husband and I are under a lot of pressure from work. Our children are really eager to get a dog. Will it work?

Depending on how old your children are, they can be counted on to take over some tasks of owning a dog, such as feeding, coat care, and washing the dishes. Still, you can't entirely escape responsibility for the dog's well-being. Occasionally that will still require a little time on your part.

Friends for Life

A dog is man's best friend. But friendship doesn't just happen—it requires a willingness to cooperate, consideration, and occasional compromises. The firm, careful training of the puppy is the start of a happy relationship between person and dog. If you get to know your dog's personality and demands, you will quickly get a grip on behavior problems and avoid misunderstandings.

3

How Humans and Dogs Came Together

Relationships often start out small. The one involving humans and dogs began with casual jobs and the prospect of some leftover prey to stave off acute hunger.

HELP WANTED. "Faithful hunting companion sought, experience preferred, food and lodging free." That's how a prehistoric hunter might have searched for a companion through an ad. The help wanted ad wasn't needed, for there was already an applicant on hand. There are some who believe that the dog willingly hooked up with early humans. There were many contact points between dogs and humans—in social structure and lifestyle, and in hunting and territorial behavior. These were the best conditions for a partnership that would bring advantages to both sides and open up new avenues.

126

An Alliance for All Times

The origins are lost in obscurity, and have been for a long time. It's now being discussed more than ever before how many millennia we have to go back to find the beginnings of the history of humans and dogs. But here's one thing that is never questioned and is always fascinating. At no time during this small eternity has either one been able to do without the other, even when roles, demands, and expectations changed.

The Mouse Hunter and the Consumer of Leftovers

Humans have made animals subservient; at least they have always tried. With some they have been defeated by their resistance to taming, self-assertiveness, and *otherness*, and with others they experienced greater success, as with cattle and sheep, for example, with goats and pigs, and later on with horses. Only with cats and dogs was the lash not required; they voluntarily sought out closeness with humans. We can speculate whether the early bonds were tied by chance, or if dogs were already solid participants in the game (DOMESTICATION, p.262). With cats there is every indication that they formed an alliance with humans and were recruited as mousers and ratters. Little has changed since their hunting days in the corn cribs of Egypt. A house cat has remained true to its nature as a free-ranging opportunist right down to our time, a charismatic character trait that evidently keeps putting more and more people under their spell. Wild dogs probably prowled around for usable scraps near the huts and sites used by our still nomadic forebears. That spared them lots of strenuous, often fruitless hunting. People gave them support, and so they gradually lost their fear of humans.

Of Wolves and Humans

The discovery of a dog's bones in a 14,000-year-old grave in northern Germany proves that dogs accompanied Ice Age hunters and gatherers. However, the association between humans and doglike animals, the CANIDS (p.260), began much earlier: during the Pleistocene, more than 200,000 years earlier, wolves and humans were sharing the same living space and hunting the same prey. Wolf bones that have been discovered near human bones indicate that wolves turned up in the vicinity of humans and ate leftovers from their meals. Wolves were first persecuted and hunted in our time. Earlier humans tolerated them as eaters of garbage and carrion in their vicinity, and they even established closer contacts through the millennia. Among primitive peoples the wolf still enjoys high esteem and often plays an important part in their life and beliefs. The North American Indians particularly prized the wolf because of its incorruptible character and highly developed social consciousness.

What Do Bone Discoveries Reveal?

Dogs and wolves are very closely related to one another. But how does a researcher know whether a set of bones comes from a prehistoric wolf or a domestic dog? One aid is the fact that the brain of house pets is significantly smaller than that of their wild prototype. There is a 30 percent difference in weight

◁
The Nordic dogs include powerful breeds with lots of stamina that still strongly resemble the wolf in appearance. Teams of Siberian Huskies or Husky mixes are always among the foremost breeds in dogsled races.

127

between a dog's brain and a wolf's brain. The smaller brain is housed in a smaller skull. And that, along with possible changes in tooth structure, tells the researcher that the subject is a dog.

New Discoveries from Genetic Research

Today, people aren't focused exclusively on bone discoveries. Molecular-genetic procedures allow exact analysis of genetic material. The degree of correspondence is an indication of a relationship between two creatures; the smaller the difference, the closer the relationship.

The difference between wolf and jackal amounts to 5 percent; between wolf and dog it is only 0.2 percent. Genetic research also shows that the wolf was probably domesticated 135,000 years ago, much earlier than previously assumed. At that time only the Neanderthals lived in the Northern Hemisphere, where the wolf was also indigenous. *Homo sapiens*, our direct ancestors, first came from Africa into Europe and Asia 40,000 years ago. The interesting question can thus be asked whether it was the subsequently extinct Neanderthals who got wolves accustomed to humans.

Little Jobs for New Friends

The four-legged helpers of the Ice Age hunters surely couldn't perform any of the tasks for which today's highly specialized hunting dogs are bred. They probably simply accompanied the hunting parties, probably at a respectful distance at first, and indicated through their behavior where the wild game was. Still, the cooperation between the new partners must have been so well established that the dogs didn't compete with the hunters for the prey.

Perhaps they regularly rewarded their hunting companions with prizes when they were successful and left some pieces of the prey for them. And yet, perhaps everything began very differently, with the raising by women of orphaned wild puppies, as the wolf and dog researcher Erik Zimen has concluded (→ Hunting Companion or Baby-sitter? p.39). The association with the family and the close bonding with the children with whom the puppies grew up would have strengthened their pack consciousness early on and increased their willingness to take on small and large jobs for their new friends.

A 12,000-Year-Old Evidence of Devotion

A gravesite was discovered in Israel that is 12,000 years old, and shows that humans and dogs were very close to one another as early as the beginning of domestication. As a gesture of togetherness the hand of the deceased lies on the body of a puppy that was buried along with the person.

Linked to us for thousands of years. Dogs were important companions of Ice Age people.

▽

A Shame to Eat

With dogs in their vicinity, early humans could count on a reserve of meat in lean times, people often argue. We know that we eat everything that's edible and moderately palatable. Dog flesh is no exception to that, even today. However, on purely economic grounds it seems improbable that domestication played a major role in storing up living provisions; raising a dog is comparatively costly and time consuming, and feeding it into adulthood costs more energy than the resulting quantity of meat it can provide.

When Humans Settled Down

It is surely no coincidence that the oldest discoveries of dog bones in the vicinity of humans are around 14,000 years old, for this is precisely the time when humans settled down. Until that time they had lived as nomadic hunters and gatherers, but now they also undertook farming and raising livestock.

Dogs were already taking care of herds, in addition to the women and children who stayed behind when the men went out hunting. Only powerful, fearless dogs were in a position to protect the sheep and goats, and later on, the cattle, from wolves and other predators.

As wolves became less common, smaller and more independent working and HERDING DOGS (❍ p.265) came onto the scene and helped the herders to keep their continually increasing flocks together. The type of intelligent and quick herding dog has survived to this day. Among the modern breeds that embody it are the Border and the Bearded Collie, the Briard, and the Berger des Pyrenees. The Pyrenees Shepherd watches over its flocks and brings wayward sheep back in, and the powerful Pyrenees Mountain Dog takes care of defending the animals from wolves.

There still exist a small handful of such imposing herd protectors, foremost among which is the very primitive Tibetan Mastiff.

❍ INFO

The Shepherd's White Helpers

They are herd defenders, and they are white: the Komondor and Kuvasz from Hungary, the Italian Maremma-Abruzzi Shepherd, France's Pyrenees Mountain Dog, and the Turkish Akbash. In the old days shepherds preferred white dogs so they could distinguish them from wolves when they forced their way into the herds. There are hardly any wolves left today, but the white fur of the shepherd breed remains.

Others have persisted in the remote mountain regions of southern and eastern Europe. These are pure working animals, which, like the Turkish breeds Akbash, Kangal, and Karabash, are not suited to life as family dogs.

All-purpose Dogs

Driving dogs were originally used for moving herds of cattle, but they soon took over many other tasks, and they even accompanied the Romans on their marches across the Alps. Even the mountain dogs of Switzerland go back to matings between these canine newcomers. The Rottweiler is still a driver, even though it's been a long time since this self-assured dog has performed its original task of driving the butcher's cattle to the slaughterhouse. Like Rottweilers, Bernese, and Great Swiss Mountain dogs, many driving dogs are also good draft and transport animals. The Newfoundland also belongs in this group of dogs. It used to help fishermen with their work, and it gained celebrity as a water rescue dog. This unique dog even has webbed toes for swimming.

As humans settled down and undertook livestock breeding, they depended on the help of quick dogs that loved to run. The Border Collie is the prototype of the intelligent herding dog that can work on its own.

A Spitz in Every Town

In the nineteenth century the Spitz was common in practically every town in Germany, and its characteristically high-pitched bark was familiar to everyone. Spitz-type dogs were presumably among the first domestic dogs. But the present-day Spitz breeds don't go back to the original Stone Age strains such as the Peat Spitz.

The similarities between the Spitzes of central Europe and the ones from the North and the East are unmistakable, so the FCI (→ Addresses, p.284) bundles them together in a single breed group. Even though the German Spitz is an enthusiastic and incorruptible watchdog and herding dog that scarcely has any hunting instinct, its northern cousins are among the most ardent canine hunters.

The Hard Life of Pariah Dogs

There are abandoned dogs all through the Orient. FERAL DOGS (○ p.263) are like the Australian Dingo; for millennia they have had to live on their own, often under the most difficult conditions. Since humans exerted no breeding influence on these Pariah dogs, they have retained many of the behavior characteristics of their wolf forebears.

Exotic Primitive Dogs

The FCI classifies exceptional, fairly exotic breeds as *primitive dogs*; they are characterized by a particularly primitive type of behavior. These include the Pharaoh Dog and the Podenco Ibicenco, which resemble the Pharaoh Dog that was widespread in the Mediterranean region during Roman times. Also included are the Canaan Dog, which was bred from Pariah dogs; the Basenji, which is related to primitive African dogs and yodels instead of barks—it also exhibits catlike behavior—and finally the Mexican Hairless or Xoloitzcuintle, which was highly esteemed by the Aztecs.

The fact that these dogs are labeled as "exotic" and "primitive" doesn't mean that they can't make perfectly fine family pets—it doesn't mean that they should automatically be ruled out in favor of the more established and domesticated breeds. However, they might perhaps require a bit more training, a bit more discipline, and a bit more supervision than some other breeds.

Novice owners should probably think about starting out with less challenging and more manageable breeds. But, for more experienced owners, breeds like the Canaan Dog and the Basenji should not present much of a problem. Indeed, many experienced owners will surely enjoy the "wild" qualities instilled in these breeds over centuries of existence apart from the typical human home.

What Do Dogs Do Today?

Dogs are multitalented. People have always benefited from their amazing abilities. And even in times of advanced technology and highly sensitive detection devices, dogs prove their superiority as drug detectors and search dogs, Seeing Eye dogs, and forecasters of earthquakes and other natural disasters. Dogs are contributors; they have a strong feeling for our well-being and our moods. They are frequently used as companions and friends to sick people, and they help psychologists and therapists who treat mentally handicapped and ill people.

Professional Hunting Assistants

Dogs have been hunting with humans for thousands of years. People long ago began breeding dogs that possessed special abilities for specific types of hunting. These include scent and tracking dogs such as the Basset, the Austrian Brandlebracke, and the unjustly ignored Bloodhound, which can use their amazing noses to pick up the trail of wounded game even after several days. Pure hunting dogs include runners such as the Foxhound, the typical pack hunting dog of the British Isles, and the Otter Hound, which formerly was used for hunting otters in the water. Water is also the preferred element of the Irish and American Water Spaniels, both waterfowl specialists. Thanks to the special structure of their waterproof fur, they can handle even ice-cold water temperatures. Even though retrievers originally were pure hunting dogs, they have all the requirements for fitting in happily as family and companion dogs. Not even the gentle and adaptable Golden Retriever can deny its hereditary passion for retrieving. Pointers exhibit quite different skills. They flush the game once the hunter gets within range and indicate where the prey is hiding. The archetype of these dogs is the Pointer.

Terriers Know No Fear

Terriers are creatures unto themselves: every one alert, absolutely fearless, and confident. The predominantly small breeds—with the exception of the Airedale Terrier—were bred specially for ground hunting (*terra* means *land* in Latin); they would catch foxes and badgers in their dens, and they also proved themselves to be very good hunters of mice and rats. The eager-to-learn, playful, devoted, and affectionate terriers long ago became lovable partners for families and single people. Their independent mind and pugnacity need to be countered with firm training and discipline. Dachshunds are similar in character. They too were originally bred for hunting in fox and badger dens.

Specialists on the Rise

It's become symbolic of the Saint Bernard: In alpine emergencies the great dog Barry saved some 40 people from certain death in ice and snow. Whether that's legend or truth, dogs have always performed inestimable services for humans. Today, specialists are developed and trained for the broadest array of duties. The most familiar working dogs (⊙ WORKING DOGS, p.275) include the German Shepherd Dog, Boxer, Doberman Pinscher, Giant Schnauzer, Rottweiler, Airedale Terrier, Bouvier des Flandres, Hovawart, and the Belgian Malinois.

All working dogs graduate from guard training. Depending on the dog's intended use, further training may follow. Dogs with an especially strong sense of smell are used as rescue dogs. Such dogs have saved the lives of countless people buried alive by earthquakes and avalanches. Here, as with dogs used in police work, the trust between the dog handler and the animal plays a decisive role. Customs dogs formerly sniffed mainly for illegally imported coffee, but today their nose is need-

3

ed for drugs and explosives. A tracking dog can even hit pay dirt when drugs are hidden in a car tire or a metal case.

Dogs for Seeing and Hearing

High expectations are placed on Seeing Eye dogs. They not only show a blind person the way, but also act as protectors and friends in all situations, and deliver exceptional results. Their training is expensive and lengthy, and it's a matter for experts.

The German Shepherd Dog and the Labrador Retriever make particularly good Seeing Eye dogs. The idea of using dogs for the hearing impaired came from the United States, where the first training facility for dogs to aid the deaf was established.

 TIP

Career Counseling

Unemployed dogs bred for running, retrieving, and tending herds need substitute jobs: Beagles take advantage of every chance to hunt, Retrievers fetch everything that fits between their teeth, and Border Collies herd cats and chickens. These dogs are happy only with lots of exercise and regular activities.

1,075 Miles (1,760 km) of Pulling a Sled

Dogs love to run. You can see that most graphically in dogsled races. The desire to run is so great that the musher has his or her hands full just holding the team back before the start of the race.

In the Iditarod, the longest dogsled race in the world, which takes place every March, the teams negotiate a 1,075-mile (1,760-km) stretch of trails through the icy wilderness of Alaska.

Earthquake Alarms and Weather Forecasters

Dogs are capable of perceiving things that are beyond the ken of humans. Like cats, they clearly react very sensitively to changes in the atmosphere and the earth's magnetic field. People have long known that their behavior changes noticeably right before a threatening natural disaster. In the regions of China that are frequently threatened by earthquakes, people place lots of importance on these observations and usually initiate a total evacuation of residents.

Dogs even have special antennas for climatic swings. The fact that they perceive even the tiniest changes in the human aura accounts for their increasing use in caring for sick or at-risk people (→ p.133).

Not Always to the Dog's Benefit

Humans have used dogs as experimental guinea pigs fairly often, in medical research and in suicide missions during war. The first living creature in outer space was named Laika. In 1957 the dog was launched into the universe on board the Soviet satellite *Sputnik II*. Return to earth was not part of the plan. Several other dogs followed Laika in similar missions.

Today, however, most people have become a lot more sensitive about the abuse inflicted on animals, including dogs, when they're made to serve as guinea pigs in human endeavors, such as medical experiments. Consequently, while many dogs continue to be harmed by people every year, the number of dogs suffering as a result of human behavior has declined significantly over the past couple of decades. Furthermore, many countries, including the United States, have enacted strict animal cruelty laws, and violators have been punished for breaking them. These are hopeful signs that should make the bond between human and dog even stronger in the future.

Social Workers and Co-therapists

Dogs are pure medicine. No risks, and a whole series of beneficial side effects; they are ideal as fitness trainers, with an unmistakable and contagious happiness, a calming influence in family squabbles, perfect as listeners and comforters, and reliable and patient buddies for the children. But dogs can do more than that. Their significance for older, ill, and handicapped people is now recognized by physicians, psychologists, and therapists.

New Life for Senior Citizens

At the end of their working life, many older people lack meaningful engagement. Often the spouse is no longer present, and people lose enthusiasm and self-confidence, let contacts lapse, and reject all advice.

The presence of a dog is something you can't ignore. It gets the attention it wants, places demands, and wants to be provided for, cared, for, and loved.

All studies in nursing homes and senior citizen housing come to the same conclusion: A dog is the best thing that can happen to older people. Even people who aren't too good on their feet needn't avoid dogs; there are small breeds that need limited exercise, and a dog-sitter can walk the dog when necessary.

Helping the Sick Get Better

In the United States and Australia people have long known of the curative effect that dogs have on sick people, and dogs have been used in treatment and rehabilitation. Reservations about risk of infection have long been dispelled, so hospitals needn't be off-limits to dogs. Dogs strengthen sick people's sense of being alive and demonstrably encourage the process of self-healing.

Dogs Break the Ice

You have to experience the effect that a dog has on mentally ill and handicapped people. A dog's presence works wonders even with patients who have completely sealed themselves off from the outside world. Their eyes fill with life, they smile, extend their hand, and stroke the fur.

Particularly friendly animals are chosen for these types of meetings, but every dog is very sensitive to the special nature of this situation.

Warning of Epileptic Seizures

There are a large number of examples, and the scientist Rupert Sheldrake is not the only one who is sure that many animals, especially dogs and cats, possess a "sixth sense" and perceive things that we can't account for.

This includes premonitions of attacks in epileptics and diabetics. A British study describes how sufferers' dogs became restless shortly before the people suffered an attack, alarming their owners by barking and whining, and even going for help. There is also talk of cases in which dogs reacted to skin changes in their owners that later developed into cancerous tumors.

3

▷

Dogs are good for people; the mere presence of a dog is calming and relaxing. For children and older people, a dog is an important contact; it provides encouragement and self-confidence to sick and handicapped people.

A Dog's Life

Young dog, adult dog, old dog—a dog presents different abilities and demands in every stage of its life.

FROM MAMA'S BOY TO A REAL PERSON-ALITY. Newborn puppies are helpless and dependent on the mother's care. But they develop very quickly, and as early as their eighth or tenth week of life, all their senses are so well developed that they can leave their birthing basket and make the transition into the new family pack.

In the following months the young dog discovers its place in society, learns to assert itself and make its demands known. The physical and mental development is complete at 15 to 24, or up to 36 months in the case of many large breeds. An adult dog possesses an independent character, has established habits, and varying degrees of close bonding with the people in its vicinity. With older dogs, fitness and sharpness of senses decline, and the dogs become more sedate and devoted.

Age and Development Stages

A dog is alone at no time during its life. In the birthing basket a puppy gets security from the closeness of the mother and the warmth of its littermates. Later on, the society of the pack, whether a pack of dogs or of humans in the family, becomes the center of its life. The dog has its established place and gladly takes on duties and tasks. An intact, stable social structure is important for the natural and proper development of the dog in every phase of its life; without social contact it becomes emotionally stunted and develops annoying behaviors.

The Mother Counts for Everything

Newborn pups see and hear nothing. Fortunately, the helpless little creatures have two skills to help them along their arduous way: The puppies know instinctively how to find their mother's teats and clamp onto them, and they cry out with their tiny voices whenever they are left alone and can't feel the warmth of their mother's body.

The peeping immediately summons the mother dog so she can pull the puppy that has fallen out of the basket back on board. A loud cry—from anyone at all—usually provokes every dog into spontaneous rescue action.

Strayed puppies need quick attention, for they are not yet able to keep their body temperature constant, and they can quickly catch cold. The temperature in the birthing room should be above normal room temperature. Or you can use a supplementary heat source (such as a heat lamp) for the dogs' basket. However, direct exposure poses risks to the puppies because of their inability to regulate heat, and it may lead to burns.

Why Are Puppies So Unprepared?

Tiny, helpless sausages with oversized heads; it seems that puppies are born too early. That's not entirely false. Dogs are runners. Hunting assures survival of their relatives living in the wild. A pregnant female is thus necessarily handicapped. The briefer her pregnancy, the quicker she returns to full capacity. But a short pregnancy also means that the puppies are born unprepared, and their development doesn't end with birth.

Everyone Healthy and Lively?

Much of life is not displayed for the first time in the basket, but a puppy's behavior and physical constitution indicate if everything is in order. If you hold up a healthy puppy, it twists back and forth, and its body is warm and firm. A weak puppy scarcely reacts, hangs limp in the hand, and feels cool and damp. It creeps around and whines or lies listlessly in a corner. If it doesn't locate a teat and get more milk, its condition deteriorates quickly. Then the case is urgent, and often the little one must be raised by hand.

Into the World on Clumsy Feet

Eating and drinking—in the first two weeks of life that's all that counts for puppies. That starts to change in the third week, when the eyes and ears open. The young dogs take in their surroundings with increasing clarity; they react to movements and noises, wag their tails to show pleasure when they get attention, and already show the first signs of self-defense by growling.

What previously was merely a forward crawl now merits the designation of locomotion. Especially active puppies test their new abilities with short excursions outside the litter basket. Their senses are not yet fully developed, but the little squirts are already having some important experiences that will influence their behavior and reactions in the following weeks.

3

135

Trust in People

The second month of the puppies' life determines where they are headed. They make giant steps in their development. They now possess nearly the complete repertory of body and vocal language, discover increasing pleasure in running, playfully improve their reactions, and filled with interest, they watch and sniff everything that goes on around them.

Puppies are open to everything that's new. Curiosity and a quickness to learn characterize the SOCIALIZATION PHASE (● p.273). Whatever makes an impression on them, excites them, frightens them, or makes them uneasy they will probably remember for their entire life. For a dog owner that means a great opportunity and a great responsibility. Intensive involvement with the puppies lays the groundwork for a trusting relationship, as it imprints the dog onto the human. Puppies that get little or no attention in this sensitive phase remain distant as adults, or confront people with mistrust. The better the young dogs get to know their surroundings, the easier it is for them to feel at ease later on. This includes early association with children and getting used to unfamiliar sounds and smells. But the most important thing for the puppy is

Chewing is part of the territory. Early contacts with people are as important for the puppy as getting used to strange noises and scents. And every new thing will first be tested with the teeth.

● INFO

How Old Is My Dog?

The young dog's development follows a stormy track: at 12 months a dog's age corresponds to a human age of 16. After that a dog ages about four times as quickly as we do. The true age depends heavily on the individual animal, however; at 10 years some are chirpy, and others are ancient.

still the association with the mother and the littermates. It plays a decisive role in later behavior with other dogs.

Ready for the New Life

The puppies won't be fully grown for a long time, but they still are strong little personalities. They know all the means of expression in dog language, eat from a dish, assert themselves in wild sham fights, and make their first contacts with people. The separation from the litter society is easiest between the eighth and twelfth weeks of life. A later separation presents problems, for the growing dogs have by that time already found a secure place in the pecking order.

Time for Teeth

Baby dogs are born without teeth, just as humans are. The needle-sharp milk teeth break through the gums between the third and the fifth week of life, and they are replaced by the permanent teeth starting in the fourth month (● TEETHING, p.273). The canines and incisors appear in a specific order. Teething can last until the eighth month, and it doesn't take place entirely without discomfort and restlessness. Many puppies temporarily refuse to eat, and many chew on hard objects. The baby teeth usually fall out and make way for the new ones.

Adolescence and Puberty

The PECKING ORDER (**○** p.269) is established between the fifth and the eighth month. That doesn't always occur without friction. The dog also tests whether its boss has the necessary authority, or whether it can take over leadership. It ignores commands and shows little interest in learning.

We can understand this puppy nonsense, but we mustn't ignore it. Firmness is particularly important in this development phase. PUBERTY (**○** p.271) is over and the dog is fully grown when a female comes into heat for the first time and a male lifts its leg. Usually this happens in the seventh to the ninth month; with large breeds, it often takes a year.

The Grown Dog

Body and behavior need more time until they are fully developed, commonly into the third year. That's when the dog is at the peak of its abilities; nothing gets past its sense perception, it is physically fit, and, depending on the breed, ready for sports. The integration into the human family is complete.

Deficient and inappropriate behaviors often can be traced back to training errors during puppyhood, or are protests against improper treatment or changed living conditions (→ p.162).

The Older Dog

Movements become more deliberate, the rest periods longer; eagerness to play diminishes, and the behavior generally becomes more subdued (**○** AGING, p.258). Most older dogs more frequently seek closeness with humans; they are more affectionate than before, and avoid frantic situations.

Male dogs show less tolerance toward other males. But there is no defined age border: with large breeds, fitness declines relatively early, yet other dogs are still playful, fit, and healthy at 12.

3

△
A handful of dog life. At 12 days the tiny puppy is still completely dependent on its mother's care.

Some typical age symptoms include rather stiff joints, declining vision, gray and white hairs, especially around the muzzle, and diminished hearing. A dog generally has no problems with aging in its familiar surroundings and in close contact with its family.

As dogs move from mature adulthood to old age, owners must be ready to adjust their relationships with their pets. For one thing, when their dogs' enthusiasm for play and exercise diminishes, owners must be ready to accept that the "good old days" of a frisbee catch or a run in the park may be over once and for all. More importantly, owners must watch their dogs carefully for signs of health problems, as these are likely to become more frequent as the years pass. And, because older dogs, of course, will need more medical attention than younger ones, owners should make sure not to miss scheduled visits to the veterinarian, especially for periodical checkups.

The Most Important Behavior Patterns

How much wolf is there in a dog? This is a question that still provides for passionate discussion among breeders and dog owners. As previously discussed, the close blood relationship between wolves and dogs is unchallenged, and with modern genetic analysis it can be documented beyond doubt. In behavior, however, there are clear differences, as the long partnership with humans has left its mark on dogs. A love of hunting and a vicious nature are not evidence of a special closeness to wolves, but rather the result of intentional breeding decisions.

Characteristics of Wolves

▷ Wolves live and hunt in packs.
▷ The pack society is characterized by a clearly defined pecking order. The highest-ranking wolf and leader of the pack is the so-called Alpha male. He is the only one that can mate with the highest-ranking female.
▷ Life in the pack is based on a highly developed, complex communication. Wolves communicate with one another mainly through body language and facial expressions. In comparison to visual signals, vocalization plays a subordinate role.
▷ The typical wolf vocalization is HOWLING (❍ p.266). Howling has a social function and strengthens the pack. Wolves stimulate one another to howl.
▷ Wolf puppies experience a fairly long puppyhood and adolescence.
▷ Wolves are very talented hunters and use various hunting strategies.

Characteristics of Dogs

▷ Like their forebears, dogs are pack animals. The social structure of a dog pack is simpler than that of wolves, however.
▷ Wolves flee from humans, but dogs have cast off the lupine shyness in the course of domestication.

▷ Dogs have learned to accept the human family as a substitute pack.
▷ Dogs have strengthened their vocalizations in communicating with us humans. Barking is a typical form of expression intended for humans. Barking has only limited significance in communicating with other dogs.
▷ The dog recognizes a human as the sole pack leader. Only with sled dogs does the team's lead dog also play a leadership role.
▷ Dog puppies have a shorter development period than wolves, and they become sexually mature at an earlier age.
▷ Most dogs still have a hunting instinct, but they are far less skilled on the hunt than wolves.
▷ As a result of turning into house pets and adapting to changed living conditions, a dog's brain is about 30 percent smaller than a wolf's.
▷ Sense perceptions have declined: Dogs hear, smell, and see less acutely than wolves, with the exception of breeds that have been developed for specific purposes, such as the Greyhounds, which hunt by sight, and Bloodhounds, with their highly developed sense of smell.

The Home Territory As a Source of Strength

As wolves travel and hunt, they cover great distances. They have a mobile territory that they defend against all intruders. With the exception of the abandoned street dogs in southern realms, their descendents are rarely infected by the travel bug. Most dogs like to stay close to home.

▷

Nothing that happens in its territory gets by dog. Every change is noted with interes

▶ INFO

How Dogs Think

A dog's brain is capable of linking various experiences together. But this association works only when the signals are given at the same time. Dogs also learn from experience and adapt their behavior accordingly. Of course they don't understand human speech, but they react very sensitively to tone of voice, posture, and gestures.

Everything that belongs to the family belongs to the TERRITORY (▶ p.274): house, yard, car, and even the garden plot at the edge of the city. The highest duty of the pack proprietor is to guard it and defend it if necessary. Only a few breeds, such as the Beagle, take a casual approach to this; other breeds have such a strong guarding instinct that strangers are often cornered at the garden gate. The homeland provides strength. Even a Yorkshire Terrier is the boss in its own territory. Visiting dogs generally respect the demands of the pack leader.

Learning Through Play

Dogs test and develop fitness and skills through play (→ p.228). Play is essential for puppies. It helps them improve their physical coordination, learn movements, and solidify social contacts.

Many elements of play come from other behavioral arenas, such as fighting, sexual behavior, and hunting. Only in play can certain types of behavior be tested without fear of injury or punishment. Playing dogs fre-

quently change roles, and every dog can have a chance to be hunter or hunted.

Ambassadors of Scent

Dogs experience the world's happenings primarily through their nose (→ p.18). But smells are also an important means of communication among dogs. A male dog uses SCENT MARKINGS (▶ p.145) in prominent places to set the boundaries of its territory, and when dogs meet (→ p.145) the sniff test determines whether they will get along or prefer to stay away from one another.

Everything That Moves

Our brain processes and evaluates the sights we see relatively uniformly. We register an uninhabited, static environment as well as movements.

A dog's perception is more selective. It registers mainly the things that move in its immediate vicinity—people and animals, objects, signals, and gestures, but also shapes and contours that change or resolve. The ball that rolls toward the dog, a balloon that's blown up, and a door that opens holds the dog's attention.

Creatures and objects that move away quickly nearly always trigger its chasing or hunting instinct. Dogs that have a marked passion for hunting take off after every "fleeing" object—from bicyclists and joggers to cars. Pack hunters such as Afghan Hounds even sprint after autumn leaves swept along by the wind.

Intelligence and Learning

Which one is more intelligent—cat or dog? Surely, fans of cats and dogs will still be searching for the answer 100 years from now. But both dogs and cats have already won the argument, provided that we understand intelligence as a measuring stick for adaptability to the respective living conditions. So a comparison of their INTELLIGENCE (▶ p.266) is about as useful as a comparison between apples and peaches.

Dogs are artists at adaptation. There are three behaviors that are responsible for this quality, and they are exhibited by puppies:

▷ **Curiosity.** This characterizes a dog's life from kindergarten on. Curiosity leads to new experiences and helps distinguish good from bad. But it can also get the dog into trouble.

▷ **Reconnaissance Behavior.** Dogs want to know what's on the other side of the fence. More knowledge and information about the living space means greater security and fosters quick, effective reactions. Again, however, this behavior can get dogs into trouble.

▷ **Opportunism.** Dogs are born opportunists. A dog will repeat on its own a behavior for which it is praised or rewarded. And undesirable behavior for which it is scolded is rarely repeated. Training and development are based on a dog's opportunistic behavior.

Behavior Basics

▷ **Sexual Behavior.** A female dog's behavior changes when she is in HEAT (**◑** p.265). Extreme clinging alternates with restlessness and a desire to search for male dogs. They are drawn like magnets to females in heat. Behavior patterns from the sexual cycle such as mounting or clamping onto a person's leg are also a dominance gesture.

▷ **Grooming Behavior.** Scratching, licking, and rolling are as much a part of grooming as shaking and gnawing the fur. Regular self-grooming is an indication of well-being. Weak or sick animals neglect themselves; breeds with long fur need our help with grooming.

▷ **Comfort Behavior.** A dog feels safe and secure in its comfortable surroundings. It lolls about and stretches and enjoys relaxing as it

3

● WHAT TO DO IF...

... the new dog turns out to be different than you expected?

We often find out how well the dog matches our expectations only as the partnership evolves. This is especially true for grown animals, but even puppies can develop behaviors that deviate from the breed's typical characteristics.

Cause: Older dogs that come to live with us already have a life history that has shaped them. They usually cling to their habits and preferences even in different living conditions. With puppies you can distinguish the confident ones from the shy ones even in the litter basket, and the most important thing for them is good socialization.

Solution: Check your expectations if you are disappointed with the new dog. Maybe your demands are too high because you have unwittingly imposed human standards. But perhaps you are also feeling overwhelmed by the daily care the dog requires. See if there are any possible concessions that will give your dog a chance. If there is no common ground, or if the dog's behavior is clearly deficient (→ p.162), you should consider therapy or corrective training. Usually that's relatively easy with a puppy, but with an older dog it will also take lots of patience and leniency.

lies on its back. COMFORT BEHAVIOR (⦿ p.261) also includes rolling in foul-smelling remains such as animal carcasses—a scent that dogs love, but humans appreciate a good deal less.

▷ **Playacting.** Many dogs are accomplished actors. They whine, limp, or can hardly run. Dipping into the list of tricks often works. The master shows compassion and the dog gets its way. Researchers see this behavior as a diversionary tactic; wild animals use it to deceive their enemies.

▷ **Compulsive Behaviors.** Continually licking its fur, chasing its tail, barking ceaselessly—sometimes behaviors strengthen themselves and become a compulsion. In serious cases the neurosis leads to mental and physical damage.

▷ **Stereotypical Behavior.** Many inherited behaviors follow a constant pattern (⦿ STEREOTYPIES, p.273). The impulse to run in a throng of other dogs is firmly rooted in the inventory of canine behavior.

Stereotypical behavior doesn't always make sense; dogs like to bury their food supplies inside the house, dig an imaginary hole, and even push imaginary dirt over it with their nose.

▷ **Contact Behavior.** Contact gestures signify belonging and compliance with hierarchical order. Among dogs that are friends, laying the paw on the back shows affection, but it can also be an expression of higher rank.

▷ **Displacement Behavior.** In conflicts a dog often reacts differently than we would expect. Instead of fighting or fleeing, for example, it yawns or licks itself. This DISPLACEMENT BEHAVIOR (⦿ p.261) shows that it doesn't know what to do.

Other animals and even people react the same way, for example, when they scratch their head in embarrassment.

Training lesson. Puppies are clumsy and bold, and they have to try everything. If things go too far for the mother, she unmistakably sends the pup back into bounds.
▽

Language and Communication

Cooperation works well in a dog pack only if communication is effective and there are no misunderstandings. When dogs meet they almost always greet each other politely and follow the other dog's lead. Even if they aren't well disposed to one another, they usually save face and avoid a confrontation. In communicating with people, dogs have developed their own style, in the hope that the master will understand everything they have to say.

A Language Guide with a Lot of Pages

The lexicon of canine language is a thick tome. Why so many pages? Dogs live in the community and for the community. In a social band there are many different behaviors and a continuous exchange of information. In order to do a job correctly and be a valuable pack member, a dog needs information. Dog language has words for every situation in life and every type of behavior. Dogs that are socialized early and regularly spend time with other dogs have no communication problems.

Dogs Speak Three Languages

Barking, growling, whimpering, whining, and howling—as far as we are concerned, these are the main features of canine communication. However, VOCALIZATION (◒ p.274) is just one of the three language forms with which dogs communicate. Body language is particularly expressive. For dogs, speaking with their body means making themselves big or small, laying back the ears, ruffling the fur, wagging the tail, and much more. The nose is the most important factor on walks, in inspecting the territory, and in meeting other dogs; scent signals and scent markings play the main role.

The Silent Language of the Body

The complex organization and the togetherness of the wolf pack follow strict rules and are based on a highly developed communication.

As animals of the wild outdoors, wolves usually are silent and inconspicuous, and they communicate mainly through visual signals. Facial expressions are especially important. BODY LANGUAGE (◒ p.259) is also the most important means of expression for dogs, even though it's not as differentiated as it is with their forebears. Vocalization thus is much more significant for dogs than for the silent wolves.

The Dictionary of Body Language

Fur, tail, ears, and facial expressions are the most important generators of signal in canine body language. A dog nearly always uses several signals at the same time and thus makes it absolutely clear what it wants; in addition to body language, those signals usually include vocal ones. The most common means of expression and "idioms" are located in the Atlas of Dog Language on page 146.

▷ **Fur.** A dog can make the hair on its neck, back, and root of the tail stand up. With short-haired dogs, the reaction is even more noticeable than with long-haired breeds and animals with a thick or voluminous pelt. Short-haired dogs can even make specific parts of their hair stand up. Dogs fluff up their fur when they perceive something that makes them uneasy, disturbs them, or threatens them, and when they want to threaten. The degree to which the hair stands up is an indication of how aroused they are.

▷ **Ears.** The condition of the ears reveals a lot about a dog's frame of mind. The position of the ears also coordinates with other vocal or body signals, especially with facial expressions (→ Dog Language Atlas, p.146).

▷ **Tail.** The way a dog holds its tail is an indication of its personality and character and provides a glimpse into its mental state. A confident dog carries its tail away from the body and often raised high; anxious personalities tuck their tail between their legs. A dog

3

that wags its tail is generally in a friendly mood; a stiff tail, in combination with other signals, indicates aggressiveness and warns of a possible attack.

▷ **Body.** A dog that is afraid or has gobbled up something would prefer to be invisible. People and dogs attempt that with the same behavior. They cringe and make themselves as small as possible. A self-assured and uninhibited dog stands up straight and presents itself full-size with head held high and legs straight; its fearful counterpart lowers its head and neck, arches its back, and moves in slow motion on bent legs (◐ IMPOSING BEHAVIOR, p.266).

▷ **Facial Expression.** Most dogs have an extremely adaptable face. The repertory of their facial expressions ranges from happy and well adjusted to threatening and ready to fight, and apprehensive and submissive. A specific ear position corresponds to every facial expression and emphasizes the mood.

Communication Problems

Wolves have everything they need for using body language: short fur, a long tail, an impressive facial mask (◐ MASKS, p.267), and erect ears. In the winter a wolf's facial expressions are even more striking. Then the packs are larger, and clear communication is especially important. Many dogs have breed- and breeding problems. The best facial expressions are of little use to the Bobtail and Komondor, because everything takes place behind a heavy curtain. There's no fur to hinder a Doberman Pinscher, but its facial skin is so taut that it is only partially fluent in facial expressions. Breeds with drop ears have a distinct disadvantage in comparison to dogs with erect ears, as they can scarcely use their ears to communicate. Dogs that carry their tail rolled over their back are as linguistically impoverished as the Greyhound and Whippet, whose breed-specific tail tuck makes them look like scaredy-cats.

The Vocalization Dictionary

We live in a world of speech. That's why we have a clearer understanding of dogs' vocalizations. Their speech repertoire is amazingly large, especially in comparison to the taciturn wolf.

Dogs are individualists when it comes to vocalizations: in addition to chatterboxes there are silent types that rarely open their mouth. Some breeds attract attention through their atypical vocalization; examples include howling sled dogs and the Basenji with its curious, yodeling singsong.

▷ **Barking.** Depending on what a barking dog wants to communicate, it modulates and varies the tone color, pitch, and sequence of

 TIP

The Personal Scent

A person's scent plays an important role for a dog. It relies on its nose so much that it will treat its own master like a stranger in certain circumstances, for example when the person uses lots of perfume. Dog owners should use aftershave, perfumes, and deodorants only in moderation and not overdo it.

notes. Of all canine vocalizations, barking has the most meanings—clean and quick as a greeting, high and expectant as an invitation to play, muffled and threatening to a stranger in the territory, regular and continuous to draw attention to itself, as when it wants to come into the house. Barking is typical dog-to-human speech; dogs rarely bark among themselves.

▷ **Growling.** This sound indicates a warning and a threat, and even novices with dogs understand it. If the growling has no effect, things can become precarious.

Puppies growl like big dogs when littermates get on their nerves. Dogs also growl when they play, but without any serious undertone.

▷ **Howling.** Dogs howl less frequently than wolves. Howling is what's known as a mood vocalization. In the pack it strengthens the sense of belonging; dogs that are left alone use howling to establish contact with other dogs or people.

▷ **Yelping.** In pain, in a threatening situation, and sometimes also in protest.

▷ **Whimpering.** Clear and high, usually soft tones; for appeasement of humans and animals, for protection, and also in begging.

▷ **Whining.** Signifies insecurity, submission, and fear of punishment. Like yelping and whimpering, it is also used by "playacting" dogs to accomplish a specific purpose.

Scent Signals and Smell Check

A male dog marks off its territory by depositing urine. The scent signals serve notice to other dogs about who is boss in the area.

Inside these boundaries, a strange dog behaves with respect and generally leaves if the proprietor of the territory is not friendly toward it.

Meetings on neutral ground take place according to established ritual (⊙ GREETING RITUAL, p.264). Strange dogs sniff each other nose to nose. Only dogs that know each other dispense with this procedure. Both dogs sniff each other in the anal region. The analysis of the scent determines further behavior.

Many dogs are interested in one another, and others prefer to go their own way; but sometimes there is also a display of might. The antagonists circle around each other and try to impress the other with erect body and hair on end. They actually come to blows only when one refuses to knuckle under.

Scents exercise an important influence on dogs' behavior. Strange objects in the house get sniffed intensively and may even get marked. If dog owners cover up their individ-

△

A clear message: with its partner in its gaze, the Basset mix uses the typical invitation to play ball. It also uses little hops and high-pitched barking to emphasize its desire.

ual scent, with perfume, for example, their dogs may become so confused that they may at first treat them like strangers.

Occasionally, the fact that dogs use their sense of smell to explore the world around them can be dangerous. In the home, for example, toxic substances that have strong odors, like cleaning fluids, may attract special attention from dogs, with potentially lethal results; therefore, these substances must be kept securely closed and out of reach. The same sorts of precautions you would take around the house if a small child were present should be taken when a dog is present.

An Atlas of Dog Language

Dogs speak in pictures, and almost always with their body. It often underlines its intent by making a sound, and sometimes through direct contact (for example, by nudging with the nose). The whole language can take on a new meaning through variations in individual elements of body and vocal language (→ p.143).

Composed and Confident

▷ **Composed.** Normal posture and facial expression, an open gaze, muzzle usually slightly open. Ears at rest, smooth fur laid back, rather than standing on end. The tail hangs down motionless. Typical in unfamiliar surroundings, but also when the dog is bored or slightly sleepy.

▷ **Confident.** Body taut, head held high, natural movements free of haste, tail motionless and either hanging or slightly erect. Free eye contact, but without fixating on the other person or animal. Typical in a territory and in living with trusted people, dogs, and other house pets.

▷ **Friendly.** Normal posture and open gaze. Minor tail wagging indicates a friendly, composed mood. Typical in meeting humans or other dogs that the dog knows and accepts, without demonstrating particularly intense behavior.

Alert and Keen

▷ **Interested.** Motionless, body slightly tense, ears held erect and pointed at the object of interest (with drop ears, the base of the ears is turned forward), watchful gaze, tail usually held high.

▷ **Very Alert.** Motionless body leaning forward, eyes and ears fixated on opponent or object, fur partly raised, tail held high.

▷ **Tense.** Body as if frozen and ready to react; the object is kept under close scrutiny, tail held high. Typical in unfamiliar situations and at the approach of strange dogs. Ears often slightly turned outward. Sometimes slight growling from uncertainty or as a warning. Depending on how the situation develops, the dog acts friendly or increasingly distrustful.

Pleasant and Playful

▷ **Happy.** Wags its tail and barks as it runs up to the person or other dog. Head held high, making eye contact with partner. Typical greeting with friends. Depending on intensity, followed by nudging, jumping, or waiting for attention.

▷ **Tumultuous Greeting.** The dog runs up to the person, wags its tail energetically, and barks loudly (generally more reserved with other dogs). The barking is often replaced by happy squealing.

▷ **Demanding.** The dog doesn't sit still for a second; continuous eye contact with the partner, and wildly wagging tail. Barking at first moderate and regular, but increasingly loud if the dog doesn't get the desired attention. Typical invitation to go for a walk. Also used in begging.

▷ **Playmate Wanted.** The body language is unmistakable: head and front part of body against the ground, hind end held high, tail wagging happily, and barking a clear invitation. Small hops in the same body position. Running away with body held sideways to initiate a chase, with the dog frequently looking back.

Lovable and Affectionate

▷ **Affectionate.** Licking the hand is proof that the dog feels affection toward very trusted people. Nudging with the nose is a sign that the dog demands attention and affection. Placing paw or head on knee shows that the dog feels a sense of belonging and devotion.

3

Alert and composed: erect posture, with raised head and open gaze the dog demonstrates strength and confidence.

Anxious and submissive. The dog would like to become invisible. The lowered body, laid-back ears, and tucked tail convey a clear message.

Alert and interested. Nothing gets by the German Shepherd Dog. It is all eyes and ears. This friendly expectant posture is typical in encounters with other dogs.

Angry and threatening. Even the uninitiated can tell that it's best not to tangle with this dog. As in this instance, aggressive behavior is also frequently mixed with fear.

▷ **Cuddling.** The dog lies on its back in front of the person, usually with direct eye contact. Slight tail wagging or thumping on the floor. Typical invitation to petting and cuddling, but also a gesture of submissiveness after bad behavior.

▷ **Begging.** Tries to attract attention to itself by offering the paw (also scratching the person's leg) and nudging (◑ OFFERING A PAW, p.268).

▷ **Anxiety Cuddling.** The dog seeks close physical contact, tries to get onto a person's lap, or creeps between one's legs. Accompanied by vocalizations: continuous whining and whimpering. Typical in storms or noisy celebrations involving fireworks.

Nervous and Insecure

▷ **Restless.** The dog runs restlessly back and forth, acts visibly nervous at every noise. Slightly crouching posture, ears in continuous movement, unsettled, wandering gaze, tail held low. Typical for dogs in unfamiliar surroundings, where they are made uneasy by strange scents (possibly from other dogs) or noises.

▷ **Ill at Ease.** Body and head lowered, tail hanging or slightly tucked. The dog moves slowly and uncertainly, or lies down in a corner. Sometimes slight whimpering. Typical for a dog that feels ill at ease, such as at the veterinarian's).

Anxious and Submissive

▷ **Anxious.** Lowered body, hunched back, head held low, slinking movements, tucked tail. Reduced eye contact. The dog seeks to creep away or get out of sight. Usually without vocalization. Typical with bad behavior, when the dog fears punishment.

▷ **Submissive.** The dog makes itself very small. Flexed knees, tail between legs, slow-motion movements. Typical humble behavior—often lies on back and presents tummy as a sign of submission, and sometimes urinates. In dogfights this posture signifies surrender.

Warning and Preparation for Attack

▷ **Mistrustful.** Body totally erect, highly focused on opponent; tail straight and motionless, fur erect, sometimes slight growling. Typical reaction when something is going on in the territory that the dog can't yet figure out.

▷ **Threatening.** The dog presents itself broadside, its fur stands on end, legs are stiff, and tail is held straight back. Mouth is open, with ears held to the side. The dog growls or barks. Typical in the case of an unwelcome visit, or strange dogs in territory.

▷ **Ready to Attack.** Body held sideways, all hair standing on end, tail pointing stiffly rearward with hairs standing out brushlike. Slow, imposing movements on stiff legs. The dog shows its teeth and stares steadfastly at the antagonist. Deep grumbling and growling. Last warning before an attack (❍ AGGRESSIVENESS, p.258).

What the Face Communicates

A dog's facial expression almost always indicates what kind of mood it's in.

▷ **Alert.** Erect ears, open, watchful gaze. The mouth is closed or only slightly open.

▷ **Threatening.** Head forward, ears turned to the side or laid back, steady, staring gaze, mouth slightly open. The teeth usually are partly bared.

▷ **Ready to Fight.** Mouth open, lips drawn back, furrowed brow and muzzle. The teeth are wholly visible. Stares unblinkingly at antagonist, and ears are held to the side.

▷ **Fearful.** Ears are pulled back, the mouth is closed, and the gaze is directed into the void.

▷ **Intimidated.** Head held low, ears laid back, no eye contact. Often the dog licks its muzzle nervously.

▷ **Playful.** The dog pulls its lips back, and the corners of its mouth upward. The mouth is slightly open, the ears are erect, and the eyes expectantly focused on the play partner. Invitation to play. A characteristic posture is also part of playful body language (→ photo, p.145).

▷ **Following a Scent.** The facial features appear frozen, the gaze goes off into the void, mouth is slightly open; sometimes the teeth click together. Typical for a male sniffing the scent of a female in heat.

What Dogs Have to Say

▷ **Howling at the Moon.** Howling serves to establish contact. Dogs howl when they feel abandoned, when males pick up the scent of females in heat, when they are triggered by specific audible signals (church bells, sirens), and when other dogs howl. And sometimes by a full moon.

3

▷ **What's Behind Barking?** When a dog barks, it is almost always intended for humans. Barking is dog-to-human speech.

Among other dogs, it's usual to growl, whimper, or howl. Only dogs that are strongly imprinted on humans bark at other dogs when they see them.

▷ **Growling Doesn't Always Mean Anger.** Like barking, growling can mean several things: softly, and without threatening undertones, it's a sign of well-being, or is intended to get the attention of a human.

Dogs often growl a lot in play fights with other dogs or in playful struggles for a ball. And dreaming dogs evidently have some neat adventures that require lots of growling.

▷ **Jumping for Love.** Nearly all dogs jump up to greet human friends. They would like to lick the people's faces as a sign of affection. Since that's not desirable or effective, we should offer to let them lick our hand as a substitute.

Like Dogs and Cats

An increasing number of dogs and cats live with us under one roof and disprove the myth of hereditary hostility. When the two grow up together, there are essentially no problems.

Animals that previously had no contact with the other party first need to become familiar with the foreign language. Here are the causes of most misunderstandings between dogs and cats:

The cat lifts a paw when the dog comes close. For the dog this is a hearty greeting and an invitation to play; but for the cat, this is the signal for "Get out of my face!"

The cat flails with its tail. Dogs that wag their tail are in a friendly mood, but in cat circles this has just one meaning: alarm and readiness to scrap.

When a cat is in a good mood it purrs. A dog perceives that as defensive growling and backs off.

Language problems are usually overcome after a few attempts, and nothing gets in the way of the friendship. There can be some problems with dogs that have a strong hunting instinct, for when the cat runs away, they see it as prey.

If you find that your dog and cat just can't seem to get along, you may want to seek professional help. Most problems can be overcome with the right behavior modification.

I really like to bite you. Direct physical contact plays an important role in the relationship between mother dog and puppy.
▽

Training and Education

Young dogs are in a rush. They are fully grown at barely a year. Their training begins on the first day. With older dogs, education requires sensitivity and patience.

NEW TRICKS FOR AN OLD DOG. A young dog goes through several developmental phases within a few months; in so doing it develops its abilities, establishes relationships, learns social behavior, and has experiences that imprint for a whole lifetime.

Grown dogs have habits and preferences, but accept changes when they are provided gently. Suppleness declines in older dogs, and old-timers need lots of attention and care. A person's understanding is rewarded with devotion and trust.

Basic Training for the Puppy

Dogs are social animals. The social environment and the relationship with humans and other dogs is as important to them as air for breathing. Dogs that live as loners atrophy and remain physically and mentally underdeveloped. A dog that was kept isolated as a puppy later finds it difficult or impossible to integrate into a communal living situation. A good pedigree changes nothing in that situation. The positive, breed-typical tendencies with which it is born must be developed and strengthened through proper living conditions and supportive influences from the environment.

It All Begins with Trust

Anxiety, mistrust, doubt, and detachment are poor teachers. Everything is strange to a puppy when it comes into a new house: surroundings, people, voices, noises, and smells. There may even be an older dog or other house pets. There is nothing to remind the puppy of its former home. It takes time for it to feel at ease in the house, distinguish the family members by their behavior and voice, and not be frightened by every unfamiliar noise. Here's what a puppy needs to develop trust quickly:

▷ **Patience and deliberateness:** Avoid frantic or sudden movements.

▷ **Love and a calm voice:** Address the dog with a soft, quiet voice. The tone of voice is the most important thing, not the meaning of the words. It's not even embarrassing to speak to it in baby talk.

▷ **Attentiveness and lots of sleep:** A puppy need lots of sleep. Pay attention to its daily rhythm and make sure that the puppy is wide awake and interested for every joint activity.

▷ **Motivation and recognition:** Pet the dog and reward it every time it participates willingly.

Avoid Expecting Too Much

Formerly, people thought it was necessary to wait until a dog was six months old before starting basic training. Today we know how important and formative the experiences puppies have between the third and sixth month of life are for them. You can start with the first playful exercises as soon as the puppy comes into the house. At the age of 8 to 12 weeks it is still a young child. It can be motivated for a short time, and then it gets interested in a thousand other things, and it tires quite suddenly. Plan a half-hour per day for training games and exercises. Start with training units of five minutes maximum; that can be increased to ten minutes starting in the sixth month. To keep your little pupil on task, never train after feeding or when the puppy is sleepy; in the summer, train in the coolness of the morning or evening. Stick to training times as closely as possible. The bones and muscles of a young dog are not yet fully developed, and mustn't be taxed too much before the twelfth month. Wild games and jumps are taboo, especially for the late bloomers among the large breeds, such as the Mastiff and Newfoundland.

Easy Learning Through Play

The puppy has tested its abilities and social status with its littermates (❍ DOMINANCE, p.262). Its motivation and enthusiasm are the perfect basis for playful basic training. The dog will grasp new play and training rules quickly as long as you are patient and firm with it:

▷ **Playtime:** The human partner is the only one who decides when and how long to play.

▷ **Course of play:** The puppy learns that exercises are repeated several times.

▷ **Time out:** A short break for rest and relaxation follows every exercise.

3

1 *Basic instruction: The puppy learns the most important commands through simple, playful exercises. When it masters "Sit," then comes the "Down!" lesson. First show a treat to the dog.*
2 *Then bring the treat slowly down to the ground in such a way that the puppy can't snap it up.*
3 *Move the morsel across the ground and away from the dog. The puppy will stretch out to get hold of the treat until it is lying down. Then it gets praise and a reward.*

▷ **Success:** If the pupil does everything correctly, praise it and pet it.
▷ **Game over:** When the puppy doesn't want to play anymore, starts to bite, or gets interested in other things, the game is over.
▷ **End of game:** After training all training aids and toys are picked up and put away. This is the right time for a little cuddling.

What Counts in Training Exercises

Puppies are easily distracted. At the outset, start them off with their instruction in familiar surroundings, preferably inside the house. Conduct your training in the yard only if a wall, hedge, or fence prevents looking to the outside.

The presence of other dogs or house pets is an interference with the exercises; with more than one puppy, each one gets private tutoring. Understandably, the tempting smell of food cooking in the kitchen, or similar distractions, doesn't necessarily add to the puppy's readiness to learn.

The puppy's basic training belongs in the hands of a family member. With a change of teachers, the dog has to get used to several behaviors, types of body language and voices, and that lengthens the school day. If the puppy is tired or ill, call off the training session.

Praise From the Leader of the Pack

Being a useful group member, providing the pack with useful services, and gaining recognition from the boss—that comes quite close to the meaning of a dog's life.

For a puppy that accepts the human as the leader of the pack, that's how it seems. Praise from our mouth carries a lot of weight in the dog's training; it amounts to validation and incentive.

In training, praise the dog only with words so you don't interrupt the progress of the exercise. At the end of the session, of course there is the obligatory petting.

3

Teaching Without an Audience

One particular member of the family should be responsible for training the dog. There should be no unauthorized spectators at the lesson, for just like a little child, a puppy is very easily distracted. It's certainly lots of fun, but the training results often fall by the wayside.

Is Punishment Allowed?

When a puppy does everything properly, the praise strengthens its readiness to learn. If the exercise doesn't succeed, there is no positive reinforcement. The dog internalizes the difference very quickly, and since its greatest desire is to gain recognition from the pack leader, withholding praise and recognition is entirely adequate for convincing it that the expectations were not met.

Corporal punishment is strictly taboo. That also applies to adult animals, as it leads only to reduced willingness to cooperate, or to trying to stay away from us.

With bad behavior you can scold with words: a long, drawn-out *"No!"* or *"Yuck!"* usually hits home quickly. Emphasize the command with a grip on the neck if the puppy absolutely refuses to obey. But use only light pressure; the important thing is for the dog to recognize the dominance gesture by the pack leader. This action makes sense only if it follows the bad behavior immediately.

The frequently mentioned slap with a rolled-up newspaper often has the opposite effect, because a cheeky puppy will perceive it as a welcome invitation to play and rip the newspaper to shreds.

How Dogs Learn

Ivan Petrovich Pavlov rang a bell every time he fed his dog. The dog quickly realized that the bell meant food. After a few more attempts, he only rang the bell and omitted the meal. Still Pavlov's dog's mouth watered. For the dog, the sound of the bell became inseparably linked to feeding.

The Russian researcher proved with his experiment on conditioned response that dogs can learn by connecting different experiences.

In addition to the learning principle of classical conditioning, so-called operant conditioning also plays a decisive role. It follows the principle of trial and error: A dog has many experiences in its life; some turn out to be useless or failures, but others make its life easier. After a short time it avoids the unpleasant situations and works hard at all actions that produce advantages. This principle is further reinforced in training through praise and recognition.

The Puppy Needs a Name

The puppy's training begins with a name. Basic training can begin only when the dog listens reliably to its name. Its name is the invisible leash that ties it to the human. Especially in the learning phase the dog should have only pleasant associations with its name. Pet and praise the puppy when it listens to its name and comes to you. Don't call it several times in succession if it doesn't react at first. The best names are short, with two syllables. The magic is in the tone of voice. Always speak to the dog with a kind, soft voice. Never use its name when a scolding is due.

House-trained from the Outset

At ten weeks old, the puppy is not yet house-trained—but it learns quickly. Bring the puppy outdoors after every nap and every meal, and of course, every time it runs back and forth imploringly. Carry it only at the beginning; later on it will run by itself and soon will know the way. Praise the puppy every time it does its business properly. If the dog has an occasional accident in the house, a stern *"No!"* will suffice. Never hit the dog or shove its nose into it. If the dog sleeps near your bed at first, you should take it out as soon as it becomes restless in the night. A corner with newspapers can help in an emergency if the puppy is alone at night. The soiled papers should be taken away as quickly as possible so the dog doesn't get used to them. Most puppies are house-trained after three weeks.

Getting Used to Collar and Leash

Collar and leash provide security and facilitate training, but the puppy doesn't need to be totally leash-trained at this point. A simple, light collar is adequate; soon it will be too small. At first the puppy will try to slip it off. Put the collar on the dog before feeding or playtime, at which times the dog is distracted and will accept the collar more readily. In the first leash tests in familiar surroundings, the dog should decide where to go. Later on you can guide the dog in the desired direction.

Basic Commands

▷ **Sit!** Hold a treat over the puppy's head in such a way that it can't jump up to get it. Usually the pup will quickly sit down so it can look up at the treat. At this instant give the command, *"Sit!"* The dog gets reinforcement from simultaneous praise and a generous reward.

▷ **Down!** The puppy has already mastered sitting on command. Hold a treat in front of the sitting dog's nose; then bring the treat down to the ground, and then slowly away from the dog. After a few tries the puppy will stretch out to get to the food. Give the command *"Down!"* as soon as the legs and hind quarters are on the ground. Now the dog gets the treat and praise. Every time before the dog stands up again, have it sit once again. Then it

will lie down more confidently. Practice this command after a good play session, when your dog is no longer full of energy (→ photos, p.152).

▷ **Come!** A puppy always wants to be with the pack, and generally will follow you on its own. Right from the beginning, call it by commanding *"Come!"* when the dog comes over to you voluntarily. To keep it from running away immediately, have it sit in front of you. A young dog also learns this most easily with a reward. If you hold the treat at hip height, the pup almost has to sit for a better view of it. It gets the treat only when it sits reliably, though (→ photos, p.155).

▷ **Stand!** Show the sitting dog the reward and move it slowly away from the dog. As soon as the dog stands up to get the treat, give the command *"Stand!"* and pet the dog on its belly to reinforce the command.

▷ **Give!** Your dog must hand over or drop on command anything it's holding in its teeth. This is particularly important with sharp or poisonous objects. If the dog doesn't cooperate willingly, the muzzle grip will help. Grab the snout from above and squeeze the lips against the upper canine teeth until the dog opens its mouth. Every time you use this action, link it with the command *"Give!"*

▷ **Heel!** Have the dog sit next to you and show it the treat. On the command *"Heel!"* walk forward. The dog should remain next to you on a slack leash. At first, practice only on short stretches, and reward the dog after stopping.

Staying Alone

A dog needs to be capable of staying alone. Begin the training while the dog is still a puppy, as it will be more difficult later on. At first leave the dog alone in a room for only a few minutes. If the dog behaves calmly, gradually increase the duration. Here are some things that make it easier for the dog to be alone:
▷ It's sleepy after playing or eating.

▷ It has a blanket or an old sweater that smells like the owner.

▷ A radio playing soft music is left on.

▷ It has something to do, for example, gnawing on a chew bone.

▷ The dog gets a special toy that's available to it only when it's left alone.

▷ Older puppies are given a bag or an old piece of clothing to guard.

Leave the house with as little ceremony as possible and avoid effusive greetings when you return.

Health Check

Get the puppy accustomed to the daily health check of fur, eyes, ears, teeth, breath, anus, and paws. Your dog has to allow this touching even in illness or an emergency.

Forbidden Behavior

Puppies try everything. Undesirable behavior can quickly turn into a bad habit. You should firmly forbid continuous barking and howling, shredding newspapers, chewing on shoes and carpets, swiping food and objects, eating filth, biting in play, pulling on pants, jumping up on people, and rolling in filth (→ When Dogs Cause Problems, p.162).

Bad behavior that isn't nipped in the bud can easily become a lifelong problem. It is much more difficult to train an adult dog to stop engaging in bad behavior like tugging at clothing or towels than it is to train a puppy not to do these things. Taking a firm stand with your dog when it's a puppy will make your relationship with your pet a lot smoother later in life.

Better Play

On page 230 you will find hints for playing with a puppy appropriately and what kinds of toys are suitable. Every puppy should take part in puppy play days (→ p.160). Play is an important part of the socialization process for puppies. If they aren't allowed to play when young, they may develop behavioral problems later in life. You can get further information from any breed association or dog training school.

1 *The dog comes to the owner on the command "Come!" and sits. In training, a reward assures that the dog will willingly obey the command. During the lesson the treat is held in the hand.*

2 *The dog's gaze is directed at the hand with the reward. It is held at belt height so that the dog has to look up, and practically sits by itself.*

3 *As soon as the dog sits calmly and attentively, it has earned its reward.*

Training and Education Goals

In the first few months of life the puppy learns the most important rules for the partnership. Basic training shapes its behavior and spirit of cooperation. It will never forget the experiences that it has during this phase of its life. Habits—both good and bad—will remain for a long time. All further training and education programs build on the puppy lessons. Conscientious basic training provides the best conditions for reaching the subsequent learning goals quickly and easily.

What Do I Expect from My Dog?

Before you even got a dog you addressed the question of which dog is right for you (→ p.24). You avoided getting a Beagle if you wanted a watchdog, or a Bernese Mountain dog to act as a jogging partner. Above and beyond breed and disposition, you really have to be sure about what you expect:
▷ the favorite of the family, which listens to everything but also enjoys its freedoms?
▷ the perfect partner that recognizes you as the absolute boss and obeys at the slightest sign?

▷ a social tiger that's always at your side and asserts itself in every situation?
▷ a pro that masters even demanding tasks with daring?
If you want to be successful in dog sports, shows, or guard duties, you will need to invest lots of time and energy.

Skills That All Dogs Need

As early as possible your dog should become familiar with all sorts of daily situations.

▷ **Traffic:** The dog is leashed and walks at heel. Have the dog stop at every street crossing.
▷ **Stairs:** The leashed dog must not pull (creating a danger of falling for the person); the dog can walk stairs without a leash only in familiar surroundings; careful on smooth stairs (such as, marble). Breeds with a long spinal column (such as, Dachshund, Basset Hounds) generally shouldn't run on stairs.
▷ **Elevators:** The dog should obey "*Sit!*" and be on a leash. It must also be leashed on moving walkways (such as, at airports).
▷ **Escalators:** There is a great risk that fur will get pulled out, or that the dog will get its paws pinched at the end.
▷ **Bridges:** Keep the dog on a short leash and at heel in narrow pedestrian passageways. Entrances and exits on pedestrian bridges are often made of metal grating that may press uncomfortably into the dog's paws.
▷ **Tunnels:** Try these first in underground walkways. In a tunnel with automobile traffic, headlights and the unaccustomed sounds reflected off the walls may frighten the dog.
▷ **Waiting Outside:** Dogs aren't allowed in most shops. Secure the leash and give the command "*Stay!*" The dog must be well socialized and remain calm when other dogs approach.

▷
Paperboy: Retrieving runs in the blood of most dogs. A dog is especially proud when it is recognized by the master for a perfectly executed task. But dogs must be forbidden to fetch shoes and other objects.

▷ **Restaurant:** Dogs aren't allowed inside, but if your dog is welcome at an outdoor café or a picnic area, secure the leash to the leg of the table or a chair.

The Watchdog's Difficult Job

Many dogs have a strong guarding instinct and voluntarily take on the job of protecting the house and yard. Zealous watchdogs can create problems, because they are on duty around the clock and allow no strangers onto the property.

The dog should report visitors properly, but consider its job done when the owner gets the message. Training requires a second person that the dog doesn't know. The person approaches the door; the dog barks, and is praised by the owner ("Good dog, Max!"), but is then returned to calm with the command "*Stop!*" Give the visitor a friendly greeting in the dog's presence. Repeat the exercise several times.

Running free in the yard is not a good idea for dogs that like to bark a lot, as they bark at passersby and cars. Good neighborly relations and regular mail delivery are also jeopardized by a dog running free.

Anxiety-free Meetings

Meetings between dogs take place according to established rules: First the dogs sniff nose to nose. If the sniff test is satisfactory, a mutual scent check takes place at the rear (at the ANAL SACS ○ p.258). Confident, high-ranking males present this region freely with tail held high in the air, but hesitant dogs are more likely to keep it hidden. Only when the pecking order is not made clear do disputes arise. Males usually scrap without causing injuries, but females fight more bitterly.

Let your dog off the leash when it greets another dog. When it's on a leash and backed up by the master, it feels strong and likes to play Rambo.

Some dogs have an avowed personal enemy that has the same effect as a red flag. Even though we generally have no idea why the two are deadly enemies, we prefer to avoid these confrontations.

An Educational Walk

Most dog owners take their walks at the same time every day. This is no secret; walking with others provides variety for dog and human and is lots of fun.

Company on the walk means even more to the growing dog: playful togetherness with other dogs of all breeds and ages provides the important social polish and teaches it manners with younger and older, stronger, and weaker dogs. The dogs practically never fight. All dogs should already have their basic training behind them. Unfortunately, females in heat must stay home.

 TIP

How Do You Pick Up a Dog?

The dog must trust you fully; strange animals resist being picked up. With smaller dogs, place one hand under the rib cage and support the hindquarters with the other one. With large dogs, place a hand or an arm under the chest in front of the front legs while the other supports the rear. Crouch down to pick the dog up.

Trial Vacation with Friends

Every dog must be able to be alone for a couple of hours (→ p.155), and it should also become accustomed early on to spending a couple of days in different surroundings (→ p.253). Arrange some visits with friends or relatives. If your dog behaves well, see if you can prolong the trial vacation. Many dogs like the variety, especially if there is another dog to play with.

The Companion Dog Test

You have already practiced the most important commands with the puppy during basic training. That knowledge is deepened in training to become a companion dog. Dogs can take part in this starting in their fifteenth month of life. The test takes place on the training grounds and in traffic.

▷ **On the Training Grounds:** To the command of "*Heel!*" the dog runs at its handler's side both with and without a leash. If the person stops walking, the dog sits without command. It must obey the commands "*Sit!*" and "*Down!*" while in motion and as the leader walks farther on. The dog is summoned by the command "*Come!*" Upon "*Heel*" it takes its place next to the companion. It is also tested for *Down-and-Stay* under distraction.
▷ **In Traffic:** The dog mustn't be distracted by passersby, joggers, cyclists, and surrounding noises. "*Sit!*", "*Down!*", and *Down-and-Stay* are also practiced.

In some places a current companion dog test is a requirement for participation in dog sports. The other version of the companion dog-training test is called Team Test. In the Team Test the dog may not be tied in the *Down-and-Stay* exercise.

Obedience—More Than a Sport

Obedience is more than complying with commands. The usually very demanding exercises require perfect understanding between master and dog and concentrated teamwork. Obedience is one of the dog sports, but it has a strong instructional component that can be used in training (→ p.246).

Versatility Test

The versatility test for working dogs is divided into sections A, B, and C, with three degrees of difficulty in each one:

Play without borders. The Golden Retriever could fetch the rope toy for hours. Unfortunately, its human partner usually tires long before that.
▽

▷ Tracking (A): the dog must follow a track while on a 3-foot (10-m) leash and point out specific objects.

▷ Subordination (B): Running exercises on and off leash, fetching (including across a climbing wall), down-and-stay, and gunsureness.

▷ Guard duty (C): Locating and cornering a suspect, who is barked at, seized by the (protective) sleeve, and then led away.

Only confident, well-balanced dogs are suitable for the demanding and time-consuming training; they must also obey their leader even in unfamiliar and extreme situations.

From Working Dogs to Elite Athletes

HERDING DOGS (○ p.265) are still at work with the herds. But for a long time the Collie, German Shepherd Dog, Australian Shepherd, and especially the Border Collie have been proving their skills in herding competitions in which sheep must be driven through a course. The winners are international stars and as highly sought after as the top Greyhounds that chase an artificial rabbit around race-tracks.

For Specialists Only

The training of rescue dogs, watchdogs, police and customs dogs, Seeing Eye dogs, and dogs for the deaf and handicapped takes a long time and is expensive, and it requires experienced professionals.

Getting into Shape for a Dog Show

A show dog (→ p.84) has to learn how to remain calm in the hubbub of the show hall. It must let itself be touched by stewards and judges and remain in show stance. The frequently intensive fur and beauty care is part of the preparation for the show, such as the trimming of an Airedale Terrier.

● CHECKLIST

Good Manners Checklist

A well-trained dog that knows its manners is welcome everywhere. Can your dog do the following?

○ It greets family and friends enthusiastically, but doesn't jump up on people.

○ It reports the presence of strangers, but stops when commanded.

○ It heels reliably.

○ It doesn't pull on the leash.

○ It listens to the basic commands: *Come, Heel, Sit, Down, Stay,* and *Stand.*

○ It doesn't bark or howl if it has to stay alone.

○ It poses no problems if it has to stay with someone else for a couple of days.

○ It has learned that the person who delivers the mail is a friend.

○ At an outdoor café it remains nearly invisible under the table.

○ It likes to ride in the car.

○ In unfamiliar surroundings it is confident and open-minded.

○ It is interested in other dogs and meets them peacefully.

○ It likes to play with children and is considerate when it does so.

○ It doesn't beg at the table.

○ It is well house-trained.

○ It knows that it mustn't chew on shoes and newspapers.

○ At night it doesn't wander around in the house.

3

Dog Training: School for Every Dog

For many dog owners, DOG TRAINING (● p.262) is the last resort when their pet causes problems. But dog training sessions provide lots more as they advise future dog owners in choosing the right dog, and guide and train the dog at every stage of life, from puppy to senior citizen. Several dogs are worked at the same time in basic and advanced training courses. Dogs with behavior problems and anomalies can get individual attention, even in their familiar surroundings, depending on how severe their disorder is.

Puppy School

Puppy play days (→ p.271) are offered by breed associations, private parties, and dog training schools. Puppies at least eight or nine weeks old are put together for play dates. The maximum age is 16 to 20 weeks. The young dogs' social status is tested and they learn the proper behavior with other dogs of their age. Through playful exercises the puppies become accustomed to different situations and noises and get to know the most important commands. Puppy schools offer a practically seamless series of beginner's courses for young dogs, in which play and sports are part of the program, along with basic obedience.

Basic Training

The most important course in every dog school is the training for growing dogs. The standard course is conducted in small groups with rarely more than 10 dogs, and it focuses on all elements and commands appropriate to basic training (→ p.154). The young dogs are trained on the practice field, in town, and in the open spaces. In many dog schools, getting to know other house pets (rabbits, chickens, perhaps even sheep) is part of the lesson plan, as well as getting used to strange noises

(sirens, firecrackers), and objects (large colored balloons). The youngest age for participation is usually six months. A complete basic course is a prerequisite for all advanced courses.

Further Training at Any Age

Dogs are curious and are interested in everything that is new and exciting. They retain their love of learning throughout their lives. There are thus no age barriers for advanced and special instruction in dog schools.

If you want to develop the breed-specific characteristics of your dog, or expect certain skills from it, you can choose specific training and develop an individualized lesson plan with the instructors. Most schools are flexible in their offerings. Practically everything is possible, from get-acquainted and weekend courses to intensive training with several hours of practice per day.

● TIP

Sniff Around a Little First

Take a look at a training lesson before you choose a dog school. Do you like the atmosphere? Are the dogs and trainers having fun? How practical are the exercises? Many dog schools not only let you take a look, but also take part in a trial lesson.

Therapy for Problem Dogs

Dealing with dogs that have behavior deficiencies is not easy for a dog school. Often, PROBLEM DOGS (● p.271) are put in school only after their owners have tried hard and are at their wits' end. It's not at all rare for the owner to reinforce the undesirable behavior without realizing it. Individual cases are evaluated; the training may be successful in the dog's familiar surroundings, but sometimes therapy is recommended in which the owner should not be present. If the behavior problems have existed for some time, a dog school may not be able to work miracles.

A Get-Acquainted Course for Athletic Dogs

Today, playing sports with dogs is one of the most popular leisure time activities. It's especially fun when done as a competitive sport, such as an Agility course or competitive dog sports (→ p.244). Many dog schools offer preparation courses in which it is possible to test the dog's (and the owner's) fitness before deciding on a competitive career.

Traffic Safety Training

Training for traffic safety is part of the basic course. For dogs with good basic training that merely need a refresher in traffic instruction, there are special practice sessions that are usually offered as weekend or daylong seminars.

The Dog School of Your Choice

Dog schools conduct training according to different criteria and teaching methods. In many schools the dog owner is with the dog throughout the training; in others, the training is in the hands of the school personnel, and the owner gets a one- or two-day practical workshop at the end of the course.

Before the start of every training session you should have a thorough consultation. You should choose a dog school only when you are won over by the program and the training methods.

Offers by dog schools to train your dog at a resort area while you are there on vacation sound appealing. Book the vacation course

△

Journey of discovery. For young dogs it is important that they lose their shyness with unfamiliar objects and strange situations. The puppies feel braver in a group.

only if it's the right one for your dog, not just because it fits into your vacation plans so nicely.

It is, in short, important to train your dog to become a member of the family in good standing. If you don't think that you can handle this task yourself, dog school offers a convenient alternative. People in the know will tell you that it's worth whatever it costs in time and money, as an untrained dog will be an endless headache for you later in life.

You can get the addresses of dog schools from professional associations of dog trainers and behavior counselors (→ Addresses, p.284).

When Dogs Cause Problems

A dog's inappropriate behavior puts a strain on its relationship with people. Therapy can succeed only if you know the cause of the problem.

THE ROAD TO HARMONY. A dog's most common behavioral problems include impatience with people and other animals, a low threshold of tolerance, and an excessive defense instinct.

The cause may be an inherited problem because of faulty breeding, or defects in training or living conditions. Deficiencies in puppies are caused by inadequate socialization, isolation, faulty imprinting, and traumatic experiences. Treatment can thus succeed only when symptoms and causes are identifiable. Therapy is always handled individually.

How to Avoid Problems

Many problems with dogs arise because we place excessively high or inappropriate demands on them, because our living situation changes, and all too often, because the four-legged partner is neglected. Mistakes in dealing with the dog usually creep in unperceived. Behavioral changes and bad habits are tolerated for too long. People who keep a sharp eye out for their own needs and those of the dog can avoid misunderstandings and correct bad behavior promptly.

Ground Rules for a Healthy Relationship

Behavior is a little like health—if you observe the most important rules, you can usually avoid problems. These ground rules are important ones in the relationship with the dog:

▷ **Respect the dog's needs:** No disturbances while eating or sleeping, regular exercise, daily play and petting.

▷ **Make the pecking order perfectly clear:** Your dog must accept you as boss. People who grant the dog equal rights endanger their relationship.

▷ **Integrate the dog into the pack:** Recognition in the community is vitally important to the dog. It must not feel neglected or excluded.

▷ **Give the dog something to do:** Dogs need tasks. Dogs that are working below capacity and bored animals develop bad habits and behavior problems.

Typical Training Mistakes

▷ **Starting training too late:** The puppy's instruction must begin right after it moves in.

▷ **Too much leniency:** Understanding is important, but continuous pampering and excessive compliance endanger the pecking order.

▷ **Excessively high demands:** Training takes patience. Dogs need time to learn from positive and negative experiences.

▷ **Too many teachers:** One reference person must be responsible for the training.

Tips for Therapy

Positive experiences encourage the dog's desire to learn. That is facilitated through positive conditioning: An exercise is set up in such a way that the dog naturally does what we want it to do. This works in behavior therapy as well as in basic training. Praise and rewards reinforce the desired behavior. The following techniques facilitate therapy and help assure success:

▷ Choose the training times so that the dog is active, attentive, and hungry.

▷ Adjust the duration of the lesson to the dog's age and ability to concentrate.

▷ Train every day and repeat every exercise several times.

▷ Set simple expectations that don't demand too much of the dog.

▷ Give lots of praise when the training is successful.

▷ Do the training in familiar surroundings to reduce distractions during therapy.

▷ Always work with the same commands and clear gestures.

▷ Give commands in a quiet voice to strengthen the dog's attentiveness.

3

◁
A tumultuous greeting. Many dogs jump up on people because they are so happy they have finally returned home. But not everybody appreciates dirty paws, and the jumping up can even be dangerous, especially for children.

Help with Behavior Problems

At first, many owners evidently don't take their dog's BEHAVIOR PROBLEMS (❍ p.259) very seriously. At some point, however, they become so severe that they tax the relationship between human and animal, and treatment becomes unavoidable. Behavior that has gone on for some time poses a major challenge to therapy. In particular, dogs that have been neglected for a long time and have not had attention and recognition need time to get beyond their defensive behavior and mistrust, and let people near them again.

Causes and Problem Situations

A flawed relationship with a dog often develops unnoticed over weeks or months. Here are the most frequent causes:
▷ Too little attention
▷ Preference shown to other pets in the home
▷ Unclear pecking order
▷ Too much coddling and shielding
▷ Lack of social contact with other dogs
▷ Lack of exercise and activity
▷ Frequently being left alone
▷ Irregular daily outings

The causes of behavior problems that seem to crop up overnight include the following:
▷ A change in the pack structure
▷ The arrival of a new house pet
▷ Moving
▷ A change in food
▷ The loss of a dog friend
▷ Revocation of accustomed privileges
▷ Coming into heat
▷ Lovesickness in a male
▷ Traumatic experiences

How Should Bad Behavior Be Punished?

Successful dog training is based on positive reinforcement—the correct behavior is encouraged through praise and recognition. If your dog doesn't achieve a training goal, repeat the training, but without rebuking or penalizing the dog. Clearly bad behavior is corrected with an admonishment such as a harsh "*Yuck*" or "*No!*" You can produce a particularly lasting effect if you ignore the sinner for a time or send it to its place and command it to "*Stay!*" The "neck bite" is also effective. The dog is seized on the neck or the shoulder area and gently pressed downward. Every dog knows what that means. It has had this experience as a puppy when its mother needed to discipline it. The MUZZLE GRIP (❍ p.268), in which the dog is grabbed on the snout from above, is also effective. This is the gesture that a superior dog uses to strengthen its status. A dog will take a scolding to heart only if it is administered during or immediately after the bad behavior, and not after its interest has turned to other things. Verbal scoldings, withholding food, and locking up are not training aids. They merely reduce the dog's willingness to cooperate.

Professional Help

In difficult cases you should describe your dog's behavior problems to an expert or enroll

▷

Overzealous watchdogs complicate life; when the house dog thinks it's a sentry, it doesn't even let family friends onto the premises, and barks at everyone who walks by the fence. Then it's time for a dog training course.

in a special training course. The first place to visit is your veterinarian clinic, where the veterinarian generally knows the dog well. The veterinarian can make sure that the behavior change is not due to illness or dysfunction. This type of support is recommended if

▷ the cause of the bad behavior is unclear,
▷ the problem has existed for a long time and gotten worse,
▷ the afflicted dog becomes a danger to you and the relationship, and
▷ you are at your wits' end and have run out of patience or energy.

The Most Common Relationship Crises

Therapy for a neurosis has a chance of succeeding when the situation that triggers it is recognized and the causes of the changed behavior are analyzed. All of the following descriptions of problems can be divided into sections dealing with the situation, the cause, and the therapy.

Anxiety over Being Left Alone

▷ **Situation.** The dog doesn't want to be left alone. It barks, howls, and yelps for hours without interruption and often destroys furniture or becomes untidy.
▷ **Cause.** Being left alone goes against the hereditary drive of a canine social creature, which always wants to be with its pack. When it's abandoned by everyone, the dog perceives it as a punishment. Separation has a particular significance for a dog, and it feels that it's permanent when the family's farewell is effusive. The dog howls and barks to reestablish contact with the lost community.
▷ **Therapy.** A therapy using small steps assures that the dog will regard being alone as something normal and no cause for alarm. In the first exercises, it is left alone in a room for only a short time. Leave it without any farewell. From outside, check to see if it starts howling or barking, but don't stand by the door, or

△

First sniffs. When a new dog comes into the house, the proprietor of the territory needs lots of attention so that it doesn't feel neglected.

your dog will hear you. As soon as the dog lets out a bark, go into the room and scold it with a "neck bite" (→ p.164). An empty tin can tossed clattering across the floor will strengthen this training measure. In so doing, say nothing and immediately leave the room again.

Repeat the exercise and increase the time the dog is left alone as soon as your dog behaves calmly. The fear of being alone is deeply seated, and relapses may occur. If necessary, shorten the separation times.

The success rate may increase if the dog is tired after sports, play, or eating, and is distracted by a toy, a chew bone, or some watchdog duty. The owner's old sweater will suggest closeness and calm the dog down. Quiet background music often helps, too. Leave the house without any farewell, preferably so that your dog doesn't even know what has happened for the first moment.

△
Swimming instructor. Many dogs have a deep-seated love of the water. However, no dog should jump into a brook or a pond without its owner's permission.

Puppies up to the age of 16 weeks shouldn't be alone longer than a half-hour. The constant closeness of the pack is important for the development of their personality.

Lack of Control

▷ **Situation:** Although everything went well in basic training (→ p.154), the puppy acts as if it's not house-trained. With an adult dog, it forgets its house-training lessons from one day to the next.

▷ **Cause:** With persistent lack of control, the veterinarian should test whether there is some organic disorder (such as kidney disease). One common cause for a change in behavior is a PROTEST (◑ p.271) by the dog. That can be triggered by jealousy toward people or other animals that get more attention, a change in food, frequent absences by the owner, a difference in the daily routine, continuous disturbances during naps, and much more. Stress may also frequently lead to lack of control. It may also be caused by frantic activity and noise, a new animal in the house, a domineering other dog, or a move. Temporary relapses in house-training may be a special case in submissive, fearful, and excitable animals. In the typical humility behavior with which a dog demonstrates submissiveness to a person or another dog, it often loses a few drops of urine. Anxious dogs, and dogs that go totally berserk when their master returns after a long absence, behave in the same way.

▷ **Therapy:** The protest is against what the dog perceives as untenable circumstances. If the triggering situation is cleared up or defused, the problem is half solved. It's important to maintain a stable daily schedule, old, familiar habits, and lots of attention in the face of perceived competition (such as a new baby or pet). The person's closeness and attention help the dog to get over its stress, as in the case of moving to a new house. Special therapy to develop more confidence may help anxious or submissive animals (→ p.175). Don't greet your dog if it runs wild with joy at seeing you again; rather, command "*Down!*" until it settles down. This type of behavior diminishes once the dog reaches sexual maturity.

Disobedience

▷ **Situation:** The dog doesn't react, or reacts only hesitantly, to commands. It expresses its own demands by growling or even biting.

▷ **Cause:** Every dog wishes for a firm pecking order with a pack leader that it can recognize. It rebels when the rank relationships are not clear, or when the owner doesn't have the authority the dog expects. Then male dogs in particular try to take over the leadership position (❍ DOMINANCE, p.262). Breeds that like to be boss include the Basenji, Chow Chow, Rottweiler, Doberman Pinscher, and Akita.

▷ **Therapy:** As long as the hierarchy remains unclear, the dog will test to see where its place is in the family pack. In the dog's eyes, a person who willingly vacates the armchair or doesn't dare to take chew bones and toys away has no leadership qualities and will be considered a lower-ranking pack member.

The course for a stable pecking order is set with firm training during puppyhood. Dealing with an adult dog that refuses to obey can be problematical. The creature knows just what its indulgent owner will let it get away with, so homemade therapy attempts are often unsuccessful.

In any case, when the relationship is put to a severe test, or the dog even becomes a danger to the person, a subordination course in a dog training school makes sense.

▶ WHAT TO DO IF...

3

... suddenly the boss isn't there?

It can always happen: A dog suddenly finds its master is not there. There are lots of reasons—professional travel, illness, divorce, financial problems. The dog reacts angrily whenever someone comes close, or it shows no more interest in its surroundings.

Cause: When a dog loses its pack leader, the trusted system that provided security and refuge comes apart. It no longer can cope. Insecurity and anxiety can lead to aggressiveness, but also to listlessness.

Solution: If the confused, anxious dog doesn't snap out of its reserve (→ Grief, p.172) despite lots of possible activities, it should be carefully integrated into a dog class by professional trainers. From the outset, the pack places clear demands on its new member, and the dog can't ignore them for very long.

Jealousy

▷ **Situation:** Suddenly your dog doesn't want to cuddle anymore and is visibly offended. Depending on its disposition it slinks into its bed, or it reacts defensively and perhaps even aggressively.

▷ **Cause:** Even dogs are capable of jealousy. When a baby arrives, or a new life's partner, a second dog, or a cat moves in, the previous central figure is often demoted to the status of an extra; rights are restricted, and attention and affection now come only in reduced doses.

▷ **Therapy:** Your dog needs a sense that nothing has changed and it is still your favorite. Your new life's partner needs to care for it and gradually win its trust by feeding it, taking it for walks, and grooming its coat. Introduce a new baby to the dog early on; feed and pet the dog in the presence of the infant. And give the dog more attention than you give to a second house pet that moves in.

Overzealous Watchdogs

▷ **Situation:** Nobody gets into the house without a problem. The dog acts distrustful even in the presence of its owner, and withdrawn with strangers.

▷ **Cause:** Most dogs exhibit pronounced territorial behavior and report the arrival of strangers in the vicinity. Normally the owner, as pack leader, decides if the visit is welcome. If the owner doesn't take care of that, the dog will.

▷ **Therapy:** Give the command "*Stop!*" and call the dog back once it has announced the visit, and greet the guest in the dog's presence. A dog with a strong watchdog and defense instinct should never be left in the yard unattended. Breeds that take their guarding duties seriously include the Dachshund, Boxer, German Shepherd Dog, Doberman Pinscher, Hovawart, Kuvasz, Rottweiler, Schnauzer, Spitz, Yorkshire Terrier, Wopfsspitz, Miniature Schnauzer, and Miniature Spitz.

Hooliganism

▷ **Situation:** Many male dogs really search out dealings with other dogs and don't go out of their way to avoid a scrap.

▷ **Cause:** Many of the smaller breeds contain ruffians. Small dogs are shielded and pampered more by their owners than big dogs are. Even little squirts such as Yorkshire Terriers feel particularly strong and attack larger dogs. Animals that grew up without contact with other dogs and don't know the rules of encounter can also cause problems.

▷ **Therapy:** With grown dogs it's difficult to overcome inadequate socialization experienced during puppyhood. If a fight starts, let the dog off the leash. The leash gives it courage, because it knows its owner is behind it. If you run 60 or 90 feet (20 or 30 m) away, some dogs become so insecure that they break off the fight. At the end of the fight, the main thing for both antagonists is to save face. Sometimes an "act of God" helps, if you spray the fighters with water or lift them by their hind legs. But don't step directly into a fight; many owners have been bitten by their own dogs. Hitting also accomplishes nothing except strengthening the will to fight.

Fighting over the Leash

▷ **Situation:** A walk turns into torture because the dog continually pulls on the leash.

▷ **Cause:** During basic training the pup was exposed to the leash too little or not at all. With an adult dog, both parties try to see which is the stronger.

▷ **Therapy:** When the dog pulls too hard, immediately stop walking. Call it back with the command "*Heel!*" Reinforce the command with a slap on your thigh, and motivate

▷

A cool distance. Even when there is no love los between dogs the human should stay out of it. The tw of them will work it out in their own wa

the dog with a treat. Train the dog firmly every time you go for a walk. You can produce the desired effect even with the most difficult dogs if you use a head halter.

Refusal to Eat

▷ **Situation:** The dog accepts only one brand or type of food or goes a long time without eating.

▷ **Cause:** Dogs are quick to grasp the easiest way to get their wishes. Usually, problems with the relationship or the pecking order are behind a hunger strike or picky eating. Every time the dog succeeds with its action, the behavior is reinforced.

▷ **Therapy:** People create poor eaters if food is always present in the dog's dish. Here's a basic rule: Leave the dish in place for ten minutes. Whatever the dog hasn't eaten by that time is taken away. Change food gradually by mixing old and new food and increase the amount of the new brand with every meal. With puppies, stick with the accustomed food for the first few weeks. As soon as possible get the puppy used to regular feeding times. Between-meals snacks are taboo for choosy eaters. A second dog as competition increases the appetite.

▷ Refusal to eat can also be caused by inflammations, foreign bodies in the throat, or teeth problems.

Barking

▷ **Situation:** The dog barks at the slightest cause, and often without obvious reason.

▷ **Cause:** Terriers and Spitzes tend to be barkers. The tendency is reinforced if vocalization is encouraged through praise and rewards during basic training. Dogs also bark from boredom and the pure enjoyment of

⊙ WHAT TO DO IF...

... the mail carrier comes

For many dogs letter carriers are a red flag. Every time they appear at the door or the garden gate the dog barks loudly, growls angrily, or even attacks. And that includes dogs that often greet other visitors nicely.

Cause: Letter carriers are always in a hurry. They can't take the time to get to know the four-legged security system so that it accepts them in its territory. They go to the mailbox on quick steps and retreat even faster. The situation is clear to the dog that barks at the mail carrier: the person is afraid. Henceforth, the uniform triggers the hunting instinct, and the dog pursues the mail carriers wherever it sees them.

Solution: The mail carriers and their intimate enemies can never patch things up without the help of the dog owner. Also, many letter carriers are uncomfortable because of unpleasant acquaintanceships with dogs. Invite the mail carrier into the house, have a conversation, and introduce the dog. To solidify the new acquaintance, you should at least speak to the mail carrier in the coming weeks to reassure your dog that the visitor is truly welcome.

3

barking. The taste for barking declines with advancing age.

▷ **Therapy:** A dog that's kept busy has no time for barking. Give your dog its favorite toy, a chew bone, or something to guard when it has to stay alone. As soon as it starts to bark, command "*Down!*" When a dog is lying down it feels less secure and usually acts calm. Praise and pet it when it quiets down. Scolding and yelling rarely help as they are far likelier to incite many dogs to bark more.

Dogs that have grown up without contact with others of their kind bark more frequently and longer than well-socialized dogs. Barkers are not tolerated in a dog community and are raised accordingly. The best therapy for dogs like this is regular association with other dogs.

Terror in the Car

▷ **Situation:** Some dogs go totally berserk when a stranger approaches the car or they see another dog on the street; for others a ride in the car is always real nightmare.

▷ **Cause:** To the dog, the family car is part of the home territory, which it is responsible for defending. Breeds with a strong protective instinct react especially aggressively. They react so strongly to strange people and other dogs in the vicinity of the car that sometimes they damage the interior.

Panic in the car often goes back to traumatic experiences. Even the very first ride to pick up the puppy may be the cause. The unfamiliar bouncing of the car and the strange sounds and smells don't lose their frightful aspect for a long time. If the dog doesn't trust the owner, the aversion often gets worse.

▷ **Therapy:** Distract the aggressive and noisy watchdog during the drive with activities and petting. Preferably it should have no view outside. Practice this with a parked car: Have a stranger walk past the car several times while you calm the dog or distract it. In stubborn cases a driving course in a dog training school can help.

Basic training for fraidy-cats: Spend a half-hour every day sitting with the dog in a parked car; cuddle and play with it until it loses its fear. In a follow-up lesson, start the motor; later, take a short ride and have a second person calm the dog. Gradually increase the duration of the trips.

Thieves

▷ **Situation:** The dog pilfers edibles, plus the owner's sweater, shoes, and socks.

▷ **Cause:** If the puppy doesn't learn what it's allowed to fetch and what's off-limits, this habit stays with it all its life. Opportunity entices food thieves.

▷ **Therapy:** The person's personal effects must be taboo for the puppy. This includes shoes and clothing, books, newspapers, and the writing utensils on the desk. Regularly train the dog to look for and fetch items expressly provided, such as dog toys, pull ropes, or its favorite squeak toy.

Here's how to give a food thief a healthy scare: Attach a treat to an empty tin can and place it on the edge of a counter. When the dog tries to snap up the food, the can clatters to the floor. The dog mustn't see when this goes on; otherwise, it will continue stealing as soon as you are out of sight.

Straying

▷ **Situation:** The dog takes advantage of every opportunity to go on tour, and often remains gone for several hours.

▷ **Cause:** Boredom, lack of exercise, and living with a dominant dog are the most common reasons for straying. (→ p.273). The impulse to seek out a sex partner is normal behavior for females in heat and lovesick males.

▷ **Therapy:** House arrest and walks on a leash are the only way to curb the will to wander of a female in heat. If you don't intend to breed the female, you should have it spayed, then you'll have one less problem.

All other wanderers need lots of attention

▷ *Backwards pecking order. Disobedience and contrariness are often tolerated for too long, especially with small breeds. By baring the teeth and growling, this little guy clearly demonstrates that it thinks it's the head of the household.*

and activity so that their closeness to the family becomes important to them again. If you have two dogs in the house, be sure one of them is not getting short-changed. If a dog with a strong hunting instinct gets away into the woods, it may be wise to notify a fish and game official.

Grief

▷ **Situation:** The dog had to be given away, or its trusted family pack has changed. The dog lies apathetically in a corner, and often refuses to eat.

▷ **Cause:** The loss of a person with whom a dog has lived for years is a real trial. The dog withdraws into grief and listlessness.

▷ **Therapy:** Speak lovingly to the grieving dog, even if it doesn't react at first. Take it on new walking routes where it can meet lots of other dogs and get it interested in playing. The change may come in different surroundings, where the dog doesn't continually miss its former owner.

Mounting

▷ **Situation:** A male dog takes every opportunity to mount a person's leg, usually with family members, but sometimes even with strangers.

▷ **Cause:** Mounting is typical for a male that has grown up in isolation and has problems being around other dogs and with sexual partners. The consequences are unhealthy fixations and anxiety with female dogs. Riding a person's leg is often a demonstration of power, when the dog considers itself superior.

▷ **Therapy:** The attempt to shake the dog off often has the opposite result, for it further goads the dog. Sharply command "*No!*" as you turn around and leave the dog alone in the room. Many wrongdoers can be distracted with treats or a toy. The affected person is the only one who should reprimand the dog. If a second person pulls the dog away, it will take that as a sign of weakness in the targeted person, and that only intensifies problems with the pecking order.

Looking for Affection

▷ **Situation:** The dog sticks like glue to its favorite human, continuously licks the person's hands, and keeps jumping up.

▷ **Cause:** In dog language, licking a person's hand means "I like you" and every dog should occasionally have a chance to do it. However, excessive licking is an expression of a one-sided fixation on the person.

▷ **Therapy:** Pet your dog on its back and push it down when it wants to lick you. If it

 TIP

Why Not Two?

Many things are easier with two dogs in the house: You can leave the two of them without feeling pangs of conscience, and they are more confident in pairs than as singles. An ideal team is brother and sister from the same litter, of course the female must then be spayed.

tries to jump up on you, give the command "*Sit!*" and praise the dog once it calms down. Never step on the paws of a dog that jumps up, and don't use your knee to push it away.

Playactors

▷ **Situation:** It's time for a shot at the veterinarian's. A moment ago the dog was fit and full of beans, but now it hobbles around the house, apparently on its last leg.
▷ **Cause:** Smart dogs are quick to register that they have more success getting their way with a little cunning than with contrariness. They howl and whine so pitifully you'd think they had a pain in every bone in their body, or they limp, or their whole body shudders. The seasoned performance rarely fails in achieving the desired effect on indulgent people.
▷ **Therapy:** If you give in and applaud an actor, you're in for trouble in a big way. The only real therapy is to ignore the dog completely; don't pay any attention. Of course the first time it happens you have to make sure the dog is not really sick. But most people who know their dog can tell at a glance what's going on.

Destructiveness

▷ **Situation:** The evildoer strikes mostly when it's left alone. It chews carpets and chair legs, shreds cushions and seat covers, and continually scratches on doors.
▷ **Cause:** With dogs that are left alone, fear of separation is often the cause of their destructiveness; sometimes the trigger is a lack of activity. During the TEETHING (◉ p.273), chewing and gnawing alleviate the discomfort.
▷ **Therapy:** Fear of separation is one symptom of lack of trust in the human. If the owner leaves the dog alone, it experiences panic that gives vent to a displacement action

3

Red handed. No dog can resist following so many good smells. The best remedy is to keep foods out of reach to deny food thieves opportunities.
▽

(○ DISPLACEMENT BEHAVIOR, p.261), biting objects. In such cases the fear of being alone must be treated (→ p.165).

Animals that are easily excited and dogs with a strong guarding instinct react to every noise outdoors. Another dog in the corridor or steps in the staircase enrage them to the point that the furnishings are used as an outlet for their anger. Restrict the dog's area while you're gone and keep it busy with guard duties, chew bones, and toys. Sprinkle endangered places with lemon, bitters, or perfume. If you catch the dog red-handed, a squirt from a water pistol may help. Give a puppy that's teething something to chew on.

Overanxiety

▷ **Situation:** The dog never goes more than a short distance away from its master, avoids other dogs, and shies away from strangers.
▷ **Cause:** There are many causes of fear in dogs: traumatic experiences such as a bad fight with other dogs, beatings by people, and accidents; inadequate socialization as a puppy and kennel life without contact with the outside world; and excessive coddling and protectiveness by the owner.
▷ **Therapy:** Fears are deep-seated. Therapy is time-consuming, and there are often relapses —especially when the experience that triggers the fear goes back to puppyhood (→ Fraidy-cats, p.176). Haste and pressure serve no purpose; you have to use lots of patience and attention to instill new trust in the dog. In such cases professional help from a dog training school or an animal therapist is required more often than with other behavior problems.

It's important for the dog to have contact with other dogs after it's involved in a bad fight. That's the only way the dog learns that not all dogs are mean.

You can get a handle on fear of the veterinarian by visiting outside office hours so the dog can meet the veterinarian when there's no stress.

Specific training can stop fear of loud noises: Start with soft noises, increase the volume gradually, and praise and reward the right behavior.

Spoiled dogs need to be around other dogs and people, but if they feel that their owner is worried about them, it won't work. Here, too, a dog training school is the right recommendation.

Torn to pieces. Fear of separation and lack of activity are the main causes when dogs become destructive. ▽

Hunting

▷ **Situation:** The dog chases after cats and rabbits, and even goes after cars, cyclists, and joggers.

▷ **Cause:** The desire to hunt appears around the sixth month of life. This instinct is a typical and deeply rooted characteristic in hunting and pack dogs.

▷ **Therapy:** Since every successful outcome reinforces enthusiasm for the hunt, puppies must not be allowed to chase after cats and birds.

A dog that has spotted something to chase or has caught a scent is usually excited for a short moment. Now is the right time to distract it and get it interested in something else. This works well with treats, toys, and items to fetch. With breeds that have a strong passion for hunting, success can be achieved only by addressing the problem during puppyhood.

Here's an alternative exercise: If the dog doesn't react to "*Come!*" or "*Heel!*" hide behind a tree, a hedge, or the wall of a house. Young dogs in particular often lose their enthusiasm and gladly turn back when their owner suddenly disappears from the picture.

If the dog takes off after joggers and cyclists, a second person takes over the role of the "prey." As soon as the dog gets close, the helper turns around with arms spread and yells at it. A stream of water can also be used to frighten the dog.

Puppy Nonsense

A puppy wants to accumulate some experience, try new things, and make discoveries; it tries out its abilities and tests its place in the community. In a dog pack, a puppy is reprimanded if it gets carried away; in a family we have to show it what's right and wrong. There is no easier time in a dog's life than its puppyhood, and a young dog never forgets what it learns.

▷ **Pants Nipper:** The puppy continually pulls on pants and stockings, nips the calves, and bites hands and feet.

For young dogs, their milk teeth are what hands are for babies; they use them to seize

▶ INFO

Compulsive Behavior

A dog continually turns around in a circle, chases its tail, keeps biting its fur, or licks itself so much that the skin becomes damaged: If compulsive behavior in a dog is not stopped, it can lead to impaired health. In many cases it is possible to distract the dog with play and activity, but severe neuroses may require medication and treatment by an experienced animal therapist.

3

and feel the new world. Don't punish the puppy for this perfectly normal behavior, but direct its activities to objects and toys that it can chew and gnaw, such as chew bars, bones, pull ropes, and perhaps even cardboard boxes that it can rip to shreds. Above all, play with the dog as frequently as possible so that it can develop its skills.

▷ **Chicken Chaser:** Puppies love to chase everything that has legs and runs away, including chickens in the yard and the cat in the house.

Puppies are curious about everything. If you catch the hunter at the beginning, it's usually possible to break it of its preference with interesting alternative choices. But never run after the dog; maybe it has already had enough, and it only eggs the dog on when the owner joins in on the hunting party.

If a leashed dog is getting ready to take off on a hunt and pulls on the leash, reprimand it with a harsh "*No!*" and call it back with "*Heel!*" But don't ever pull the dog back to you by the leash, or it will connect coming with a punishment.

▷ **Fraidy-cats:** Dogs that are overly sheltered often fail to learn the normal manners toward other dogs, because their owners have kept them away from all encounters. The results are predictable: Around the person the dogs feel strong, but they bark constantly and act aggressively to all strangers (❍ BITING, p.258). But without a protector they are little milksops.

A young dog should be let off the leash as frequently as possible when it meets other dogs. The vast majority of grown dogs are tolerant of young dogs, but will make it clear in an appropriate way where the limits are.

Experiences that plunge a puppy into fear and anxiety can mark it for its entire life and endanger its development.

Carefully confront the dog with the situation that causes anxiety so that it connects it with positive experiences. This applies to problems with a car, elevator, or running up stairs, but also when the puppy is afraid of individual people or is fearful of certain noises.

It's especially important to cure the dog of its irrational fears if it's routinely going to be confronted with situations that bring out those fears. For example, if your dog is afraid of cars, but you live in an urban area, then both you and your dog are going to have a very rough time if the problem isn't dealt with early on.

If you don't know how to "cure" your dog of its fears, seek the assistance of an animal behaviorist. Your local breed club or association should be able to put you in touch with a behaviorist if you don't know how to find such an individual.

▷ **Begging:** Whenever the family is seated at the table, the dog is there and gives no one any peace until it gets a couple of morsels. Begging once is once too often; even the most lovable puppy gets only its dog food, and only in its dish. Feed the dog before your own mealtime. If the dog still begs, it's put into its place with a firm "*Stay!*"

Teaching puppies proper food etiquette is important not only to curb their propensity to beg, but also to keep them healthy. Human food just isn't right for dogs, especially growing puppies. Many foods that humans eat can't be digested easily by dogs (e.g., certain types of vegetable matter), and some foods are simply toxic (e.g., chocolate). The latter, of course, should never be given to dogs, even in very small quantities.

Furthermore, consumption of human food can promote obesity in dogs. You may think that you're giving your dog a welcome treat by feeding it human food every now and again, but you're actually contributing to a bad habit that can really hurt it later in life. As in humans, obesity can trigger a variety of very serious health problems.

It's best to keep your dog on a steady diet of dog food. If you can't prepare your own, then use one of the many commercially available brands. Doing so will give your dog the best chance of avoiding food-related health problems down the road.

▷ **Nuisance:** Young dogs sleep a lot. The rest of the time they are full of beans and need something to do. Frequently they besiege their owner and whine and whimper if the person doesn't take pity on them.

Set firm playtimes. Your dog will quickly understand when you have time for it. After the play session pick up most of the toys; then playing together takes on a special value. End the play session by saying, "*Sit!*" and praise your dog for being a good playmate.

As with other types of bad behavior, it's important to get on top of poor play behavior early in the dog's life. If you don't set firm limits on when, where, and how your dog plays, it may come to believe that it can do so whenever, wherever, and however it chooses. Such poor socialization could, for instance, turn your home into a disaster area, as the dog romps around at will, knocking over plants, breaking furniture, and engaging in other acts of destruction. It could also lead to injuries among family members or other people, as a rambunctious dog, even a small one, could end up biting or scratching because it had never been taught the rules of play.

Research and Practical Application

Training and Communication

In dog training, desirable behavior is encouraged and reinforced. An important factor is the close sequencing of behavior and reinforcement. CLICKER TRAINING (⊙ p.260) makes that easy. The clicker is a type of noisemaker that makes a "click-clack" sound when it's pressed. It is used simultaneously with a desired reaction and a reward. Dogs quickly understand what the clicker is all about.
A clicker enables even beginners to experience visible success in training and educating their dog.

In the English Pedigree Center, a trainer is forbidden to use any kind of punishment in dog training. People don't even use the word "*No!*" There is praise and reward for every positive behavior; undesirable behavior is simply ignored. The dogs know exactly how to get recognition.
Only a dog that has no fear of punishment and neglect is self-confident, composed, and enthusiastic. It doesn't become discouraged and develops great trust in its owner.

Every year there are thousands of incidents and accidents involving dogs. These include injuries from biting and scratching, and falls caused by a dog jumping up on someone.
Many times dogs express joy and enthusiasm with powerful movements, for example, when they greet someone. Dealing with large dogs can be a challenge for physically impaired or older people and may pose a risk of injury.

Dogs add to our well-being and strengthen our immune system. American researchers have discovered that babies are up to 50 percent less susceptible to allergies when there is a dog in the house.

Since many parents are concerned about their children's health, they don't permit house pets. However, the positive, healthy effects of pet ownership far outweigh the risks. In addition, a pet helps with a child's social development.

◁

Getting a grip. The muzzle grasp makes it perfectly clear to unreasonable dogs who the boss is. Superior dogs also use this dominance gesture with other dogs to show that they're the ones that call the shots. This grip should be used sparingly.

As early as age 10 or 12, depending on their knowledge and maturity, children can train their dogs to be obedient with expert guidance in a dog club. That's the best way for them to learn about the animal's personality and behavior.
Responsibility for a dog sensitizes children to the needs of others. They are more attentive to their surroundings, and they are more willing to put aside their own needs than children of the same age who don't own a dog.

Ten Questions About Training and Education

I don't feel up to training my dog myself; it should be trained by professionals. How can I find a good dog training school?
Set up appointments with two or three dog training schools so you can watch a lesson. Many dog training schools also offer practice lessons that you and your dog can participate in without obligation. Here's one thing to consider: The fewer the dogs enrolled in the course, the more intensive the training. The training ground must be large and fenced in, but practical training also takes place in the city and in the woods. The atmosphere has to be right: everything harmonious and low-key. Parade-ground commands have been passé for a long time.

When we play together my Bobtail gets so wound up that he won't give me his toy. How can I get him to do it?
When your dog protects its toys it is undermining your authority. The pup has to be forbidden to do that. Show your playmate a treat, give the command *"Give!"* and praise the dog when it drops the toy. Then wait a couple of seconds before you reward the dog

with the treat. After a few repetitions, it will connect the reward with the command and willingly give up the toy when you say the word. With dominant males, avoid contests and rope pulling so that you don't get into competitive situations.

When I lift up my nine-month-old Dachshund, I grab it by the back of the neck. A friend tells me that's wrong. Is he right?
Mother dogs use the neck bite to carry her offspring back to the litter basket, but you shouldn't pick up a dog that way. The neck grasp causes pain and can lead to injury in an adult dog. The Tip on page 157 tells you how to pick up a dog properly.

When it's on the leash, my Poodle snaps at every dog. The dog training school recommends an obedience class, but without my being there. Does that make sense?
In dealing with problems that the dog owner consciously or unconsciously causes, a separation between master and dog during therapy can make sense. If you have coddled the Poodle too much, it may play the tough guy with respect to other dogs. It may learn some manners only when its protector is no longer right behind it.

A puppy needs lots of exercise outdoors. How can I tell if I am overtaxing it on walks?
Up to the time the dog is nine months old, it would be best to take several shorter walks every day and undertake longer expeditions only thereafter. With puppies the most important function of a walk is to solidify the relationship. Call a halt to the walk when the puppy becomes tired and doesn't want to go any farther.

▷

Digging deep: It's hard to keep most dogs from digging. If you set aside a special digging spot for the earthmover, the rest of your yard generally will be spared.

3

Nip it in the bud. A puppy generally learns quickly what's allowed and what's not. Puppies are generally forbidden to chew shoes.

My Collie is driving me nuts. He's a real garbage chute, and rolls in all kinds of filth. I'm at my wits' end.

Leftovers and garbage smell very tempting to dog noses. Once a dog discovers these "alternative feeding places" it is difficult to keep it away. The only way that promises success is never to leave edibles lying around and keep the dog on a leash near dumps and compost heaps. The search for substitute food can also be triggered by improper nutrition.

My dog growls when it's eating and I get close to its dish. Should I accept that?

In principle a dog shouldn't be disturbed while it's eating, but the owner gives the dog permission to eat. Your dog must allow you to take its dish away. Lure it away from the dish with a treat, take away the bowl, and praise the dog. Only then may it continue eating.

Our puppy has one trick down pat: rolling in filth. How do we get it to stop?

Rolling in cow manure or bird droppings is an instinctive behavior. The dog is covering over its own scent, or "perfuming" itself.

Train your puppy on a leash at an appropriate location. The first time it tries to roll, tug briefly and energetically on the leash as you say, "*Yuck!*" or "*No!*" After several repetitions

the dog should have the command memorized. Now you can test its behavior off leash. After a proper bath, the impulse to roll is especially strong. Keep the dog away from particularly seductive places.

Our Labrador Retriever is not really disobedient, but it simply ignores many commands.

Disobedience is typical for dogs that feel neglected. They create an inner distance between themselves and the owners. Provide your Labrador with opportunities for play and activities and give it a chance to meet new surroundings, people, and other dogs. Always going for a walk in the same place is stultifying, and a real tour of the town is the best therapy. You will be able to renew the dog's obedience as soon as it feels that it's a valued member of the family again.

I have signed my puppy up for a basic course at the dog training school. Should it take part in puppy play days before the course?

Look into my eyes. As soon as a dog hears a command, it should make eye contact with its owner.

At puppy play days the young dog will learn how to play with other dogs of the same age, lose its shyness, and soon find out what it can do. Dog training school will be a lot easier for puppies that have become well socialized at puppy play days. The puppy will be easier to motivate and will learn more quickly.

Feeding, Care, and Health

The right amount of food, regular care, knowledgeable health checks, and a complete shot program are the basis for proper dog ownership. That takes no more than a few minutes every day, and you can be sure you are doing everything possible to keep your four-legged friend healthy, fit, and happy. In this chapter you will find all the necessary information, practical tips, and most important rules on care, feeding, and disease prevention.

4

Healthy, Appropriate Food

The dog has long been a full-fledged member of the family, but it's not a human on four legs. It places very special demands on its nutrition.

THE BEST WAY TO THE HEART IS THROUGH THE STOMACH. Today it's easier than ever to feed a dog properly. But just because feeding also signifies attention and affection, that doesn't mean there aren't some mistakes in the food dish. Your dog shouldn't have to live like a dog, suffering outdated feeding practices.

How to feed a dog properly is something that can be learned. The demands that the dog places on its nutrition depend mainly on its origins and life style. Whether it is fed properly or improperly depends not only on the quality and amount of food, but also on its living conditions.

A Dog's Nutritional Requirements

The dog is descended from the wolf but in the course of domestication, it has distanced itself from its wild forebears. Its behavior is imprinted on humans, and its appearance has changed through selective breeding. From a physiological standpoint the dog is no longer the wolf it once was.

But a dog still gulps down its food hastily in big hunks, often regurgitates its food, and puts aside provisions for lean times. Still its nutritional requirements have changed a lot—it needs much less meat (protein) and less fat than a wolf.

The Most Important Nutritional Building Blocks

Every dog food must contain the three basic nutritional categories: proteins, carbohydrates, and fats.

▷ **Proteins.** High-quality proteins come from both animal and plant foods. Dogs utilize both types of protein; of the two, animal protein is generally more valuable to them. Very good sources of protein include meat, fish, milk, cheese, and cottage cheese.

▷ **Carbohydrates.** A dog's stomach can digest the carbohydrates in rice, oats, and vegetables only after they have been broken down by heating. Indigestible carbohydrates such as cellulose are referred to as roughage. They don't provide the body with any energy but they are important for digestion and they facilitate intestinal activity.

▷ **Fats.** Food from meats contains a certain percentage of fats. Even plant oils supply high quality fats. Fats make energy available and are as important to dogs as proteins and carbohydrates.

The fat content of dog food should fall between 10 and 25 percent (of dry mass); less will lead to signs of deficiency. Enzymes are important for digestion of fats.

Vitamins and Minerals

A dog's body needs some minerals such as sodium, calcium, phosphorus, and potassium in fairly large quantities; others, such as zinc, iron, and iodine, like the vitamins, are needed only in trace amounts.

▷ **Vitamins.** These are vitally important to many metabolic activities:

Vitamin A: Protects against infections, supports growth and vision, and keeps skin and mucous membranes healthy

Vitamin B_1 (Thiamin): Nervous system and carbohydrate metabolism

Vitamin B_2 (Riboflavin): Protein and fat metabolism, growth

Vitamin B_6 (Pyridoxin): Blood production and glucose and protein metabolism

Vitamin C: Provides for connective tissue

Vitamin D: Building bones

Vitamin E: Various defense functions, important for fertility and pregnancy

Vitamin H: Skin and Hair

Vitamin K: For normal blood clotting

Biotin: Important for breaking down fats

Niacin: Metabolic functions

Pantothenic Acid: Energy utilization

Folic Acids: Blood and protein metabolism

A healthy dog produces biotin and ascorbic acids (Vitamin C) itself. A lack of biotin causes skin problems and leads to hair loss.

▷ **Minerals.** The right amount of minerals in the food helps keep a dog healthy.

Sodium: Fluid balance in the body

Calcium: Bone building, blood clotting, muscle and nerve functions

Phosphorus: Many metabolic functions, skeletal development

Calcium: Water balance, nerve functions

Magnesium: Nerves and muscles

Zinc: Skin and fur

Iodine: Muscles, fur, hormone balance

Iron, Copper, Manganese: Blood production

The dog gets a little reward after a job well done, or when it has learned a training lesson. To keep the dog from losing its slender figure, every treat is subtracted from the daily ration.

Sodium is available in abundance in the table salt in food. The relationship between calcium and phosphorus is crucial (ideally 1.2–1.5 to 1). Although a dog needs only tiny amounts of zinc, iron, iodine, manganese, and copper, these trace elements are essential to its health.

What About Meat and Bones?

By nature, dogs are not purely meat eaters. Their wolf forebears ate their prey with skin and hair, bones, innards, and the mostly plant-based stomach contents, which provided balanced nutrition.

▷ **Never Meat Alone.** People who feed their dogs only meat make them sick. Meat con-

tains much less calcium than phosphorus, and a diet of only meat disrupts the building of teeth and bones, and thus leads to severe skeletal problems.

▷ **Never Raw Meat.** Raw meat may contain dangerous disease pathogens that could lead to severe illnesses or the animal's death. The virus that causes the always-fatal Aujeszky's disease (pseudorabies), for which there is still no cure, is transmitted mainly through raw pork. Other pathogens such as salmonella and worm larvae are reliably killed only when meat is boiled or roasted. Cooked meat loses none of its nutritional value, and furthermore, it is easier to digest.

▷ **Never Bones.** Even if dogs and bones go together in our minds: bones are not a food source for dogs. The canine stomach is durable, but it's not meant to handle large bones. Sharp bone fragments can cause serious injuries, and many dogs have lost teeth by chewing on hard bones. In addition, bones produce hard, dry excrement that is hard to get rid of. Dried beef ears are good for chewing.

Water and Nothing Else

The dog's water dish must always be full. The water mustn't be too cold, and must be changed every day. How much a dog drinks depends on its food, the temperature and humidity, its physical activity, special conditions (such as, pregnancy), and body size. If the dog eats mainly dry food, it will have to drink more, as about 90 percent of the natural moisture has been removed from the food.

Energy Expenditure and Daily Rations

A dog's nutritional needs depend on its age and body size; they are also related to its activity and output. The basal metabolism, which indicates the energy expenditure of an organism at rest, serves as a quantitative reference. The basal metabolism of smaller dogs is greater than that of larger ones. The former also have a relatively high energy requirement. The nutritional need is especially great in puppies.

▷ **Adult Dogs.** The energy usage of a Miniature Poodle that weighs 11 pounds (5 kg) amounts to 380 kj (kilojoule: see note below) per kilo of bodyweight, so its daily requirement is about 1900 kj. The basal metabolism of an Airedale Terrier weighing 44 pounds (20 kg) is significantly lower at 260 kj per kilo; the daily requirement is about 5,200 kj. A Borzoi that weights 88 pounds (40 kg) uses 210 kj per kilo, for a daily requirement of 8,400 kj. The energy requirement can be two to three times higher with dogs that do performance sports, and with working and hunting dogs. Pregnant bitches have a daily requirement 1.5 times higher than normal; nursing mothers of pups need three to four times as much.

Note: As a unit for measuring energy usage, the joule has superseded the calorie. To convert from kj into kcal, the number of joules is divided by 4.2.

▷ **Puppies.** A puppy's energy and nutritional requirements are twice as high as those of an adult dog. The puppies are nursed by their mother for four to six weeks, but starting in the third week of life they may also be given special puppy food. This is also the time to get the young dogs used to the feeding dish by putting small portions of food onto a saucer. Because of their tiny stomachs and sensitive digestion, puppies must be fed several times a day in regularly spaced intervals, and at first even during the night (→ Feeding Rules, p.187).

▷ **Older Dogs.** Agility and enthusiasm for exercise decline noticeably in older dogs. They use less energy than a middle-aged dog, so their food should be about 20 percent lighter in calorie content. Food for older dogs must contain high-quality protein to avoid straining the kidneys and liver, which become more sensitive with age. Reducing the daily ration usually is not welcomed whole-heartedly. A better idea is a special, reduced-energy com-

mercial food for senior dogs, which still contains all the vitamins and minerals that are important to an older dog's health.

Commercial Food—Everything a Dog Needs

Of course you can prepare the food for your dog, but it's not such a simple matter: You have to pay attention not only to the amount of food and the caloric content, but also the right relationships among all the nutritional elements and additives. You should already be somewhat experienced in nutritional science to do that.

 TIP

How to Weigh a Dog

Every dog should be weighed regularly. Checking the weight is essential, especially for dogs on a diet, and for puppies. Puppies and small dogs can be weighed on a kitchen scale, but larger dogs require the use of a bathroom scale: First weigh yourself alone, and then once again with the dog in your arms. The difference is the dog's weight. A veterinarian or a breeder can help you weigh a very large dog.

It's easier and quicker to use mainly commercial food. There is a type of commercial dog food today for every age group from puppies to older dogs, for pregnant and nursing bitches, for performance athletes, for overweight animals, and for dogs that have to stick to a special diet. There are three basic categories. All three can be used alone or as the main food source:

▷

Too spicy, too sweet, too fatty. Even if it smells so appealing in the basket, human food is not for a dog's stomach. Only commercial foods contain all the important nutritional building blocks in the right proportions.

people who treat their dogs to snacks between meals must reduce the rations accordingly. The freshness date is the producer's guarantee that all ingredients will remain fresh up to the indicated time and can be consumed without concern. Out-of-date commercial food should not be used, as special vitamins and minerals lose their effectiveness.

The Most Common Feeding Mistakes

▷ **Human Food.** People who feed their dogs leftovers from lunch, with spicy food or sweets, are setting them up for illnesses and deficiencies. Cat food is not for dogs, because it is too high in protein and fat.

▷ **Feeding from the Table.** The dog gets the wrong nutrients and is taught to beg.

▷ **Treats.** Too many treats are unhealthy and make a dog fat. Low-calorie snacks especially for dogs provide chewing fun. Between-meals snacks must be deducted from the daily ration.

▷ **Too Hot or Too Cold.** Dog food must be given neither straight from the refrigerator nor from a hotplate. Since smell plays a major role for dogs in eating, lukewarm food is ideal.

▷ **Adult Food for Puppies.** For healthy development, young dogs need special mixtures of nutrients and specific vitamins and minerals. Food for adult dogs doesn't meet this need.

▷ **Wet Food.** This consists of a mixture of meat such as heart, liver, and lungs, and plant protein from various grain types and all-important vitamins and minerals. The moisture content is around 80 percent. Wet food is sold in cans, packets, and dishes.

▷ **Partially Wet and Dry Food.** The formulation of both products is similar to the wet food, but the moisture content is reduced to 20 percent in the partially dry food, and to 10 percent in the dry food. The resulting higher energy content must be considered in the daily feeding. With both partially wet and dry food, drinking water must always be available so the dog can satisfy its noticeably higher fluid requirement.

What's on the Dog Food Can?

The purpose for which the commercial food is intended is indicated on the can or the packaging—for example, as the sole nutritional source for a grown dog, puppy food, reduced-calorie food for elderly dogs, or a supplemental food for nursing females.

The feeding quantities are merely guidelines. Depending on a dog's age, size, weight, and activity, the amount of food really required can vary. With single-source food the recommendations are for an entire day's requirement;

● INFO

Stomach Problems

Dogs cannot be properly nourished with human food. Furthermore, many foods that taste good to us disagree with dogs and frequently lead to serious digestive problems. This applies to such things as milk, raw egg white, and raw plant starches.

▷ **Sudden Change of Food.** Many dogs—especially puppies—react to a sudden change of food type or brand with stomach and digestive problems and diarrhea. Mix the new with the existing food and increase the percentage gradually. Diet foods in particular are often rejected (→ p.191).

What to Watch For

▷ **Bowel Movements.** Your dog should excrete well-formed, medium-brown droppings several times a day. Dark, foul-smelling stool indicates too much meat; light and hard, along with danger of constipation: bones; diarrhea: too much liver. The stool check is important also in case of worms (→ p.208).

If, after several bowel movements, your dog's stool hasn't returned to normal, it's a good idea to consult a veterinarian as soon as possible. Prolonged constipation or diarrhea may be a marker of a more serious health problem. And, of course, if you spot worms in your dog's droppings, a veterinary appointment is indicated immediately.

▷ **Eating Droppings.** Generally a very bad habit. It may also be the result of a pancreas malfunction, or exclusive feeding with meat.

▷ **Eating Grass.** Not entirely clear. One possibility is stomach acidity, which the dog tries to neutralize with grass.

It's not a good idea to let your dog eat grass. Many lawns and fields, after all, are treated at certain times of the year with dangerous chemicals to protect them from insects and invasive plants. Eating grass could make your dog sick; therefore, if you suspect that your dog has been eating grass, it would be a smart idea to take him to the veterinarian in order to alleviate the underlying problem.

▷ **Loss of Appetite.** Many different causes: inadequate exercise, too many treats, pregnant female or lovesick male, summer temperatures, changing puppy teeth, toothache and tartar in older dogs.

Consult a veterinarian in cases of persistent loss of appetite with diarrhea, constipation, or vomiting. Information on the causes and cures of food rejection is found on page 170.

The Most Important Feeding Rules

Dogs are creatures of habit. Even with puppies, fixed feeding times should be adhered to. A dog's digestive system adjusts itself to these times. Naturally every dog has its own food dish (→ p.93) and should be disturbed as little as possible during mealtimes.

When and How Often to Feed

▷ **Puppies:** A puppy will nurse for four to six weeks, but it can be given supplementary food starting in the third week of life. Start with small quantities so that its stomach can gradually get used to the change from mother's milk to a different type of food. In licking food a puppy learns how to use its tongue. The food ration is divided into several feed-ings (including during the night at first):

Second month of life: five to six feedings (in the course of 24 hours)

Third month: three to four feedings

Fourth to fifth month: two to three feedings

Sixth to seventh month: two feedings

Eighth to twelfth month: two feedings

From the twelfth month on: one or two feedings

Small dogs under 22 pounds (10 kg) are grown at 10 to 12 months; medium-size dogs are grown by 18 months; and large dogs over 88 pounds (40 kg) are fully grown only after two years, some even later. Smaller breeds are thus switched over from puppy food to adult food much sooner.

4

▷ **Adult Dogs:** Adult dogs are well provided for if they have one main meal and an additional small snack. After eating, every dog needs time for digestion in an undisturbed siesta. Because of the danger of gastric torsion (→ p.210), large breeds in particular must avoid sports and games for at least two hours. The feeding times should be set according to the dog's habits and preferences, but that's not always possible for working people.

▷ **Older Dogs:** With dogs in the second half of their lives, the organs become less efficient. The stomach and digestive system are taxed less when the daily ration is divided into two meals. After eating, elderly dogs need more rest than young dogs. There are significant individual differences when a dog becomes old. With small breeds, that begins in the tenth year; with medium breeds, the seventh or eighth; and with very large breeds, starting with the sixth year of life.

▷ **Pregnant and Nursing Females:** Becoming a mother and raising offspring entails stress and saps the strength. At this time a bitch needs a particularly energy-rich food. The energy requirement of a nursing mother dog is three to four times greater than normal.

Feeding Tips

▷ The meal is over in ten minutes. Take the

▶ NUTRITION AND CALORIE ADVICE

Large dogs need more food than small ones. The food requirement per kilo of body weight is much higher with small dogs, however. In addition, the needed amount of energy depends strongly on the dog's activity level. Commercial food guideline: The standard can of wet food (approx. 14 oz. / 400 g) contains about 1,500 kj (360 kcal); dry food about 1,400 kj (340 kcal) per four ounces (100 g).

Energy Requirement of a Grown Dog

Size	Weight	Daily Energy Requirement in kj (kcal) per kg of bodyweight	total
very small dog	5.5 lbs./2.5 kg	416 (100)	approx. 1,040 (250)
small dog	11 lbs./5 kg	308 (72)	approx. 1,540 (360)
medium dog	33 lbs./15 kg	233 (56)	approx. 3,500 (850)
large dog	66 lbs./30 kg	200 (48)	approx. 6,000 (1450)
very large dog	132 lbs./60 kg	167 (40)	approx. 10,000 (2400)

Energy Requirement of a Puppy

Age in Weeks	Feedings Per Day	Daily Energy Requirement in kj (kcal) per kg bodyweight
4	6	approx. 1,050 (250)
10	5	approx. 840 (200)
14	4	approx. 590 (140)
24	3-2	approx. 550 (130)
30	2	approx. 420 (100)
adult	1 (2)	see above

dish away; that will teach your dog good table manners.

▷ Remove leftovers immediately. They crust over, may go bad, and attract flies.

▷ Wash out the food bowl with hot water, using no soap.

▷ Provide fresh drinking water every day.

▷ When more than one dog is present, each one should have its own food dish.

▷ Feed adult dogs at mealtimes to reduce begging at the table.

▷ Dogs may have snacks and treats as a reward for good performances. They are important in training the dog. The calories must be deducted from the daily ration.

▷ Cover open food cans with a plastic lid (available in stores). Keep opened cans of food fresh in the refrigerator.

▷ Take portions out of the refrigerator early; cold food can lead to vomiting.

▷ Your dog must allow you to take away its dish.

▷ Keep a puppy from playing with its food right from the beginning. After ten minutes the food dish should be taken away.

▷ Chew bones are ideal for care and cleaning of the teeth.

▷ Puppies become house-trained sooner if they are brought outdoors after every meal.

▷ When using commercial food, a healthy dog needs no vitamin or mineral supplements.

▷ High-energy food is for only high-performance dogs such as sled dogs and hunting dogs. A dog is not taxed excessively in jogging, hiking, and trotting alongside a cyclist.

▷ Older dogs are more susceptible to tooth problems, and may thus have some problems eating. Consult a veterinarian in any case.

▷ Refusal to eat can be caused by hot summer temperatures, and also by health problems (throat, teeth, gums, general weakness). In case of doubt, always consult a qualified specialist.

△
Table manners. A puppy quickly learns that it is fed at specific times, its food is served in a dish, and that it's taken away after about ten minutes.

The Eating Habits of Dogs

Dogs instinctively want to bury leftover food. For their forebears, which had no food dish filled daily, this was a sensible storage of provisions (◖ EATING BEHAVIOR, p.262). Your dog demonstrates that this legacy is still in effect today when it tries to bury an imaginary prey animal in the house. When raw meat is buried in the ground, it usually doesn't go bad. It actually remains edible longer, even though it appears spoiled. On the other hand, food that has gone bad in the refrigerator is dangerous. Many dogs rarely drink indoors, but pounce on every puddle on a walk. You shouldn't permit that on busy roads or in the vicinity of sprayed farm fields. Eating snow is equally harmful to dogs. Often the cold food produces severe stomach discomfort and vomiting.

DIET FOODS AND SPECIAL DIETS

There are high quality dietetic foods for four-legged patients, and the ingredients are tailored to particular illnesses.

High demands are placed on diet foods, and people who would like to prepare such foods themselves won't succeed without a knowledge of nutrition, and will have to invest a lot of time. Every diet for a dog must be discussed with a veterinarian.

A Quicker Recovery with the Right Diet

Carefully controlled diet food improves the quality of life for a sick animal and fosters recovery.

▷ **Gastrointestinal Diet.** The typical symptoms of a gastrointestinal disease are vomiting and diarrhea. The diet is easily digestible and low in fat.

▷ **Kidney Diet.** Kidney damage can lead to ammonia poisoning. The diet has a high energy content but little protein and phosphorus.

▷ **Diabetes Diet.** Even diabetic dogs can't do without carbohydrates entirely. The diet food contains lots of raw fiber.

Ninety percent of diabetic dogs are unneutered females; overweight dogs are also particularly susceptible.

▷ **Allergy Diet.** Skin ailments and diarrhea may point to a food allergy. The diet food is free of most allergens.

▷ **Pancreas Diet.** An important feature is the high proportion of easily digested fats.

▷ **Liver Diet.** Easily digested diet food that takes the strain off the liver

▷ **Bladder Stone Diet.** Reduced-mineral diet food. Prevents formation of new bladder stones; also used to support treatment and after surgical removal of stones

▷ **Building Diet.** A diet rich in energy and nutrients for special demands, such as following operations and for weak puppies.

Who Needs Special Diets?

With chronic diseases such as diabetes and kidney insufficiency a dog must often stick to a strict diet for its entire life. A veterinarian usually prescribes a special diet for a dog for a specific time period to get it back onto its feet quickly after diarrhea, vomiting, operations, or poisoning symptoms. You can prepare a tasty menu for your dog with easily digested meat (chicken) and rice. There are commercially prepared special diet foods for various applications and in several different tastes; most are available right from the veterinarian.

Danger for Overweight Dogs

Being overweight is not only unattractive, but also a serious health risk for a runner such as a dog. Every extra pound strains joints and tendons. As weight increases, a dog's love of exercise and agility deteriorate; inadequate training in turn diminishes the performance of the heart and circulatory system, so the dog has less energy and puts on even more weight—a vicious circle. At the same time, the susceptibility to secondary diseases such as diabetes, bladder stones, and tumors increases dramatically.

Nearly one of every three dogs is too fat, and many of them tend to obesity, with a weight significantly over 20 percent above normal. At the top of the list of causes are faulty feeding habits and inadequate or irregular exercise. In addition to the excessive food rations, treats and rewards add to the problem. Only rarely are disorders such as thyroid or adrenal gland malfunction responsible for the excess weight.

Is My Dog Too Fat?

One small test is all it takes to see if your dog has packed on too much bacon: Run your hand over its ribs. If you can't feel them, the little chubby chops will have to go on a diet. With short-haired breeds you should simply be able to see the bulge of the ribs. If you want to keep your dog's weight under control, you'll have to check it regularly (→ Tip, p.185), and in your evaluation take into account sex, age, breed characteristics, and individual traits.

Problem Cases

Decreased activity and changes in hormone balance are responsible for the tendency of older dogs to gain weight more easily than young ones. Hormone changes in neutered animals may also favor weigh gain. Especially in the first few weeks after the operation it's important to stick to the daily ration. Finally, there are some breeds that have more trouble keeping their slender figure than others. These include the Beagle, Longhaired Dachshund, Cocker Spaniel, and Labrador Retriever.

Fighting Pounds

Even among dogs there are good and bad utilizers of food. For some the recommendations on the dog food label are just right, but for others they are clearly excessive. Also, constitution, temperament, and physical activity play a role.

The basis of every therapy is increased exercise. At first the amount of food is reduced about 20 percent, and later on, a further 10 percent. Energy-rich food should be replaced with a lower-energy mixture. Nourishing between-meals snacks must be eliminated altogether. Weight-reduction diets, which you can get from the veterinarian, are lower in calories and often contain a higher proportion of plant fiber.

Making sure that the extra pounds stay off of your dog will not only keep it looking good, but will also contribute to its health. Obesity in dogs, just like obesity in humans, can lead to all kinds of health problems; therefore, pay attention to your dog's weight. If you see it becoming overweight, take steps to correct the problem before it becomes overwhelming.

▶ **WHAT TO DO IF...**

4

... my dog won't stick to its diet?

The overweight dog stubbornly refuses its diet food, until the owner suddenly gives in and goes back to the accustomed food.

Cause: Diet food tastes different, and not always as good as the accustomed food. Small dogs in particular flex their muscles when a new type of food is dished up.
Solution: An overweight dog doesn't get hungry that fast. If it doesn't touch the special food, take the food dish away after 10 minutes. The next time give the dog a smaller portion. Keep repeating the exercise and offering less, until the dog eats it all. Especially at the beginning of the slimming program, make sure your dog gets plenty of exercise and keeps busy. The dog will often forget about begging and whining. Divide the daily diet ration into two meals. A medium-size dog should lose about a pound (500 g) in a week.

The Most Important Dog Care Tips

Regular care is important for keeping your dog looking good, but in addition, it requires a lot of attention and is the best way to detect illnesses early.

COAT CARE STROKES THE DOG'S SOUL. A dog's fur should repel all kinds of weather, protect against injury, and exhibit breed-specific traits. Because that works only when the fur is well cared for, long-haired breeds especially need our help.

Brushing and combing is an important sign of attention for a dog. Daily coat care also means dependable disease prevention: Parasites don't have a chance; colds, and other indispositions can be cured quickly; and in the case of serious illness, the early symptoms provide the veterinarian with valuable information for an effective cure.

Coat Care Basics

Some dogs have retained the thick all-weather fur of their forebears, and breeding has pre-scribed wirehair, shorthair, curls, and opulent silky coats for others. Dog coats are a theme with many variations. Despite different fur structure and fullness, the various types of fur resemble one another in their need for care— a dog's fur should be free of dirt, dust, and dead hairs; knots and tangles must be removed; and the protective, water-resistant oily layer on the skin should not be disturbed. The demands are necessarily much greater for show dogs in which the length of the hair and the finish play an important role.

A Dirty Slob? No Way!

If a dog goes out in the rain, its fur takes on a certain smell; it "smells doggy." It smells much stronger, and much worse to our noses, when the dog rolls in some foul remains. The fact that a dog's cleanliness is often called into question is surely due to its natural smell and its desire to "perfume" its fur ($\rightarrow$ p.179). But that's not fair, as the dog can't compete with a tidy cat, but it does keep its fur in good shape. Especially after a long walk a dog will often nibble its fur and get the dirt out of it. It's true of both cats and dogs that neglected coat care is the first symptom of illness.

Shedding

Dogs shed in the spring and fall, and in four to six weeks they lose a large amount of their hair. Depending on the breed, it may take up to three months to complete the renewal of the summer or winter fur. During shedding the need for coat care is greater than usual. Since the dead hairs itch, some breeds need to be brushed daily.

The Most Important Care Measures

A comb and brush are essential to coat care

($\rightarrow$ The Right Grooming Accessories, p.195). Handwork is just as important: The hand is used to loosen up the fur, undo tangles and knots, and get rid of dead hairs, often in whole bunches from the insulating fur of the winter coat. Scissors are used to trim the hairs from sensitive or hard-to-get-to areas; wire-hair is brought back to shape with a trimming knife, and curls are trimmed with shears. Trimming and SHEARING ($\circledcirc$ p.273) require experience, and if you have any hesitation you should let the pros in the dog styling salon handle it. On various parts of the body the hair grows in different directions; you can feel

⊙ INFO

Trimming and Shearing

In TRIMMING ($\circledcirc$ p.274), dead hairs are plucked out and living ones are short-ened. That requires the use of a strip-ping knife or thumb and forefinger. Shearing is done with haircutting or clipping shears. Terriers such as the Fox Terrier, West Highland Terrier, and Scot-tish Terrier are trimmed; Bedlington and Kerry Blue Terriers are shorn.

the direction with your hand. Brushing is usually done in the direction of the hairs; brushing in the opposite direction produces a stimulating massage effect.

Special Grooming Instructions

▷ **Longhair.** Regular combing and brushing at least twice a week with thick undercoat, and daily during shedding season. Typical for Spitz, Bobtail, German Shepherd Dog, New-foundland, and others.

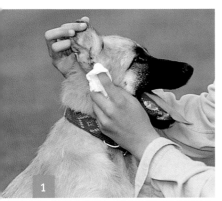

Ear care. Clean away dirt with a moist cloth, check ear canal for wax, and check the smell. A strong smell indicates an infection. All breeds with drop ears are particularly susceptible.

Eye care. Wash away secretions from the corner of the eye with a paper towel. Check the eyes every day with dog breeds that typically have problems (Basset Hound, Lhasa Apso, King Charles Spaniel, and others).

Paw and claw care. Check footpads for cracks; protect with Vaseline in the winter. Remove splinters and pebbles from between pads. Claws that don't get worn down enough must be trimmed back.

▷ **Shorthair.** With easy-to-care-for breeds such as the Boxer, Doberman Pinscher, and Mastiff, a dog glove can be used to remove dead hairs, dirt, and dust easily and quickly. Breeds such as the Corgi and Labrador Retriever must be combed and brushed once or twice a week, as under their thick outer coat they have a soft undercoat, which in the case of the Labrador Retriever repels water.

▷ **Wirehair.** The tough guard hairs of the Schnauzer and many terriers must be trimmed every 10 to 16 weeks. The fur around the eyes and ears is trimmed with scissors. With the Schnauzer the trimming produces the typical beard. The complete TRIMMING (❍ p.274) of an Airedale Terrier, for example, is very time consuming.

▷ **Silky Hair.** Because of the thin hair structure, the coat tends to tangle. If Afghans Hounds and Irish Setters are not combed and brushed regularly, it becomes very difficult to untangle their coat. Also, with spaniels at least the ears must be trimmed. Some small breeds

such as the Pekingese and Maltese also have silky fur.

▷ **Curly Hair.** Poodles, Bedlington Terriers, and Kerry Blue Terriers lose no hair and are a good alternative for people who have allergies to dog hair. The fur grows continually and must be shorn every eight weeks. A comb and brush are also required once a week. A dog should get used to shearing when it's a puppy so that it stands still during the procedure. This also applies to trimming.

▷ **Special Cases.** The fur of the Komondor and Puli consists of cords and tangles, and taking care of them requires special knowledge. Even the skin of the bald Mexican Hairless requires special care.

Care Requirements by Breed

▷ **For People Who Don't Care for Grooming.** Breeds that require minimal care include the Appenzeller Mountain Dog, Basenji, Beagle, Boston Terrier, Bull Terrier, Coton de Tulear, Dalmatian, German Mastiff, Doberman Pinscher, Entlebucher Mountain Dog, Smooth-haired Fox Terrier, French Bulldog, Irish Wolfhound, Labrador Retriever, Malinois, Rhodesian Ridgeback, Rottweiler, Sloughi, Whippet, Xoloitzcuintle, and Miniature Pinscher.

▷ **For Enthusiastic Groomers.** The fur care for the following breeds is time consuming: Afghan Hound, Bearded Collie, Bobtail, Chow Chow, Fox Terrier, King Charles Spaniel, Komondor, Lhasa Apso, Maltese, Pekingese, Poodle, PON, Puli, Samoyed, Scottish Terrier, Shih Tzu, Yorkshire Terrier, and Miniature Spitz.

A Bath for the Dog

A special grease-cutting dog shampoo should be used in giving the dog a bath about every three months—more frequently if the dog is very dirty. Dogs are relatively clean animals; however, they do require a good scrubbing at regular intervals.

Set the dog in the bathtub or the shower; a second person should hold the dog and a rubber mat underfoot keeps the dog from sliding on the bottom of the tub. Run a gentle stream of warm water onto the back, sides, and legs and massage in the shampoo. Keep the shampoo from contacting the eyes. Rinse thoroughly and dry the dog with towels.

In the winter keep the dog indoors as long as its coat and skin remain damp. Otherwise, you risk the dog's health. It will be vulnerable to various respiratory illnesses.

1 *Showing the teeth. Dogs rarely get cavities, but it's important to check for tartar. This is a threat especially to small dogs with teeth that are close together.*
2 *A good choice for grown dogs is a special chew snack that provides a mechanical cleaning of the teeth and reduces buildup of deposits and tartar on the teeth.*

The Right Grooming Accessories

The right accessories are necessary for grooming a dog properly and adequately. The basic equipment (→ p.93) should be on hand even before the dog moves in.

The earlier it gets used to the utensils and to being held for grooming, the more cooperative it will be in daily practice. This applies especially to breeds that have to undergo fairly long trimming or shearing sessions.

If the dog resists grooming, it can easily be injured. Be sure to use the grooming tools carefully. It takes many dogs months to get over shrinking from the scissors or wire brush that caused them pain through careless fiddling around.

Brushes and Combs

▷ **Hair Brush**. Soft, short, and thick natural bristles are fine for short-haired breeds. The bristles have to be longer and spaced farther apart for longer fur so that the hair can be worked down to the skin. Many brushes have metal teeth on one side and bristles on the other. Bristles made of nylon or other synthetic materials are not a good choice because they get charged with static and can break the hairs.

▷ **Wire Brush**. Brushes with stiff wire bristles require a skilled hand and are not a good choice for all breeds. Models in which the wire bristles are mounted in a flexible rubber bed are easier to use.

▷ **Currycomb**. The fine metal teeth of the currycomb are good for removing dead hairs from the undercoat (→ photo, p.199). Currycombs usually have two brush surfaces, one with metal teeth and the other with natural bristles.

▷ **Untangling Comb**. The rotating teeth make it easier to untangle the fur of long-haired dogs.

▷ **Dog Glove**. A dog glove is recommended for short-haired dogs such as the Doberman Pinscher. The short wire bristles and rubber knobs remove dead hairs and make the fur shine. The glove is not effective with longer fur.

▷ **Rubber Comb**. The comb removes dust and dirt and massages the skin.

▷ **Comb**. A plastic comb usually doesn't last long; a metal comb is a better choice. Basic equipment includes a comb with teeth spaced about 5/64 inch (2 mm) apart. It keeps firmly attached hairs from coming out with the dead ones during combing. A comb with teeth close together is used for fine fur that tangles easily. When you buy a comb, make sure that the teeth don't end in a point, but rather are rounded.

Scissors and Knives

▷ **Haircutting Scissors**. Scissors are used to shorten or remove hairs from sensitive body parts, such as the ears, around the eyes, near the muzzle, and around the anus and genitals.

Short scissors make it easier to remove hairs between the toes and footpads. The rounded points of the scissors reduce the risk of injury.

▷ **Thinning Shears**. Thinning shears make it possible to thin out the fur or even just the undercoat without changing the overall structure.

Thinning shears have either two toothed cutting edges or one normal one and one toothed one. Since they are not easy to use, beginners should get some instructions from an expert. The shears are used primarily for show dogs.

▷ **Claw Clippers**. A clipper is easier to use than scissors in shortening claws. The claw clippers should have a safety catch, and the cutting edges must be sharp to avoid painful bruising of the claws (→ Technique, p.198).

▷ **Stripping Knife**. The toothed, sharpened blade of the knife removes dead hairs and thins out living ones (→ photo, p.199).

Other Accessories

▷ **Dog Shampoo**. Alkali shampoo that reduces oil. Shampoos for people are inappropriate, as they destroy the acid protection layer of the dog's skin.

▷ **Dry Shampoo**. The powder is massaged into the fur and brushed out. This does not replace a bath with normal dog shampoo.

▷ **Massage Glove**. The strong knobs on the glove stimulate circulation in the dog's skin.

▷ **Toothbrush**. Tooth care with special toothbrush and dog toothpaste in various flavors.

▷ **Paper Towels**. Lint-free cellulose, essential for care of eyes, ears, nose, and anal region.

Daily Physical Care

On walks your dog sniffs at thousands of interesting things; it rolls in unidentifiable remains, and digs in the ground. Parasites settle in its coat, it can injure its eyes and ears in the underbrush, and get snagged by a claw. Careful attention assures that your dog remains fit and healthy and is protected from injuries and illness.

Eyes and Ears

With many dogs, secretions build up in the corner of the eyes that are easy to remove with a paper towel (→ photo, p.194). Dab encrusted secretions with a cloth moistened in lukewarm water and then carefully wipe them off. Excessive secretions may be the result of illness or foreign bodies. Usually the conjunctivas are also irritated and red. To check, gently pull the lower eyelid down. You should clean the eyes every day and check your dog's ears once a week (in the case of drop ears) or every two to three weeks (for erect ears). Remove earwax with a soft, damp cloth or a special ear cleaner; this can be difficult with ears covered in thick hair (→ photo, p.194). Because of the particular anatomy of a dog's ear, you should not use swabs, because they might push a piece of earwax down toward the eardrum. Redness in the ear canal is an indication of infection; hard, brown deposits indicate mites. A sniff check will confirm this; mite infestations are signaled by an unpleasant odor. With either symptom your dog belongs in the hands of a veterinarian. Heavily furred drop ears are more vulnerable and require more care than erect ears.

Nose

You can usually tell if your dog has been digging by noticing the dirt on its nose. Cleanup involves water and a paper towel.

Make sure the nostrils are clean, and if the dog's nose is cracked, apply a greasy, odorless salve (such as Vaseline), especially in the winter.

Teeth and Gums

Healthy teeth are almost more important for a dog than for us. Fortunately its teeth can withstand a lot. A couple of teeth may become wobbly in advanced age, usually among the incisors. The danger to a dog's teeth lurks elsewhere: tartar. Dogs that don't regularly clean their teeth mechanically with chew bones or hard food are particularly susceptible to tartar, which forms as a brownish layer around the base of the teeth. If the layer

The price of beauty. The long, sensitive silky hair of a Yorkshire Terrier requires daily care to keep it from becoming matted.

▽

becomes excessive, it must be removed by the veterinarian.

Severe tartar causes tooth pain and inflammation of the gums. One unmistakable indication is the dog's bad breath. To keep things from going that far, every dog should get used to regular teeth checks and tooth care from the time it's a puppy (◉ TOOTH CARE, p.274; also, photo, p.195). You can get toothbrushes and special dog toothpaste in pet shops.

In brushing the teeth, the chops are lifted up and the brush moves carefully in a circular motion over the teeth and gums. If your dog categorically refuses to have its teeth cleaned, you must give it hard food so that at least the top surfaces of the teeth will get cleaned in chewing.

Paws and Claws

Many dogs are very persnickety about their paws. It may take words of comfort, patience, and a couple of treats to get the dog to stop pulling its feet away immediately.

After every walk inspect the footpads for foreign bodies, leftover tar, salt, and rubber (→ photo, p.194). Dirt, pebbles, and splinters can get caught between the toes and lead to injuries and infections. After walking in the rain and snow, rinse the paws off in water and rub them dry. With long-haired breeds, trim the hair between the footpads with blunt scissors so that it doesn't become matted. Cracks and cuts on the footpads heal slowly, and commonly must be treated by a veterinarian. Make sure that the claws are not brittle, torn, split, deformed, or too long.

Cutting the Claws

With a dog that runs a lot on paved streets and roads, the claws naturally get worn down by themselves. However, excessively long claws have to be shortened, as the dog could get caught by them.

There are blood vessels and nerves in the claws that mustn't be injured when the claws are clipped. With light-colored claws you can

◉ TIP

Checking a Puppy's Teeth

Get the puppy used to regular teeth and gum inspections early on. It must consent without resistance and let you open its mouth. Holding the head and muzzle is a dominance gesture, but it also gives a puppy confidence.

see where the veins are, but not with dark ones. If you're not certain, you should have the claws clipped by a veterinarian or in a grooming parlor. Your veterinarian will gladly show you the right technique.

Claw scissors require more practice than a clipper. Shorten the claws a maximum of about 1/32 inch (1 mm) at a time; they can be cut back again if necessary. A claw is the right length when it doesn't reach beyond the surface of the footpad.

It is exceedingly painful for a dog if the nerve or blood vessel is cut. Keep a styptic pencil handy just in case, for an injured claw bleeds a lot.

One advantage of regular trimming is that it becomes normal to the dog, and the nerves and blood vessels retreat somewhat, thereby reducing the risk of injury. A dog that is injured when its claws are being cut often goes into a panic at the mere sight of the clipper.

Dewclaws

The fifth toe on a dog's foot is atrophied. In running, the dewclaw doesn't touch the ground and doesn't get worn down. Dewclaws are also present on the back legs of many large breeds.

4

If the claw grows inward toward the pad, it must be shortened or removed as it presents a high risk of injury to the dog. This is especially true for the Briard and the Lundehund, which have double dewclaws. If the dewclaws are covered by hair, it's easy to forget to check them.

Anus

The dog's anus may become matted with secretions from the anal glands or excrement. Use lukewarm water from the shower hose to wash away the dirt and matting; otherwise you can use a damp cloth. The care is easier with long-haired dogs, for the hairs around the anus can simply be trimmed. The genital area must likewise be free of dirt and secretions.

Emptying the Anal Sacs

The anal sacs are slightly low and left and right of the anus. A dog uses the secretions that are mixed with its droppings to mark its territory. Normally these sacs empty by themselves; however, sometimes the anal sac becomes plugged with thickened secretion and may become inflamed.

Plugged anal sacs cause itching and pain. The dog indicates plugging by "sliding" and it keeps dragging its bottom over the floor, continually licks its anus, or turns around in a circle. The unpleasant situation should be taken care of quickly. In cases of chronic plugging or inflammation of the anal sacs, the dog needs to see the veterinarian, who also knows the right technique to squeeze out the sacs.

1 *Basic care. The short teeth of the currycomb make it easy to remove dead hair from the undercoat of short-haired dogs.*
2 *Stripping. A stripping knife is used to shorten and thin out live hairs and pluck out dead ones. An expert should show you how to use the knife.*

Caring for Older Dogs

▷ As you groom an older dog, carefully feel its body for warts, knots, and tumors. If you find any lumps, you should consult a veterinarian to rule out the existence of a malignant tumor. Like humans, dogs are very susceptible to cancer, and it can be just as deadly for them. Such a condition can't be left untreated.
▷ Dogs are more susceptible to tartar in old age. Regular tooth care and chew bones provide effective preventive care and prevent receding gums and tooth damage. If tooth damage has occurred, you should consult a veterinarian.
▷ Discharges and growths that you notice in cleaning the anal and genital areas may be the first symptoms of illness. Again, if you find any problems, consult your veterinarian as soon as possible. Illnesses that are discovered in their earlier stages can often be treated more effectively than if they're discovered at advanced stages.

How to Keep Your Dog Fit and Healthy

Even dogs sometimes get sick. Every owner should know how to recognize illnesses early and how to get the four-legged patient back on its feet quickly.

TAKING CARE OF A FRIEND. One comprehensive health measure for the dog presumes that you know its physical constitution and behavior well enough so you can react quickly to changes.

Many illnesses lose their terror and can be combated more effectively when they are treated in the early stages. Every dog owner should know what to do if the animal is injured, seriously ill, or has to have an operation.

The success of the veterinarian's therapy also depends largely on active support by the owner.

Health Precautions and Early Detection

Dogs live in closer association with us today than ever before. Their continual nearness also guarantees that we immediately notice when their behavior changes—reluctance to go for a walk, indifference to playing with the children, and leaving half of its favorite food in the dish. In daily care the owner palpates the little knots under the fur and detects the inflamed conjunctiva in the eye. Along with knowledgeable precautions, early detection of illnesses is the dog's best protection against health problems.

The Healthy Dog at a Glance

▷ Dogs are curious creatures; a healthy dog is interested in everything that goes on around it.

▷ The dog stands straight, head erect, and its body has a natural tension.

▷ It moves easily and regularly, without holding back with one leg or limping.

▷ Its ears are in continuous motion (visible at the base of the ears with drop ears) and react to every sound.

▷ Its eyes are clear, with no discharge, and the conjunctivas are pink.

▷ The nose is moist.

▷ It has a good appetite, no problems eating, and no mouth odor.

▷ It drinks regularly, but not too much.

▷ It does not continually shake its head or scratch its ears.

▷ The fur is free of bald patches, and the hair is neither dull nor brittle. It doesn't scratch excessively, and doesn't continually gnaw or lick its fur.

▷ It does its business several times a day. The stool is well formed, the urine normal in color, and free of blood.

▷ The anus is neither matted nor smeared, and the genital area is clean.

The Most Important Preventive Measures

Preventive health measures begin when the dog is a puppy, even before it comes to your home. Knowledge of the bloodline and possible breed-specific diseases are just as important for its future health as are the proper living conditions, knowledgeable care, healthy food, and regular shots.

▷ **Bloodline.** Illnesses that occur in certain breeds are usually inherited (→ Research and Practice, p.223). Usually it's not possible to identify hereditary problems in puppies. The breeding guidelines of breed associations specify which bloodlines may mate in order to prevent hereditary problems. The breeder of a recognized breed association uses a Breeding Evaluation (→ p.223) that spans several generations to document the puppy's ancestry and health risks for the purchaser. Today there are effective preventive and detection examinations for the most common diseases, such as early detection of hereditary hip- and elbow malformations, or eye diseases such as glaucoma and progressive retinal atrophy.

4

◁

Keeping a cool head. Dogs are sensitive to heat. The grate in a car window keeps the inside temperature in the summer bearable, and simultaneously keeps the dog from climbing out of the parked car.

▶ CHECKLIST

What's Going On?

Frequent symptoms of illness in a dog, which every dog owner should take seriously:

- ○ Persistent diarrhea: possible food problems; go to the veterinarian promptly
- ○ Continuous vomiting: often stomach and intestine; consult veterinarian
- ○ Loss of appetite: along with high temperature, possible sign of infection
- ○ Fever: usually a sign of serious illness. See the veterinarian
- ○ Halitosis: tartar, inflammation of stomach lining; gastritis
- ○ Cramps: poisoning, epilepsy, calcium deficiency in a nursing female
- ○ Hard stool: improper nutrition (too many bones), lack of exercise
- ○ Shaking of head: ear inflammation, mites, or foreign matter
- ○ Hair loss: intestinal parasites, fungus, kidney problems, infection
- ○ Itching: allergies, diabetes, fur and skin parasites
- ○ Dragging the bottom: plugged anal glands, matted anus, tapeworm
- ○ Blood in urine: inflammation, bladder stones, penis injury
- ○ Blood in stool: dietary indiscretions, HGE, and clostridial colitis
- ○ Runny eyes: inflammation of conjunctiva, allergy, foreign matter
- ○ Dull fur: general disease symptom; consult with veterinarian

▷ **Shots.** Only a complete series of shots provides certain protection against infectious diseases. This includes the basic puppy shots and yearly boosters (→ page at right).

▷ **Nutrition.** Appropriate, balanced nutrition strengthens the immune system and encourages recovery. Nutritional deficiencies and inappropriate food lead to poor physical development, favor parasite infestation, and cause teeth damage and problems with fur and skin. Overweight dogs are disproportionately susceptible to frequent illness.

▷ **Living Conditions and Care.** A dog needs a pack. The closeness and care of the owner or the family are essential to its well-being. Dogs kept in kennels and neglected animals become ill in body and mind. Proper care is the basis of health maintenance.

▷ **Identification.** In addition to a dogtag, every dog should have a tag with the owner's phone number and address, and be identifiable through a tattoo or a microchip. In case of accident or other emergency the owner can be notified using the identification.

Things That Make Dogs Sick

When dogs suffer mentally they become sick. Depending on their psychological stability and personality, dogs react with fairly noticeable behavior deficits and symptoms of illness. The following situations can lead to bad behavior and disease:

▷ **Living Habits.** Frequent absence of the owner, irregular daily outings, friction in the family

▷ **Pack Structure.** Divorce, arrival of a new baby or pet

▷ **Living Conditions.** Moving, inadequate exercise, cage confinement, no area set aside for the dog, dominance by other dogs

▷ **Animal-human Relationship.** Coddling, physical abuse, lack of attention and care, poor training

4

Early Detection of Disease

The first indications of illness in a dog are often nonspecific. Carefully observe every deviation from the accustomed behavior and every physical change; so much the better if it later turns out to be a false alarm.

▷ Loss of appetite
▷ Excessive thirst
▷ Restlessness (especially at night)
▷ Weariness and apathy
▷ Continuous panting
▷ Reclusiveness
▷ Fear of bright light
▷ Fear of loud noises

Are Dogs a Threat to Our Health?

ZOONOSES (● p.275) are diseases that can be passed directly from dogs to people and vice-versa. The risk to us is minimal; cleanliness is the best defense. Roundworms and tapeworms (→ p.208) are communicable; infestation through a dog's whipworms and hookworms is extremely rare. Dogs and people are both susceptible to skin fungi, and the treatment is time-consuming. The only defense against rabies is having the dog inoculated regularly. People who are allergic to dog hair usually have to avoid direct contact with dogs.

● SHOTS AND WORMING

Basic shots and boosters protect dogs from the most dangerous infectious diseases. Regular worming is just as important. This chart is just a guideline; your veterinarian may suggest an alternative plan.

Age	Worm Cure for Round-, Hook-, and Tapeworms	Shot
2 weeks	●	
4 weeks	●	
6 weeks	●	With great danger of infection, preliminary shot for distemper and parvovirus
8 weeks	●	First basic shot for distemper, hepatitis, leptospirosis, and parvovirus
12 weeks	●	Second shot for distemper, hepatitis, leptospirosis, and parvovirus
16 weeks		Rabies, possibly kennel cough
6 months	●	
9 months	●	
16 months	●	Booster shots (multipurpose) for distemper, hepatitis, leptospirosis, parvovirus, and rabies
18 months	●	
28 months	●	Booster shot (multipurpose)

The multipurpose shot containing five vaccines is repeated over time. The shot for distemper and hepatitis is good for two years. Adult dogs are wormed twice a year, or more often when necessary. Worming is done two weeks before any booster shot.

The Most Dangerous Infectious Diseases

The only protection for a dog against the most common infectious diseases is preventive shots (→ Chart, Shots and Worming, p. 203). The treatment possibilities with a pre-existing infection are limited. INFECTIOUS DISEASES (❍p.266) are caused by bacteria, viruses, or one-celled pathogens. Transmission occurs from dog to dog, and through other infected animals such as foxes, rats, and mice, and frequently through indirect means involving objects that have come into contact with infected animals.

Distemper

▷ **Description:** High-grade infectious viral infection that can affect dogs of all ages. Young animals are particularly vulnerable. Intestinal distemper with vomiting and diarrhea, lung distemper with lung inflammation, and nerve distemper with paralysis and cramps.

▷ **Means of Transmission:** Usually by sneezing and coughing, directly from dog to dog, but also indirectly through droppings, food dish, clothing, and shoes. Danger of infection from wild animals such as martens and ferrets.

▷ **Course of Disease:** Very high fever, diarrhea, loss of appetite, and apathetic behavior in the first stage of the disease, approximately 7 to 21 days after infection. Additional inflammation of connecting tissue and highly infectious discharge from eyes and nose. After apparent recovery of several days comes a second fever phase, accompanied by discharge of pus from eyes and nose, diarrhea, violent vomiting, and continuous cough.

Is my dog healthy? Apathy, lacking or excessive appetite, unkempt fur, vomiting, and diarrhea are the first symptoms of illness.
▽

Because the distemper virus affects the whole body, often, several symptoms follow in succession: with the intestinal strain; these especially include vomiting and bloody diarrhea; with lung distemper, coughing, difficulty breathing, and inflammation of the lungs; with nerve distemper, cramps, loss of balance, muscle convulsions, and paralysis.

▷ **Treatment:** There is a hope of saving the infected dog with an immunization serum only in the early stage of the disease. In the case of an afflicted pup under the age of six months the formation of tooth enamel is usually disrupted. The damage leads to stunted teeth with brownish spots that persist for the dog's lifetime as "distemper teeth." Further possible long-term damage includes nerve disorders and cracked paws.

▷ **Prognosis:** Generally, dogs with nerve distemper can't be saved; to keep them from suffering they should be put to sleep. The survival rate with the other disease strains depends on their severity.

▷ **Preventive Shot:** Yes.

▷ **Danger to Humans:** None.

Hepatitis

▷ **Description:** Liver inflammation.

▷ **Means of Transmission:** The virus remains infectious for a long time. Transmitters may thus be dogs that have recovered from a liver inflammation and outwardly appear healthy.

▷ **Course of Disease:** With severe illness, hepatitis leads to death within a few hours. High fever, apathy, and eye and nasal discharge are typical symptoms. Disrupted blood clotting leads to bleeding in mouth and eyes. The stomach is distended and taut. Animals that recover from hepatitis often suffer from lasting kidney damage or chronic inflammation of the liver.

▷ **Treatment:** None.

▷ **Prognosis:** Slim chance of recovery.

▷ **Preventive Shot:** Yes.

▷ **Danger to Humans:** None.

▶ CHECKLIST

A Drugstore for Dogs

A pet store has everything necessary for first aid and treatment of illness and patching up minor injuries.

○ Thermometer

○ Blunt tweezers

○ Bandages

○ Curved scissors

○ Tick tweezers

○ Plastic syringe (with no needle) for dripping medications and liquid foods

○ Spatula for applying salves

○ Elastic wraps in various widths

○ Gauze compresses

○ Band-Aids

○ Absorbent cotton

○ Tissues

○ Lint-free paper towels for cleaning eyes and ears

○ Disinfectant for wounds

○ Salves for cuts and wounds

○ Vaseline for footpad care

○ Flea-prevention products

○ Worming supplies

Replace all medications after expiration date (such as eyedrops).

4

Parvovirus

▷ **Description:** Viral infection that can affect all dogs; especially dangerous for young dogs up to the age of six months.

▷ **Means of Transmission:** Principally through the excrement of infected animals. Parvoviruses are exceptionally long-lived and can cause disease even after years. Dogs that are under stress (for instance, because of cage confinement) are particularly vulnerable. Parvovirus is related to feline panleukopenia, but infection from a cat is not possible. In exceptional cases, however, transmission can occur from dog to cat.

▷ **Course of Disease:** First symptoms are dullness and fever alternating with low temperature, followed by bloody diarrhea and vomiting, trembling, and loss of appetite. The disease damages intestinal mucous membranes. The infection is often fatal, especially in puppies up to ten weeks old; often dogs die of acute heart failure without showing typical symptoms.

▷ **Treatment:** Medications have no effect on the virus itself. Increasing the dog's defensive powers through serums, a special diet, and antibiotics for diarrhea may save the dog's life. Comprehensive hygiene is especially important with parvovirus to keep other dogs from becoming infected.

▷ **Prognosis:** If an animal survives the first week of illness, its chances of survival improve, but frequently, the heart suffers long-term damage.

▷ **Preventive Shot:** Yes.

▷ **Danger to Humans:** None.

Leptospirosis

▷ **Description:** Bacterial infection that damages mainly the stomach, intestine, and kidneys. Other designations: Stuttgart disease and canine typhus.

▷ **Means of Transmission:** Leptospires include various bacteria that are transmitted mainly by rats and mice. Danger of infection

▶ TIP

Tropical Diseases

In the tropics and subtropics, and in the Mediterranean region, dogs can become infected with diseases that cause serious health damage and often are diagnosed late. These include leishmaniasis (→ p.208) and especially ehrlichiasis and piroplasmosis, both of which are transmitted by ticks.

in dogs is through puddles and other standing water, in which the pathogens can survive for quite a long time. The urine of infected animals is highly infectious.

▷ **Course of Disease:** Leptospirosis leads to fairly severe general illness, so at first the symptoms are often nonspecific: vomiting, fever, diarrhea, increased fluid intake, difficulty breathing, loss of appetite, sometimes jaundice. Sick dogs don't like standing. Eventual result: kidney damage.

▷ **Treatment:** Antibiotics and medications to reduce inflammation.

▷ **Prognosis:** Good, with mild case and early treatment.

▷ **Preventive Shot:** Combination vaccine for two leptospirosis pathogens.

▷ **Danger to Humans:** Leptospirosis can afflict humans as well as animals.

Rabies

▷ **Description:** A viral infection that must be reported to authorities; it follows various courses, and the symptoms are not always the same. Incubation times last up to a year. This is the most dangerous viral infection for humans and animals. Anther designation: Hydrophobia.

4

▷ **Means of Transmission:** The virus is excreted through the saliva of afflicted animals and usually gets into the body through bite wounds. All warm-blooded animals and humans may be affected. The main source of infection is foxes.

▷ **Course of Disease:** The first symptoms of a rabies infection are behavior changes. The dog becomes restless, reacts fearfully or overly friendly, but sometimes also aggressive and vicious. Later there is a distinction between "furious rabies" and "dumb rabies." In the former instance, restlessness and aggressiveness increase; the dog bites objects indiscriminately, howls, and salivates heavily. Its movements become increasingly random, and epileptic seizures occur.

Apathetic behavior with an indifferent gaze and pupils dilated to different sizes are typical of the dumb strain of the disease. The dog salivates constantly, and its lower jaw hangs down. In both forms of rabies, paralysis may result in the final stages.

▷ **Treatment:** No possible treatment. Unvaccinated animals that are suspected of having rabies must be killed.

▷ **Prognosis:** Incurable.

▷ **Preventive Shot:** Yes. Travel overseas with a dog is possible only with a valid rabies shot noted in the vaccination record. It must be at least four weeks but less than one year old (→ Vaccination Record, p.252). With the establishment of immunization codes for foxes, the principal carriers, the disease has been contained in some areas. Affected areas are sometimes marked with warning signs. Rabies vaccination for cats is also important to dogs.

▷ **Danger to Humans:** The infection is fatal in humans. Only with inoculated dogs can we be sure that the pathogen will not be transmitted.

Kennel Cough

▷ **Description:** Infectious disease caused by viruses and bacteria.

▷ **Means of Transmission:** Infection through saliva droplets from coughing. Spreads especially quickly in animal shelters and wherever many dogs live together.

▷ **Course of Disease:** Typical symptoms include hoarse barking, dry cough, and nasal discharge. Whistling sounds indicate inflammation of throat and larynx. Despite the persistent cough, afflicted dogs usually look perky. With a high concentration of cases, even inoculated animals may become infected.

▷ **Treatment:** A veterinarian attempts to quell the cough stimulus with medications containing codeine. Treatment with antibiotics prevents lung damage.

▷ **Prognosis:** Good. The "dog flu" is curable in nearly all afflicted dogs with no aftereffects.

▷ **Preventive Shot:** Part of the combination shot; however, the shot is not always reliable.

▷ **Danger to Humans:** None.

Other Infectious Diseases

▷ **Tetanus.** Tetanus bacteria are very widespread and remain viable as spores. They too can lead to illness in a dog if they get into the body through cuts and scratches and produce nerve poisons. The results include fever, mus-

◁

Annoying pests. When a dog scratches itself constantly, the cause is usually parasites, most commonly fleas. The saliva that a flea injects when it bites can lead to allergic reactions. The flea infestation is particularly bad in the summer.

▶ TIP

Infections That Must Be Reported

Every injury to a person caused by a rabid or suspected rabid animal, and contact with such an animal, must be reported to the health authorities (▶ REPORTING REQUIREMENT, p.272). If the pathogen *Echinococcus* (dog and fox tapeworm) is discovered, it too must be reported.

cle cramps, especially in the head area, a stiff gait, increased fearfulness, and sensitivity to noise.

Treatment involves serums and penicillin. Because of severe swallowing difficulties, afflicted animals must often be tube fed. Dogs and cats are rather insensitive to the tetanus pathogen, and serious illness is rare. There is no required tetanus shot for dogs.

▷ **Toxoplasmosis.** The toxoplasmosis pathogen is a tiny parasite (▶ PARASITES, p.269) that reproduces sexually only in cats. There is a danger to humans and dogs through eggs in cat excrement, and through raw meat (mainly pork) that contains toxoplasmacytes. Especially in young dogs the disease leads to nasal discharge, coughing, heart damage, and jaundice, and later also to meningitis.

Antibiotics lead to improvement in the early stages of infection.

▷ **Tapeworms.** A dog can become infected with tapeworms by eating raw meat containing tapeworm larvae, or through contact with rats, mice, and fleas. Symptoms include diarrhea, loss of weight despite normal appetite, and unkempt fur. Whitish segments of tapeworms are excreted with the droppings and are easy to identify on sight. Dog tapeworms

and dwarf fox tapeworms can be transmitted to humans. The fox tapeworm afflicts mainly foxes and rarely occurs in dogs. It's important to combat fleas, since they transmit the most common dog tapeworm.

Worming a dog regularly also protects people from infection.

▷ **Roundworms.** Transmission occurs in the womb. The worms (nematodes) are identifiable in a puppy's stool as early as the fourth week of life. Symptoms include diarrhea, weight loss, and developmental problems.

Administer worm cure starting in the second week of life (→ Chart, p.203).

About 12 percent of dogs are afflicted; nearly all young dogs are. High risk of infection for humans. Most susceptible are children—for example, through infected dog stool in the sand at playgrounds.

Prophylaxis through regular worm cures and thorough disinfection of the dog's bed is thus extremely important.

▷ **Leishmaniasis.** Dogs can become infected with leishmaniasis through travel in southern countries. The pathogens are usually transmitted by sand flies. Symptoms include weakness, weight loss, and changes in the skin.

It can be treated successfully only with early detection. Danger of infection also to humans.

▷ **Canine Coronavirus.** The virus is transmitted through the excrement of infected dogs and is related to the feline infectious peritonitis virus (FIP). The pathogen causes intestinal inflammation, but only rarely serious disease symptoms.

The symptoms can usually be treated successfully with antibiotics. No vaccine is available.

If you suspect that your dog has been infected by a parasite, you should bring your pet to the veterinarian. It is important not to let any parasitical condition persist, as it will only become worse over time. A veterinarian should be able to treat most infections with medication, and the problem should clear up quickly.

Research and Practical Application

Nutrition and Care

Calcium and phosphorus are important for a dog's bone formation and metabolism. A dog requires more calcium than phosphorus; an ideal ratio is 1.2 to 1. The ratio is 0.05 to 1 in meat, liver, and kidneys; in plant foods, 0.2 to 1. These food portions must also be enriched with calcium.
You can rarely achieve the right mineral content with food you prepare yourself; only commercially produced food is designed to supply the requirements of the animal organism.

A dog that moves its bowels frequently and excretes large amounts is not digesting its food adequately. A large amount of food passes through the large intestine and is excreted undigested. Intestinal bacteria that produce harmful metabolic products place a burden on the organism. High-quality food is largely utilized in the stomach and small intestine. It places no great demands on the dog's digestive mechanism, and it excretes less.
A dog is much more restless and less relaxed when it doesn't digest its food well, because it has a continuous need to relieve itself. Regularly check the quantity of the dog's stool.

Depending on the brand, commercially manufactured food contains between 40 and 70 percent meat, plus plant ingredients such as grains, vegetables, and high-quality organic soy. The meat percentage indicated on the label refers to the meat contents that determine the taste (for example, 4 percent wild game).
Your dog can detect the finest nuances of taste in its food, even when a preparation of beef and fowl contains only 4 percent wild game. Let the dog try several recipes and decide which one it likes.

Small dogs are more demanding than large ones; they don't accept just any food and usually eat slowly and with enjoyment—almost like cats. The larger a dog, the faster it gulps its food down.

◁
In the pink. A healthy dog that gets balanced nutrition is perky and alert; it has thick, shiny fur, no weight problem, and good digestion. This is what the veterinarian wishes for all his patients.

For a very large dog, divide the daily ration into at least two meals to avoid straining its digestive system (risk of gastric torsion).

Even short-haired dogs need regular care. They enjoy the ritual as long as they get used to it from an early age.
A dog lies on its back to get its tummy brushed. This is also a gesture of trust toward the owner.

Healthy teeth are vitally important to a dog. Special chew snacks cut the buildup of tartar and tooth deposits by more than half.
Chew snacks are an alternative for dogs that don't like having their teeth brushed.

4

Help with the Most Common Illnesses

Appropriate living conditions, healthy nutrition, a complete vaccination series, and regular worming protect a dog from illness. But even with the best care it may fall ill and depend on our care. People who observe their dog closely make it easier for the veterinarian to diagnose and treat the dog and protect it from serious health consequences. Because the susceptibility to certain diseases also depends on the breed, you should get information about your dog's possible tendencies.

Stomach and Intestines

▷ **Gastritis.** Serious vomiting frequently points to gastritis. Frequent, possibly bloody vomiting, and vomiting after drinking, are almost always signs of serious illness. Possible causes include intestinal parasites (often roundworms in young dogs), indigestion, poisoning, allergies, and spoiled food. Diarrhea usually accompanies gastritis or intestinal inflammation. Gastritis can also be caused by foreign matter and by infectious diseases (→ p.204). Attendant manifestations include stomach cramps, sagging posture, and a painful stomach area. With acute gastritis the dog should be taken to the veterinarian as soon as possible. Treatment with home remedies is rarely helpful, and in the worst case it costs valuable time that the veterinarian needs.

▷ **Gastric Torsion.** This life-threatening malady requires quick veterinary intervention, and usually an emergency operation. Causes of gastric torsion can include many factors, including, in many breeds, a weakness in connective tissue. If the food is not digested adequately and quickly enough, gases build up that distend the stomach. It becomes twisted along the long axis, thereby blocking the entrance and the intestine. The dog becomes restless and has great difficulty breathing. Its circulation collapses, and the situation requires immediate treatment. All large breeds are particularly susceptible. Smaller food portions reduce the risk. The dog must not play for at least two hours after eating.

▷ **Intestinal Blockage.** Foreign bodies that get stuck in the intestine, a strangulated hernia, or intestinal paralysis resulting from poisoning or infection may be the causes of intestinal blockage. Stomach pains, vomiting, loss of appetite, and apathetic behavior are characteristic signs. The dog can't evacuate its bowels. As with gastric torsion, the patient needs immediate help from a vet. An emergency operation is almost always unavoidable.

▷ **Peritonitis.** Peritonitis can have many causes: internal injuries after an accident, infection of the abdominal cavity after an intestinal rupture, or an inflamed pancreas. The dog has a fever, vomits, breathes quickly and shallowly, and suffers severe abdominal pain. The vet treats the condition with antibiotics and medicines that reduce the inflammation. An operation is often necessary.

▷ **Constipation.** Dogs that eat lots of bones experience hard stool. The animals can relieve themselves only with great exertion, if at all. The excretion problems are accompanied by increasing restlessness and continual licking of the anus. Paraffin oil in the food can provide relief in fairly mild cases. If the condition doesn't improve, the veterinarian must step in. Bones are not appropriate food for dogs, and not just because of the risk of constipation. Older dogs suffer from constipation more frequently than younger ones.

Skeleton and Muscles

▷ **Arthrosis.** Overweight dogs are especially vulnerable to chronic skeletal changes. Arthrosis can be caused by inborn deformations (→ Hip and Elbow Dysplasia, p.211), and through strain and dislocations. Inflammations in the joints are very painful, suppleness declines, and the dog limps. Further symptoms include loss of appetite and apathy. If the limping persists, take the dog to the veterinarian to relieve its pain. X-rays can be used for diagnosis. Chronic arthrosis often requires an operation. Some special food additives have proven useful. With acute pain the dog should not move much, especially if painkillers have been prescribed and the joint feels normal, because the dog can't feel the pain.

▷ **Slipped Disk.** Problems with disks afflict most breeds that have a long back and short legs. One example is Dachshund paralysis. Other dogs that are affected are Schnauzers, Spaniels, Poodles, and Basset Hounds. The cause is deterioration of the disk cartilage; the first symptoms appear at the age of four or five years. The dog becomes lame, can no longer jump, and experiences pain when it's picked up. This condition can progress to paralysis of the fore- or hind legs. Treatment involves medications that reduce pain and inflammation; an operation is required in severe cases. Take precautionary measures with susceptible breeds—avoid jumping and wild games as much as possible, and carry the dog on stairs.

▷ **Hip Dysplasia.** Large, heavy breeds in particular have a hereditary tendency to hip dysplasia because of malformations and changes in the hip joint. Depending on living conditions and the severity of the deformation in previous generations, HD eventually occurs. Mobility is reduced, it becomes difficult for the dog to stand up and lie down, and the condition may lead to lameness and loss of control over the hindquarters. Pain medication can alleviate acute discomfort, but chronic pain must be corrected surgically. An artificial hip can give afflicted dogs a nearly pain-free life. Have the dog X-rayed for HD starting in its twelfth month of life. Breeders use selective breeding (→ p.223) to prevent inappropriate mating and the risk of HD.

⊙ WHAT TO DO IF...

4

... there's no more hope?

The dog was a loyal friend to us for its whole life. And like a friend, we should be with it in its last hours and say good-bye to it.

Situation: The dog will never recover from its severe illness and is suffering visibly. Even the veterinarian can do nothing to assuage the pain.

Recommendation: This is the most difficult decision in all the years that we have lived with our dog, and during which it has grown in our hearts. But if it is suffering and there is no hope of recovery, it should be set free. The veterinarian can put the dog to sleep with progressive anesthetic. The dog will feel nothing and will peacefully drift away in sleep. You should be with it in the last minutes. If you have a yard and there are no restrictions (such as a watershed protection area), you can bury your dog. You can find more information about PET CEMETERIES in the quick reference guide on page 270.

Health barometer. With a healthy dog the nose is moist and cold; a dry, warm nose often indicates fever or illness. The moistness of a dog's nose holds scent matter and conducts it into the olfactory surfaces inside the nose.

▷ **Elbow Dysplasia.** The elbow joint may develop abnormally starting in the sixth month of life, especially among large breeds. This leads to stresses, bone separations, and lameness in the front quarters. An operation can stop the degenerative process. As with HD, animals at risk must not breed.

Skin and Fur

▷ **Dermatitis.** Severe itching is the typical symptom of dermatitis (skin inflammation). Continual scratching and biting leads to hair loss, eczema, festering infections, and susceptibility to further disease pathogens. Causes of dermatitis can include fleas, allergies, fungi, improper nutrition, worms, hormonal imbalances, stress, poisoning, injuries, and insect bites (○ PARASITES, p.269). Skin and blood tests make a precise diagnosis possible. With all types of illness, the dog must be kept from scratching and licking, either by means of bandages or a neck brace. Cortisone combats inflammation and itching; antibiotics are effective against bacteria. Circular bald spots in the fur are typical of many fungal infestations. The veterinarian can perform a fungus culture to identify the pathogen. The treatment is lengthy; in addition to special medicines, liniments, baths, and thorough disin-

fecting of the surroundings are required. Skin fungi can be transmitted to humans.

▷ **Mange.** This is an illness caused by two different types of mites. The symptoms of sarcoptic mange are severe itching, hair loss, lumps, scabs, wounds caused by scratching, and infections. Sarcoptic mange is communicable to humans. Symptoms of demodectic mange are red spots on head and legs, infected pustules, scabs on eyes, ears, and paws. The mites reside in the hair follicles of many dogs without causing harm. They take over only when the host's immune system becomes compromised, such as when worms are present. Young dogs are at risk. Treatment involves washing with special solutions and antibiotics.

▷ **Fleas, Lice, and Ticks.** These can be detected with the naked eye; flea droppings are tiny black dots. Fleas cause allergic skin irritations, and the dog flea is a carrier of canine tapeworm. Other mites form reddish nests on the legs, paws, and throat; in a fully developed state they are strawberry-size and easy to locate. They communicate diseases such as borreliosis and meningitis, which is dangerous to humans. Fleas and lice can be treated with sprays, shampoo, powder, topical preparations, and flea collars. Treating the surroundings is important. Insecticide tinctures can help with chiggers. Tweezers are the best way to get rid of ticks. To prevent infections, they must be removed carefully.

Heart and Lungs

▷ **Bronchitis.** Persistent cough, wheezing sounds from breathing, and breathing difficulties are indications of bronchitis. Bronchial inflammation is often caused by infections, foreign bodies, and hypersensitivity. Expectorants give the dog some relief and hasten recovery. If there is a risk of pneumonia, antibiotics must be prescribed.

▷ **Pneumonia.** Foreign bodies in the lungs, incompletely cured bronchitis, allergic reactions, and infectious diseases such as distemper can lead to pneumonia. Typical symptoms are a high fever, short, shallow breathing, coughing, and nasal discharge. Treatment is with antibiotics.

▷ **Heart Defect.** Coughing after physical exertion or resting at night, swollen paunch, and breathing problems may be signs of a defective heart valve. At first there is often an infection. A problem with a heart valve may lead to water in the lungs or the abdominal area. Sick dogs must often be treated medicinally for their entire lives to prevent subsequent illness. A heart defect can't be cured. Animals with a bad heart must not exert themselves too much or become excited. Inborn heart defects are usually breed-specific, but they are rare among dogs.

Liver, Spleen, and Pancreas

▷ **Acute Hepatitis.** Acute liver disease can be caused by poisoning, but it is often the result of an infectious disease (→ p.204). The symptoms are varied: sluggishness, loss of appetite, fever, vomiting, and jaundice in the eyes. Quick help can save the dog's life. Treatment involves antibiotics and infusions, plus a strict diet.

▷ **Chronic Hepatitis.** The causes and symptoms of chronic hepatitis are complex and difficult to assess. It may be caused by liver inflammation, infections, poisoning, improper nutrition, obesity, and diabetes (→ below). The afflicted dog is apathetic, drinks a lot, has diarrhea, and often a distended paunch. Loss of appetite, light-colored stool, and weight loss despite normal food consumption may point to chronic liver damage. The underlying disease is usually treated with antibiotics; simultaneously the dog is given cortisone and vitamins and placed on a strict liver diet.

▷ **Spleen Tumors.** The spleen in susceptible to cancer. A distended paunch, pale gums, and general weakness may be indications of spleen tumors. Benign growths cause no problems, but malignant ones often lead to the formation of metastases in other organs. If the

tumor bursts, the dog bleeds internally. If the spleen is removed in a timely manner, the dog can lead a normal life, as other organs will take over the functions of the spleen.

▷ **Diabetes.** The pancreas produces the hormone insulin, which is crucial for the energy supply in the body. With diabetes mellitus, the organs are undersupplied. This leads to damage to heart, kidneys, liver, and eyes. Symptoms include thirst, fatigue, and weight loss despite ravenous hunger. When diabetes is suspected, the veterinarian will check the blood sugar level and determine the insulin dosage that must be injected daily. Diabetic dogs have to stay on a diet for their entire lives.

TIP

Taking the Temperature

Lift the dog's tail and insert the Vaseline-lubricated thermometer about 1 inch into the anus. Don't let go, and withdraw it after a minute. A fidgety dog must be held by a helper. The body temperature of a healthy dog falls between 99.5° and 102.2°F (37.5–39°C).

Kidneys and Reproductive Organs

▷ **Nephritis.** Inflammation and infections can damage the kidneys permanently. Apathy, halitosis, altered drinking habits, weight loss, vomiting, and unkempt fur are signs that the entire organism is affected. The dog's breath smells bad, and the animal produces only a little, often dark-colored, urine. Acute kidney damage can also be caused by inflammation of the peritoneum, poisoning, sepsis of the uterus, and other diseases. Antibiotics, infusions, and a kidney diet can slow the progress of the disease.

▷ **Pyometra.** Six to ten weeks after coming into heat, a bitch often experiences a fever and severe thirst, vomits, and emits a vaginal discharge. The veterinarian determines that it's *pyometra,* an accumulation of pus in the uterus, which is often caused by a hormonal imbalance. Often (but not always) the ovaries and uterus must be removed surgically.

▷ **Prostate Enlargement.** Older male dogs are particularly prone to experiencing an enlarged prostate. It presses on the cecum, and the dog experiences pain upon excretion. The urine is often bloody. The disease can lead to blisters and kidney inflammation, and to the formation of cysts. A treatment with female hormones brings temporary relief, but the only lasting cure is by neutering.

▷ **Bladder Stones**. Bladder stones arise from bacterial infections and are encouraged by high mineral content in food. However, they are often genetically linked, as with Boxers, Shepherds, Dachshunds, and Poodles. Male dogs are more susceptible than females. Fairly small stones are removed by irrigating the bladder; larger ones require surgery. Diets can prevent new recurrence.

▷ **False Pregnancy.** Eight to nine weeks after coming into heat a bitch may exhibit false pregnancy (**◯** FALSE PREGNANCY, p.263). She behaves as with a normal pregnancy, produces milk, treats toys like her young, withdraws, and usually also builds a nest. Take the substitute puppies and the nesting material away. The only remedy for recurring false pregnancy is spaying (→ Info, above).

Eyes, Ears, and Teeth

▷ **Conjunctivitis.** Allergies, infections, dust, sand, and many other causes can lead to an inflammation of the conjunctivas in the eye (conjunctivitis). The symptoms are redness, tearing, sometimes a discharge of pus. In addition to eyedrops, a chamomile solution

 INFO

Neutering

In spaying (**◯** p.268) the ovaries and uterus are removed. Spaying prevents coming into heat, pregnancy, and false pregnancy, and protects against mammary cancer and inflammation of the uterus. The operation is performed usually before the dog first comes into heat. In male dogs, neutering can reduce aggressiveness and heightened sex drive, and usually the urge to roam also declines noticeably. Recent research indicates that unfavorable effects on the male's character are very rare. Because of hormone changes shortly after the operation, a neutered dog may experience increased appetite, and may become sluggish for a while. Carefully controlled feeding can prevent this problem. The operation is useful in preventing uncontrolled reproduction.

helps, but it should be used for only two or three days to keep from irritating the eye further. With bacterial infections eye salves containing antibiotics are prescribed.

▷ **Glaucoma.** Cloudy spots that affect the vision develop in the lens of the eye. Glaucoma is an age-related disease, but it can also be caused by an illness.

▷ **Ear Infection.** A dog scratches its ear, shakes its head, and experiences pain in moving. A foul-smelling discharge is typical for an inner ear infection. There are many causes: mites, bacteria, fungi, foreign matter, and excessive earwax. A veterinarian can prescribe eardrops and irrigation solutions. Foreign matter must often be removed under anesthesia. Careful attention to the ears, especially with breeds that have drop ears, helps prevent inflammation.

▷ **Periodontal Disease.** Tartar causes gum inflammation. If it is not removed promptly by the veterinarian, it leads to periodontosis or receding gums and may produce infection and loss of teeth. Hard food and chew bones slow tartar formation. Smaller dogs are particularly susceptible to tartar. Regular tartar control at the veterinarian's is important.

Nerves

▷ **Epilepsy.** Epileptic seizures often come out of the blue: The dog falls down and has cramps or passes out. This can be caused by a malfunction of the kidneys or liver, by tumors, low blood sugar in the case of diabetes, blood and oxygen deficiency in the brain, infections (such as distemper), and injuries. In many cases the cause of the attack can't be ascertained with certainty. Especially susceptible breeds include the Dachshund, Poodle, and Schnauzer. Usually the attacks occur between the age of one and three; they are more severe in older dogs. Long-term treatment involves sedatives (→ Emergency Aid, p.217).

Age-related Illnesses

▷ **Incontinence:** Many older dogs lose urine, often while sleeping. Tumors in the anus can contribute to uncontrolled defecation.

While incontinence is not one of the most serious of age-related illnesses, it can be a real nuisance in the household. People don't want their floors, rugs, or furniture soiled by their pets; therefore, it's a good idea to consult a veterinarian about this problem.

▷ **Constipation:** Older dogs get less exercise. Divide the food rations into several smaller portions.

Like incontinence, constipation is not one of the more serious age-related illnesses; how-

ever, it can be quite uncomfortable for a dog. Therefore, watching your dog's food rations as well as its general diet is highly recommended.

▷ **Tooth Problems:** Having the veterinarian remove tartar and taking care of the teeth retard tartar formation.

▷ **Vision:** Eyesight declines, often as a result of glaucoma. Many animals become blind. Still, with loving care most dogs can lead a nearly normal life.

If your dog loses its ability to see, you can make its life easier around the house by keeping things in order. For example, don't move furniture around unnecessarily. A dog that is familiar with its surroundings should be able to compensate to some extent for its lack of vision through memory. A stable household, in short, should help to avoid accidents.

▷ **Arthrosis:** The bones become weary, the limbs stiff, and the joints frequently arthritic. Pain-killers from the veterinarian provide visible relief.

If your dog suffers from bone or joint problems, do what you can to make its life more comfortable. Don't ask your dog, for instance, to engage in strenuous physical activities if they're going to cause pain. Also, you should think about arranging your house so that the dog can move around as easily as possible.

◁

Old-age aches and pains. The bones don't work so well anymore, the muzzle is gray, and the eyes and ears have become weaker. But even the old dog needs moderate exercise. And sometimes it even plays enthusiastically, like a young dog.

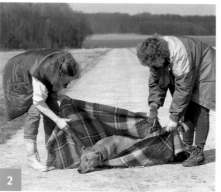

First Aid. Approach an injured dog carefully and speak to it reassuringly. Check the pulse and breathing, note any bleeding, and feel the body over for broken bones.

Carrying an injured dog. A blanket or bed sheet can be used to transport an injured dog. The help of a second person will be needed with large dogs. If necessary, first put on a muzzle and a leash in case the dog resists or becomes panicky.

Bandaging. Cover wounds with clean cloths or gauze pads and wrap with a gauze bandage. An elastic wrap can be wound on gently and will keep the bandage clean.

Emergency First Aid

Valuable time often goes by before an injured dog gets into the hands of a veterinarian. Quick help and the proper emergency care can save the animal's life. You should be familiar with the most important measures.

Important in Case of Accident

All it takes is one moment of inattention—your dog runs into the street and gets hit by a car. After making sure the accident site is safe, take stock of the situation; is the dog unconscious? Does it have visible injuries? Is it bleeding heavily? Does it react to you when you approach it?

▷ **Conscious Dog:** Remain as calm as possible and soothe it with a calm voice. A dog that is experiencing pain or is in shock may even bite its owner. Put a temporary muzzle on the dog before you touch it. A shawl, scarf, or a gauze wrap will work well; tie the cloth in the middle, place the knot under the lower jaw, and place the loop over the muzzle, cross the cloth under the muzzle, and tie the ends behind the head. The muzzle should not be used with an unconscious dog or in the case of chest injuries.

▷ **Bleeding:** To stop leg bleeding, tie a stocking, cloth, or elastic wrap above the wound. First cleanse a foot injury that's bleeding badly, then cover with tissues or cellulose and wrap with a bandage. Similar compresses can also be used to treat injuries to ears and eyes.

▷ **Broken Bones:** Avoid touching the area of the break so the bones don't move. Wrap a broken leg with a cloth and cushion it with a bandage. In addition, apply splints of twigs or sticks and secure with a wrap.

▷ **Panic Attack:** Place leash or cord around dog's throat or upper body to reduce the risk of getting bitten.

▷ **Unconscious Dog:** Be sure breathing passages are clear (foreign bodies, vomit), and place the tongue to the side between the teeth.

▷ **Shock:** Quick breathing, pale mucous membranes, elevated pulse, and unconsciousness or apathetic behavior are typical indications of shock. Lay the dog on its side, check for free breathing, and cover it with a blanket to maintain body temperature.

Transportation to the Veterinarian

In all emergencies the injured dog must be taken to the veterinarian or the animal clinic as quickly as possible. If possible, call ahead to be sure someone is there. A strong blanket makes a good stretcher; with large dogs two people will be needed. If a spinal injury is suspected, the dog must lie on a firm surface.

Quick Help in an Emergency

▷ **Epilepsy.** This is the most common cause of seizures fits in dogs. Symptoms include collapse, foaming at the mouth, cramplike movements in the legs, continual chewing, and loss of excrement and urine. Lay the dog in a dark, quiet place and keep it warm with blankets; check for free breathing; clean up droppings, urine, and drool; and offer drinking water as soon as the dog is feeling better.

▷ **Heatstroke.** Dogs usually withstand cold easily, but not heat. It gets especially hot in the car in the summer. Symptoms of heatstroke include circulatory collapse, panting and salivating, often fainting.

Spray the dog's body with water and get the dog to the veterinarian as quickly as possible.

▷ **Poisoning.** Symptoms: cramps, vomiting, collapse, bleeding, shortness of breath, apathy, pale mucous membranes, severe salivating, muscle twitches.

Get to the veterinarian's immediately. If the dog has ingested pills or chemical products (household cleansers or solutions), or nibbled poisonous plants (⚬ POISONOUS PLANTS, p.270), be sure to bring some of the questionable material or plant to the veterinarian when you go.

▷ **Foreign Bodies.** A twig, wood splinters, or a small ball can block the throat or windpipe.

Immediate first aid: Lift the dog up by its hind legs, open the mouth, and press rhythmically on the chest. For a large dog, get help from a second person. Deeper foreign bodies must be removed under anesthesia by the veterinarian.

▷ **Burns.** Symptoms: burned or singed hair, red- or white-colored skin, and blisters.

Cool the affected areas under flowing cold water or with ice cubes. Cover serious or large burns temporarily with a cloth or apply a bandage and get the dog to a veterinarian immediately.

▷ **Bite Wounds.** Inspect your dog for injuries after any fight. Apply a pressure bandage to bleeding bite wounds. Even wounds that are scarcely visible at first glance can become

 TIP

Help with Bee Stings

Dogs frequently step on bees and wasps. If they get stung they limp and lick their paw. Cool the painful area with ice or cold water and try to get the stinger out. Young dogs like to snap at insects. Cool a stinger in the mouth or throat and get the dog to a veterinarian quickly.

abscessed if they are deep.

Every bite wound should thus be treated by a veterinarian.

Quick help in an emergency just may save your dog's life; therefore, you should know what to do in each of these situations beforehand. Don't wait to learn until it's too late. Your veterinarian or local breed clubs or associations can provide you with information about emergency care. You should consult these resources at your earliest opportunity.

Taking Care of a Sick Dog

A dog that's sick or injured, or that has recently had an operation, is entirely dependent on our care. Instinctively, most sick dogs want to be close to their owners, swallow pills, and allow themselves to be bandaged without a murmur of protest. If you know the most important measures for caring for a dog, you spare yourself and your dog annoyance and assure that it will soon be back on its feet.

Hand-feeding

A dog weakened by illness often shows little appetite, or doesn't even touch its food. Without regular nutrition its body doesn't have enough resistance to get better. Offer your dog treats with your hand or let it lick small portions of food from your fingers. If it doesn't cooperate, you have to feed it. That's easier if a second person helps by placing one arm or hand around the dog's throat and the other around the muzzle, simultaneously pulling the chops upward. You can now use a spoon to place some food in the cheeks or dribble liquid nutritional supplements into its mouth with a syringe (with no needle!). Many dogs refuse diet food. Mix diet food with the accustomed food and increase the amount of diet food by about half with every feeding. Clear broth or meat juices make the food tastier, as long as they are not excluded from the diet.

Drinking a Lot

Even more important than the food is getting enough fluids into a sick dog. Especially with vomiting and diarrhea, the body dries out quickly when the dog drinks too little. Ask your veterinarian if you can offer your dog thinned milk or broth.

Pills and Drops

Medicine often tastes unpleasant. Dogs are not always cooperative when they have to swallow pills or drops.

▷ **Pills.** The surest method requires a little practice, and at the beginning maybe even help from another person. Grab the dog by the upper jaw and draw the chops upward. As soon as the dog opens its mouth, place the pill far back on the tongue. Use both hands to hold the muzzle closed until the dog has swallowed the pill, or hide the pill in a piece of sausage or cheese. Pills that are mixed in with the food usually get avoided. You shouldn't divide or grind up pills, for that sometimes releases bitter-tasting ingredients.

▷ **Drops.** As with liquid nourishment, introduce into the side of the mouth with the syringe.

Ointments, Baths, and Injections

▷ **Ointments.** With skin ailments (such as a mite infestation), the veterinarian will prescribe an ointment. Often the fur must be shorn from the affected body part. After applying an ointment, distract the dog with a game or a walk so it doesn't lick it off.

▷ **Bathing.** Sometimes the only effective treatment for parasites is a special active ingredient from the veterinarian. Here it is even more important than usual to keep the shampoo from contacting the dog's eyes and ears. Often the preparation requires some time to take effect. At the end, rinse thoroughly. Fungi and other skin ailments can be transmitted to humans. After each treatment, wash the hands thoroughly.

▷ **Shots.** Dogs with diabetes have to have an insulin shot every day. Pull up the skin on the neck or along the back like a tent, and insert the needle into the skin. Change the injection site daily.

Changing Dressings

Dab at seeping wounds with cotton moistened with disinfectant. Then apply wound powder, lay on a packet of gauze, and wrap with a bandage. Your veterinarian will tell you if air should be allowed to reach a seeping wound. A stocking or a T-shirt will protect a bandage on the dog's body from getting dirty, and the dog can't pull it off. A neck brace keeps a dog from licking off ointments, nibbling at wounds, or shredding dressings.

Care Following Operations

After neutering or other operations, a dog may still be anesthetized or very weak. Wrap it up in blankets to keep it warm during the drive home and set its bed near the heater at home, maybe even with an additional heat source (such as a heat lamp). The dog must lie relaxed on its side and be able to breathe freely. It mustn't drink after waking up, and should not be fed for at least eight hours after the operation.

An Appointment with the Veterinarian

The veterinarian can't ask a dog about its complaints, and must depend on your help. Take note of every change in behavior and every physical symptom. When did you first notice the problem? Has it gotten worse? Does the dog vomit, have diarrhea, or pass blood in its urine?

If there's any doubt, bring a sample, especially if poisoning is suspected. The veterinarian also needs to know if you have already given the dog medication, especially one that was not prescribed. You should also bring your dog's vaccination record to the veterinarian, even if it has not yet had any shots or been wormed.

If you can provide accurate information about your dog's condition to the veterinarian, he or she will be able to render a diagnosis—and come up with a treatment—that much more quickly. In extreme cases, a dog's life may actually depend on the rapid diagnosis and treatment of a problem; therefore, when you see your veterinarian, you should be prepared to provide him or her with as much information as you can possibly gather about any problem.

4

Take it easy. In the first few days after a fairly long illness or an operation, avoid spurring your dog on to physical exertion.

▽

How About Alternative Animal Medicine?

Natural treatments are popular even in veterinary medicine. Whereas classical medicine treats the symptoms of illness, alternative medicine works with the whole body, mind, and soul. Natural treatments are intended to strengthen the body's self-curing powers without causing any undesirable side effects.

Possibilities and Limitations

Natural cures can't be used to cure a dog of a hereditary disease or mend a broken bone. The limitations of alternative veterinary medicine end where broad-reaching organ changes make self-healing impossible. Natural remedies can foster the healing process, however, by stimulating the functioning of a diseased tissue organ. Especially in dealing with infections, allergies, and chronic pain, it is possible to visibly improve a dog's quality of life. Alternative veterinary medicine uses curatives and physical and behavior therapies that on a case-by-case basis may complement conventional treatment methods.

Homeopathy

The basis of homeopathic treatment methods is the similarity rule: Like can be cured by like. Active ingredients are not used as antidotes, but rather as specific stimulants to induce the process of self-healing in the body. Mineral, plant, and animal substances in highly diluted concentrations are used. The rule specifies that the smaller the dosage, the stronger the effect. The degree of dilution is given in potency grades: D1 means a dilution in a ratio of 1:10, D2 indicates 1:100, and so forth.

The dog's disease symptoms are less the focus of homeopathic treatment than its nature and individual constitutional type. Is it a sensitive loner that doesn't like to be touched by strangers? Such dogs are strong-willed, confident, and good performers, but they bond with just one person. They like salty food, and in homeopathic treatments, they respond to salt preparations. Or is the dog rather of the timid glutton type, and excitable and very sensitive to pain, that gulps down everything edible and tends toward digestive difficulties? This type can be helped with preparations of nux vomica. In classical homeopathy the veterinarian chooses the appropriate medication for the individual dog based on a thorough report from the dog owner. There are also combination preparations that a dog owner with a little experience can use in cases of cold, diarrhea, or nervousness in the dog.

Bach Flower Therapy

The English doctor Edward Bach discovered flower therapy as a gentle healing method, in which the focus is not on the physical illness symptoms, but rather on the patient's emotional state. Bach flower therapy has been used successfully with dogs in recent years. In all there are 38 flower essences available that are administered to dogs in highly diluted, watery form either directly onto the tongue or mixed with its drinking water. They exert a positive influence on mental disturbances such as impatience, lack of confidence, timidity, and aggressiveness by strengthening self-confidence. Bach flower therapy has proven its worth especially with dogs under stress, such as before a visit to the veterinarian or in giving birth.

The Bach flower mixture "Rescue Remedy," which contains essences of cherry-plum, touch-me-not, white clematis vitalba (traveler's joy), yellow rock rose, and star of Bethlehem, can help in an emergency, and if a dog is in shock or panic, as after an accident. The drops alleviate pain after operations and are

1

Relieving pain. Pressure is applied to specific points in the body through acupressure. This healing system is used successfully in treating chronic pain.

2

Improved well-being. Massages stimulate the circulation and relax the muscles. They are used therapeutically after muscle injuries and with mobility problems.

effective in treating wounds—but even these healing methods have their limits. A dog's behavioral tendencies due to breed and breeding are scarcely treatable with Bach flowers.

Acupuncture

The acupuncture method is an offshoot of traditional Chinese medicine. Illness is viewed as an imbalance between the two opposing but complementary forces of Yin and Yang. They contain the life's energy Qi, which flows through the body along meridians.

When the Yin and the Yang are in equilibrium, the body is in harmony and the organism is healthy. If it is sick, in classical acupuncture small needles are inserted at certain acupuncture points (670 in a person, 112 in a dog) along the body's meridians, in order to stimulate or dampen the energy flow.

Veterinarians who are oriented toward western acupuncture place the needles in places where the dog is feeling pain. The needle pricks are intended to stimulate receptors and free up endorphins (pain-killing substances) from the brain.

Acupuncture replaces neither urgent, necessary medicines nor operations; however, it is a pain therapy for dogs with back pain, arthritis, or tendon damage, and for various diseases of the nervous system. If the treatment is performed in a relaxed manner, calm dogs even fall asleep. Dogs that become excited or resist the treatment should be spared acupuncture.

Acupressure and Shiatsu

Acupressure and shiatsu, like acupuncture, work on the principle of meridian flow. Instead of needles, acupressure uses the fingers to apply pressure or rub the acupuncture points and the neighboring tissue. Acupressure is recommended especially for dogs that resist the needles, and it has the additional advantage that the dog owner can administer the treatment at home after receiving instructions from the veterinarian. Acupressure and acupuncture work well together; the veterinarian can first relax the dog with acupressure so that it doesn't resist inserting the acupuncture needles.

With shiatsu therapy the entire body of the dog is worked with finger pressure. It should bring on muscle relaxation that increases the blood supply and promotes healing.

Tellington-Touch

Within the framework of horse training, the Canadian horse trainer Linda Tellington-Jones developed a gentle form of body therapy. Her basic idea comes from the Feldenkrais method, which helps people to become more aware of their body.

Today, the so-called Tellington Touch (TTouch) is also used with dogs. The body is worked using certain circular and stroking motions of varied intensity. It is intended to activate cell functions, stimulate the nervous system, and encourage the dog's simultaneous relaxation and powers of concentration.

TTouch strengthens the bond between master and dog. The dog must perceive the touching as pleasant. It may even serve to alleviate behavior problems such as aggression and excessive nervousness.

TTouch therapy is the means of choice for calming anxious animals. It is used successfully in soothing pain and chronic suffering in dogs, accelerating the healing process, and stimulating self-healing.

One advantage of the gentle healing method is that every moderately patient dog owner can learn to use it. There is no doubt that the treatment is good for dogs; reportedly there are animals that demand their TTouch regularly and emphatically.

Therapeutic Massage

Massage doesn't just make your dog feel good. It can soothe indisposition and pain, relax muscles, and stimulate the circulatory system. That increases the amount of oxygen in the tissues, and harmful metabolic products are carried away more quickly.

Various techniques are combined in therapeutic massage and are carried out as far as the dog permits. The massage begins with gentle stroking motions in one direction (effleurage), which is intended to calm the dog. Then certain skin and muscle regions are drummed, kneaded, gently wrung, and rolled (pétrissage).

Therapeutic massages are used for illnesses of the movement apparatus and for treatment of muscle injuries. But they should never be used in case of a slipped disk, inflammations, and in the vicinity of broken bones and tumors. A massage should also be avoided if the dog has a fever or has injured itself in the back or throat.

Massages also strengthen the bond between master and dog and make it easier for the owner to detect the dog's physical problems earlier.

Hydrotherapy

Water is an ideal medium even for dogs. It gives the body buoyancy and takes the strain off limbs and joints after injuries or with degenerative diseases. When the water is cold, it causes the blood vessels under the skin to contract, and that can be helpful with inflammations, but warm water dilates the blood vessels and increases the blood supply.

Whether you take your dog to a trained hydrotherapist or let it swim in a pond or river, it's best to let the dog decide for itself how it wants to come into contact with the water.

Dogs are naturally strong swimmers; however, if you allow your dog to swim in a pond, a river, or the ocean, you should supervise it at all times, just as you would a child. Pond, river, and ocean waters can be treacherous, and your dog may get into trouble and need assistance to get back to shore.

Furthermore, pond, river, and ocean water contains minerals—and, sometimes, harmful substances—that could affect your dog's health; therefore, you should clean your dog thoroughly after it comes out of the water.

A day at the beach, in short, can be great fun for you and your dog. Swimming is a very good way for both you and your dog to get your required exercise. However, because there are dangers involved in going into the water, you should take the appropriate precautions to make sure that a fun day at the beach doesn't turn into a tragedy.

Research and Practical Application

News About Dog Health

In both city and country, dog ownership poses no health risks to humans. This is the conclusion of research by the microbiologist D. Anton Mayr. Sixteen families with children and fifteen older couples who live with dogs participated in his study. No fungus or parasite infestation could be detected in any of the animals.

A few simple rules assure safe hygiene in dealing with your dog: Prompt inoculations, preventive worming, and regular cleaning of the sleeping area to keep parasites away.

The skin makes up 12 percent of a dog's organism and is the largest organ. Since it is extremely metabolically active, up to a third of the dog's requirement of protein and other nutrients are used for maintenance of skin and fur.

The dog's health, well-being, and nutrition are reflected in the condition of the skin and fur. Balanced, healthy nutrition provides for a vital, shiny fur; unkempt, rough fur is the first indication of indisposition and illness.

Up to 40 percent of fungal infections in dogs are caused by the skin fungus *Microsporum canis* (with cats the figure reaches 95 percent). Even dogs with healthy skin can be infested with up to 10 percent *M. canis*. The skin fungus is one of the transmittable skin fungi that can affect humans.

Infection with skin fungi usually occurs through direct contact. Children who cuddle with dogs are at particular risk. The first symptoms are bald spots on the head. Careful washing (wash hands after contact) can prevent transmission.

Swedish researchers have determined that a reaction to animal allergens can be caused by the clothing of people who have had previous contact with animals.

Before you buy a dog, check to see if you or your family have any allergies by visiting dog owners or an animal shelter.

◁
Playing it safe right from the beginning. A puppy can become infested with worms even in its mother's womb. It needs to be wormed every 14 days from the second through the twelfth week of life, and later every three to four months (→ Vaccination Schedule, p.203)

The BREEDING SUITABILITY EVALUATION (◉ p.260) makes it possible to assess the dog's genetic baggage and the risk of genetic diseases, such as hip dysplasia (HD). With HD a dog's breeding value is determined based on its HD grade and those of its parents, littermates, and other offspring. The value is compared to the average for the breed. If it is higher, the hereditary risk is greater than the average; if it's less, the risk is lower.

When you buy a puppy, be sure that the parents are as free as possible of hereditary diseases. Even in mild cases you should consider the purchase carefully.

Ten Questions About Nutrition, Care, and Health

Raw pork is taboo for dogs. But I have also read that all raw meat can be dangerous. Is that right?

It's mainly through raw pork that a dog can become infected with the pathogen for the fatal Aujeszky's disease. But even other animal foods in the raw state can transmit bacteria, viruses, and parasites. They should be cooked, to play it safe.

We have a Mastiff and a Dachshund. The little guy goes to the water dish more frequently than his big friend. Is there something wrong?

In fact, small dogs drink proportionally more than large dogs. A different need to drink depends on lots of factors, though, and can be caused by the Dachshund's higher activity level.

My Beagle is seven months old and is still getting puppy food. When should I change it over to food for adult dogs?

An adult beagle weighs 26 to 33 pounds (12–15 kg) and is one of the medium-size dogs. You can keep feeding your dog puppy food up to about the age of 12 months and then switch over to food for adult dogs. Proceed gradually and every day mix in more of the new food with the accustomed food for about a week, after which it will get only adult food. A dog's sensitive digestive system will often react with diarrhea to a sudden change in food.

Our Cairn Terrier is thoroughly healthy, except for the continual buildup on its teeth. The dog won't have anything to do with tooth brushing. What can I do?

There are three causes for buildup of tartar and other deposits on the teeth: an inborn tendency, too little crunchy food, and even inadequate exercise.

What does exercise have to do with the teeth, you ask. A lot, for whenever a dog is in motion, the tongue and chops rub against the teeth and automatically perform a mechanical cleaning. An active dog thus generally has healthier teeth than a stay-at-home.

The size of the dog also evidently plays a role. Small dogs have a greater susceptibility to tartar than larger breeds. Dog researchers believe that the smaller jaw area of small dogs is responsible. The teeth are closer together than with large dogs. The bacterial tooth film finds the best conditions for taking hold in the tight spaces between the teeth.

If your Cairn Terrier wants nothing to do with tooth brushing, you should at least regularly give it tooth-cleaning dental sticks or other chew snacks. The daily tooth care snack helps reduce tooth deposits by up to 60 percent.

Totally relaxed. Not only the physical constitution, but also the behavior says a lot about a dog's health. It's obvious that a puppy that lolls about feels fine.

Spic and span. The fur of these two tidy little fellows wouldn't be so neat without the daily care by their owner.

One of our Bearded Collies frequently vomits his food and then eats it again. Can we cure him of this?

Like their wolf forebears, dogs gulp down their foot hastily and later regurgitate it for consumption at leisure. Divide the daily ration into two meals if the dog frequently shows this behavior. Divided feedings will also keep your Bearded Collies from coveting each other's food.

It would be good for our Newfoundland to lose a couple of pounds. Does a day of fasting make any sense?

One day of fasting per week is no problem for the dog, but usually the human has a guilty conscience and eventually gives in. Here's how to reach the goal sooner: Instead of a single meal per day, divide it into four small ones, with no snacks in between, and provide lots of exercise. Or, have your veterinarian prescribe a special weight-loss diet.

At what age do puppies become susceptible to worms?

Every newborn dog already has worms from its mother. Puppies thus need to be wormed for round-, hook-, and tapeworms starting in the second week of life and continuing in 14-day cycles.

Besides neutering, are there other means of preventing reproduction?

The veterinarian can suppress a female's coming into heat with hormone treatment consisting of either shots or pills. The hormone cure is not a long-lasting one, though.

I can't get my Kromfohrlander into the bathtub. How can I convince it to bathe?

Few dogs willingly take baths. If they get shampoo in their eyes or slip in the bathtub, the aversion becomes even stronger. Start with a gentle wash cycle outside the bathroom, for example in a warm cellar or outdoors in the summer. Moisten the legs and flanks with warm water and a sponge or hose, massage in grease-cutting dog shampoo, and carefully rinse. Clean the head area only with a damp cloth. Finally, rub the dog dry with a towel. Praise your dog when it stands still.

Our dog has been free of fleas for barely a week, and they are back again. What can we do?

A good grip. To pick up a puppy, place both hands under the body for secure support.

There are effective products such as dog shampoos for combating fleas and lice. You can get collars, drops, sprays, and powders in pet shops or from your veterinarian. Since fleas go onto the dog only to suck blood, it's very important to disinfect the dog's bed and the surrounding area. A vacuum cleaner is also useful. Before using it, spray the vacuum cleaner bag with flea spray.

Sports, Games, and Travel

Most dogs love to play throughout their lives, preferably with their human partner. If you want to get your dog into good physical condition or be active with it, there are many appealing choices, from Agility and Obedience to demanding competitive dog sports. Of course, today, dogs naturally go traveling with us. The main thing is to travel safely and get home healthy.

5

Playing Makes Dogs Strong

Playing is no afterthought for a dog. It uses play to discover its surroundings, test its abilities, and establish social ties. Play is part of its personality.

A LIFE OF PLAY. Everything is a game to a puppy: testing its strength with its littermates, discovering the new world, and the first training steps with the master. Dog experts and behavior researchers have known for a long time that nearly every dog can be motivated to cooperate by means of playful learning exercises that they make it possible to reach training goals more quickly. The lessons learned are retained better than with formal instruction and training.

Playing strengthens the relationship between human and dog. Whether tricky combination and thinking games, hiding games in the house, or power play with Frisbee and ball outdoors, playing keeps body and mind fit. Little, low-key games are great therapy for bored animals, encourage recovery after illness and operations, and help get little fatties back into shape.

Appropriate Play and Meaningful Activity

A dog's world is in continual motion. Every dog is enthusiastic about playing sports. At the top of the list are chasing balls and Frisbees, fetching games, chasing and hunting games. Dogs have a phenomenal memory and powers of observation that are ideal for thinking, puzzles, and digging games. And in hide-and-seek games they are the champs, and they beat their human partners by more than just a nose.

The Ten Commandments for Playing with a Dog

▷ **Established Playtimes.** Set firm times for playing with the dog. Dogs are creatures of habit and quickly learn when it's time to play and when it's not.

▷ **You Are the Boss.** In all games together with the dog, you are the one who decides what, when, and how long to play. Especially after wild games, indicate the end of the play session by telling your dog, "*Sit!*" or "*Down!*"

▷ **Keep the Toys Put Away.** Certain toys are reserved exclusively for playtime and are put away at the end of the game. This toy will have special significance for the dog, and it will retain its interest for a long time.

▷ **Don't Overdo It.** The duration, intensity, and demands of a game have to be tailored to the dog's abilities. Take a break if your dog starts to lose interest. (→Types of Players, p.231); thinking games and combination tasks should not be too complex. The most important incentive for the dog is praise and recognition for tasks performed well.

▷ **Facilitate Learning.** Puppies learn through play, so play with a puppy only when it's focused on the task. Stick to short playtimes as a young dog tires quickly.

▷ **Taboo for Dominant Males.** Strong males often try to test their superiority over humans through competitive play. Allow physical contact only with dogs that are well trained. This type of play is inappropriate for children.

▷ **Stop Anytime There's a Danger of Injury.** Fetching stones: wearing down the teeth; playing with small objects: danger of swallowing; playing tug with puppies: jaw problems; playing on icy ground: sprain from slipping, playing on a surface that's been salted: chapped paws; playing on road surfaces softened by heat: clumps of tar retained in pads; swimming in unfamiliar water: possible injury. Injury is possible also from playing on stairs, tiles, or wooden floors.

▷ **Cut Back on the Playing.** For puppies and old dogs, for pregnant bitches, after illness or an operation, and in summer, especially for breeds that are sensitive to heat.

▷ **Rest Time.** After feeding and whenever the play becomes serious, or when the dog has overexerted itself. The symptoms: extreme panting, restlessness, vomiting, and lameness.

▷ **Do Not Disturb.** Play with your dog only when it's in the mood for play. Don't wake it up and invite it to go play.

◁

Under control. Nobody should have to work too hard at sports and games with the dog outdoors. Be mindful of people who are afraid of dogs. The dog must always be kept on a leash in areas where there are wild animals.

THE BEST TOYS

Balls, squeak toys, and tossing rings are at the top of the list of preferred dog toys. Many creatures have their personal favorites such as an old blanket, a stuffed toy, or a rubber bone. All toys must be bite-proof and free of chemicals.

BALL

Appropriate for   Ball: Finding and fetching games, toss and catch; Also for indoor games and for playing alone. Large ball: nudging, pushing, "soccer"; especially for playing together outdoors

Recommendation   Ball: Firm and not too small; large ball: As light as possible

FRISBEE

Appropriate for   Fitness training and incidental games on walks. Not appropriate for puppies or young dogs as jumping after the Frisbee puts a lot of strain on the hip joints.

Recommendation   Choose lightweight disks (approx. 4 ounces. / 120 g); replace shredded ones.

TOSSING RING

Appropriate for   Toss and catch, carrying while on walks; ideal for fetching exercises during training.

Recommendation   Match size and weight to size of dog; make sure the ring is bite-proof.

SQUEAK TOY

Appropriate for   Fetching, guarding, and carrying around, favored by dogs of all ages, and good for a teething puppy.

Recommendation   Look for a durable rubber shell to keep the squeaker from getting swallowed; take away chewed-up toys.

FETCHING DUMMY

Appropriate for   Fetching and carrying around. Dummies and fetching logs are used in many facets of training and education.

Recommendation   Choose a version in the right size and weight for the dog.

TUG ROPE

Appropriate for   Playing tug and chewing games, develops the chewing muscles and is particularly important for puppies getting their adult teeth.

Recommendation   Look for strong material (usually cotton) when purchasing.

Come Play!

Dogs are articulate. There are many ways in which they communicate their desire to play:

▷ **Playful facial expression.** This facial expression is unmistakable: the top of the nose wrinkled, teeth bared, wide-open gaze fixated expectantly on the play partner; often coupled with an invitation to play.

▷ **Invitation to play.** Crouching forequarters, front legs flat on the ground, hindquarters raised, friendly tail-wagging. The dog usually makes little jumps and barks loudly and clearly in this posture.

▷ **Showing the toy.** The dog picks up its favorite toy and shows it to the person.

▷ **Nudging.** The dog nudges a person's hand or leg with its nose.

▷ **Paw contact.** Touching with a paw invites a person to notice and pay attention to the dog.

▷ **Growling and barking.** Dogs that are ready to play tell us with a loud, high-pitched bark; puppies typically growl when they want to play.

▷ **Play-biting.** The play partner is grasped very carefully with the teeth.

Types of Players

Terriers are crazy about playing; the wilder it is, the better they like it. Their favorites are balls and Frisbees. Herding dogs such as the Bernese Mountain Dog, Bobtail, Collie, and Shepherd love to fetch and are good at games of skill and hiding. Bassets, Beagles, retrievers, and spaniels have the best nose for following a trail in hide-and-seek games. Boxers, Hovawarts, Poodles, and Doberman Pinschers are ready for any kind of game, as long as their owner is involved. The midgets such as the Chihuahua, Papillon, Pekingese, and Miniature Poodle prefer to play indoors. They are perfect partners for thinking-, puzzle-, and combination games.

Dogs that love children and are always ready to play: Beagle, Bobtail, Boxer, Cocker Spaniel, Dalmatian, Eurasier, Fox Terrier, Golden Retriever, Poodle, Spitz, and West Highland White Terrier.

△
A top athlete. Playing with a Frisbee is great fun, and it requires total physical involvement on the part of the canine player.

The Right Toy

Choose toys made of safe materials—and nothing that has been painted, glued, or chemically treated.

▷ A chew toy is particularly important for puppies: tough, durable pull rope, strong cotton cloths, a pure rubber tossing ring, or a splinter-free chew bone.

▷ Balls excite all dogs. Knobby or smooth pure rubber balls, a large ball of fairly stiff leather or tough plastic. Beware: Balls that are too small, such as golf balls, can get stuck in the throat.

▷ Squeak toys with a strong rubber shell so that the squeaker can't be swallowed. Squeak toys are fun for a long time, and they strengthen the chewing muscles.

Little Indoor Games

Games inside the house are more than a stop-gap measure when the weather is bad or there's not much to do outside:

▷ There is always a little time for a quick ball- or searching game in the house.

▷ Playful training exercises work better indoors, as there are fewer distractions for the dog than outside. This is especially true for puppies.

▷ With dogs that aren't obedient, there is no danger of their running away.

▷ Older animals whose bones no longer cooperate are not overly taxed by low-key games.

▷ After an illness or an operation, beginning to play carefully indoors is the right way back to fitness.

▷ There is less risk of injury to puppies that are still stumbling over their own feet.

▷ You can play inside a cool house even in the summer with dogs that are sensitive to heat.

Hide and Seek

Things that your dog especially likes, or that it recognizes by scent (its favorite toy or a blanket, respectively), are good choices for hiding. A hidden treat also provides the right motivation. A successful outcome is important for the dog, so set up easy tasks. To keep the dog from following on your heels when you're hiding something, it must obey the command "*Stay!*" or be held by a second person. The simplest version involves placing an object in plain sight in a room while the dog watches you. The game starts with the command "*Find it!*" When the dog is successful, praise it generously. Variants for experienced players: Bring an item into an adjoining room and put it under the couch or an armchair, or hide it in a box or under a blanket. A sharp dog will find every hiding place, even when it's inside a coat pocket. End the game while your dog is

still enthusiastic about playing, then the next time it's guaranteed to be totally involved.

Fetching Games

Practice with balls or toys that are easy for the dog to pick up in its mouth. At first the fetching won't always work; puppies, in particular, usually drag the item to a secure place. Move into a position where the dog has to run past you. Encourage it by commanding, "*Come!*" as it comes to you, and show it a treat. If the dog drops the object, give it praise and a reward. The anticipation of getting treats and praise will soon turn the dog into a reliable retriever (◑ FETCHING, p.264). Link the exchange of object and treat with the command "*Give!*" After a few repetitions the dog will voluntarily bring the item even without a reward.

Running and Jumping Games

Action games indoors are feasible only for miniature and small dogs; there's usually not enough room for larger dogs. In any case the area needs to be large enough for playing and running. There is a danger of injury on slippery floors (wood or tile), on stairs, unsecured terraces and landings, and on rugs that slide easily.

▷ **Mini-slalom.** A long hallway free of furniture is a good place for slalom training. Start with three poles (such as broom handles) and expand the course later on. At first, guide the dog with a leash and knee contact. This is good training for Agility (→ p.246).

▷ **Hurdles.** Start with small jumps. Place poles on piles of books about 8 inches (20 cm) high. Hang a cloth over the pole to cover the area beneath it and keep the dog from simply running under the hurdle. The pole must simply lie on top of the books to avoid danger of injury. Stand on the other side of the hurdle and use a treat to encourage the

△
Ready for the circus. There are no limits to the imagination while playing indoors. Some good games don't require much space and keep the dog physically and mentally fit.

dog to jump over it. If you increase the height of the jumps, do so slowly.

▷ **Door Jump.** Cut a hole about 8 inches (20 cm) from the edge of an old bed sheet. Measure the diameter so that your dog can easily jump through the hole. Set up the sheet in a doorframe. There is no risk of injury, so the jump is something that even dogs that aren't very athletic can do. Here too begin with a modest height.

▷ **Tunnel Run.** Using blankets, set up a small tent that's open on both ends. This is a good training aid to rid a puppy of its fear of the dark.

Ball Games

Nearly all dogs like balls. Stay away from small balls that could get swallowed (golf and Ping-Pong balls), and balls made of soft materials that can't stand up to the dog's teeth.

▷ **Roller Ball.** Every dog will chase after a rolling hard rubber ball. They strengthen a puppy's movements and physical coordination.

▷ **Ball Push.** A large ball that's not too light is pushed forward with muzzle and paws; use an uncluttered surface.

▷ **Chew Ball.** A ball that's fine for the mouth and has a squeaker, usually with a knobby surface. Look for durable, bite-proof plastic. Many dogs just love their squeak ball. It's a good choice for fetching games.

▷ **Catch.** Throwing and catching game using a ball indoors; only for small dogs and at short distance. With large dogs there is a high risk of injury against furniture in jumping for the ball. A ball for playing catch must be the right size so that the dog can snap it up easily.

▷

The old shell game. Many dogs are keen on combination and mind games. The tasks must be easy to perform. The important things for the four-legged mental gymnasts are success and recognition from the human.

minutes, and encourage the dog to find it.

▷ **Intelligence Test for Experts.** As in the beginners' test, place the object in a box, but before beginning the search, leave the room with the dog for five minutes.

▷ **Intelligence Test for Pros.** After hiding the item, rearrange the boxes. It's OK for the dog to watch.

Games to Combat Boredom

When a dog is alone and bored in the house, it quickly gets crazy ideas into its head. At such times, the dog may become destructive—chewing up clothing, knocking over plants, smashing furniture, and generally disrupting the home—as many owners can readily testify to. You can avoid problems with little games for dogs that have to stay home. Get some toys out of the box that your dog is otherwise not allowed to play with, such as an exciting squeak toy, balls that rustle and clatter, or a new fetching dummy. After you come home, the exclusive toy is put away again. A dog with a strong urge to guard will take its job seriously if you give it something like a bag or a basket to watch over. Whatever you decide to do, you should make sure that your dog has something to occupy its time while it's alone in the house.

Roughhousing

Wild roughhousing is part of the puppy's daily schedule. Later on, the human will be a welcome partner. Allow rough play only if your dog knows how to play gently, refrains from using its teeth, and never forgets its good training in the excitement of the skirmish. If the playing becomes too wild, put a stop to it with the command *"No!"*

Mental and Combination Games

▷ **Detour Game.** Use chairs, boards, or a gate to set up a barrier that the dog can't jump over. Roll a ball under the closed gate. In order to get it, the dog has to run around the obstacle. Even more demanding: build the obstacle in a U-shape and show the dog the U. When it wants to get the ball, it first has to run in the opposite direction.

▷ **Hocus-pocus.** Pull a toy or a treat tied to a string through a pipe at least 3 feet (1 m) long, or under a tent made of blankets. It's OK for the dog to watch you. After several demonstrations, leave the object inside the tunnel so that the dog has to go after it.

▷ **Intelligence Test for Beginners.** In the presence of the dog, place a toy or a treat in one of three different-colored or different-sized boxes. Put a lid on, wait for two or three

Playing with Puppies and Senior Citizens

▷ Avoid games of tug with puppies before they get their adult teeth (usually at the age of 20 weeks).

▷ Training a puppy not to bite; if it bites too hard during play, roll it onto its back and pinch it lightly.

▷ Don't expect too much of the dog with difficult tasks, or repeat the same game endlessly.

▷ A puppy tires quickly. End the game when its interest falls off.

▷ Little games strengthen an old dog's self-confidence. An old dog knows that it's no longer so agile and fit. It is especially appreciative of success in the game (such as intelligence games) and its owner's recognition. Give older dogs easy tasks.

The Best Outdoor Games

Going for a walk is nice, but playing is the best. Playtime—with other dogs on a joint morning walk, or with the human playmate—is the highlight of a dog's day. Dogs of all ages love to play—puppies, practically as soon as they can hold themselves up on their legs, and old-timers, even if the old bones can't do everything the dogs would like. Everyone has a favorite game outdoors, from running full speed with ball and Frisbee to more sedate games of skill and searching.

Ball Games

▷ **Chasing and Fetching.** The dog runs after a tossed ball and brings it back. Accomplished players can catch the ball in the air. Many dogs are fanatical ball players who can go on for hours. Take regular breaks so the dog doesn't overdo it.

▷ **Soccer.** The dog plays with muzzle and paws, and the human and the dog try to get the ball away from one another. The ball must be large enough so that the dog can't grab it. Take a break if the game becomes too heated.

▷ **Ball Boxing.** The dog runs after the ball thrown at a medium height and boxes it back using taps with its muzzle. Choose a light ball that's not too small.

▷ **Water Ball.** A swimming dog pushes the water ball forward with its nose. Keep a safe distance to avoid injury from the claws of the swimming dog.

▷ **Transport.** Sturdy balls the right size for fitting in the mouth are good for carrying on a walk.

5

The human is always the activities director. Stop or take a break any time a strong, dominant dog tries to get the upper hand in games of pulling and roughhousing.

▽

Wild Games

▷ **Frisbee:** (→ also p.247). Throw the Frisbee at a shallow angle so the dog can catch it with its teeth on the way down. Never aim directly at the dog. Frisbees that have been chewed up and bitten through can injure a dog.

▷ **Tug-of-War.** Use a branch, a rope, or an old blanket. Play this only with obedient dogs, not with dominant males and puppies. Make sure the dog doesn't pull on its leash.

▷ **Cops and Robbers.** A chase game with changing roles. Stop if the dog pulls on your clothing or jumps up on you. Calm down impetuous and excited dogs with the *"Sit!"* command between games.

Hiding Games

▷ **With Objects.** Use the command *"Sit!"* or *"Stay!"* and hide a ball, chew bone, or the fetching dummy behind a tree, in the leaves, in the ground, or under a branch.

▶ **TIP**

If the Dog Suddenly Runs Off

Never run yelling after the dog if it runs away from a game. It's better to quickly run and hide behind a tree or a hedge. When the dog notices that you are no longer there, it loses its enthusiasm and turns around. Praise it effusively so that coming back is a positive experience for it.

▷ **With People.** A companion holds the dog until the main person has hidden. Then the dog is commanded to find the person. At first the dog is allowed to watch where you hide; later on it can be distracted by the other person. Give the dog lots of praise when it finds the hiding place.

▷ **Putting Down a Trail.** The dog smells an old sweater or its favorite toy. Drag the item over the ground and hide it. A dog with a very fine nose will be able to follow even convoluted scent trails.

Games of Skill

▷ **Balancing.** Choose thick logs that aren't too slippery. Have the dog jump up onto the log (using the command *"Jump up!"*), and pat the log; lift up smaller dogs.

At first, practice with the leash and stay close to the dog. Balancing develops a sense of self-confidence.

▷ **Jumping.** Appropriate obstacles for high jump and long jump include branches, low bushes, ditches, and small streams. Check the landing area behind the obstacle in advance.

Water Games

▷ **Fetching.** Throw a branch from the shore into the water. Make sure the area is safe for swimming. Be careful in unfamiliar waters, and don't let the dog swim in rivers with a strong current. The dog must come out of the water immediately when commanded.

▷ **Water Ball.** (→ Ball Games, p.235)

Little Games While Walking

Appropriate toys include a fetching dummy, a squeak toy, a ball, a ring, a pure rubber ball, and a rope.

Between-times, games prevent boredom, encourage bonding, and can even be played on leash. A carrying duty involving a stick, fetching dummy, or other item fills every dog with pride and is a cure for leash biters.

Yard Games

A fenced yard is the best playground for a puppy. It can safely discover the world, romp around to its heart's content, accumulate Agility experience on a miniature course, or get its first training lessons in playschool.

It's More Fun Together

Things almost always go well on walks involving neighborhood dog owners and their pets. The dogs race each other, go on wild chases, dig in the dirt, and scrap over the best branches.

But all dogs need to be obedience trained. Regrettably, dogs in heat have to stay home. To avoid friction, don't bring along any toys from home. These same rules apply to the dog training ground, where dogs can mingle freely.

Important Considerations for Outdoor Play

▷ **Basic Obedience.** Your dog has to be familiar with the most important commands.
▷ **Amicability.** A dog must not be aggressive in group play. Sexually hyperactive, overly high-strung, and spoiled dogs can cause problems (→ Overanxiety, p.176).
▷ **Supervision.** Interrupt the game and call your dog back when joggers, children, or cyclists are in sight.
▷ **Control.** Dogs with a strong hunting instinct must be on a leash in areas that are home to wild game. Stay with your dog at all times on forest paths to avoid disturbing the wild animals.
▷ **Inspect the Terrain.** Before starting the game, inspect the terrain for dangerous objects, sharp stones, and holes in the ground.
▷ **Sight Contact.** In all activities your dog should remain in sight.

Tips for All Kinds of Weather

▷ **Heat.** In the summer, put off playtime to the cool morning or evening hours, and avoid wild, active games. Watch out for tarred surfaces that have softened in the sun.
▷ **Cold.** Nearly all dogs can withstand below-zero temperatures well, but they have to remain active. After a walk in the damp cold, dry the fur with a towel. Vaseline protects the footpads.
▷ **Rain.** After a walk in the rain, rub the fur

△
Jump training. You can use homemade obstacles to turn your yard into an Agility course. Here the athlete develops the fitness required for taking part in official competitions.

thoroughly dry and let the dog lie in a warm, draft-free spot.
▷ **Snow.** Watch for a dog that continually eats snow, vomits, and experiences diarrhea. Keep snow eaters on the leash and say *"No!"* every time they try; emphasize the command by pulling back strongly on the leash.
▷ **Ice.** Even dogs can fall and hurt themselves on slippery, icy surfaces. Wash clumps of ice and salt from the paws with warm water.
▷ **Tick Season.** Ticks can infest the dog from the spring through the late fall. After a walk, check over the head, chest, and legs for ticks; use pincers (from a pet shop) to remove the PARASITES (⊙p.269).

Sports Activities

A dog that is challenged athletically on a regular basis is self-confident, fit in body and mind, and has a happy and stimulating relationship with its owner.

EXERCISE IS THE MAIN THING. Running, preferably at top speed, is in a dog's blood. The aimless stroll that cats prefer is not a dog's cup of tea. Sports keep muscles in shape, sharpen the senses and reaction time, and strengthen the body's resistance to infections. Athletic dogs rarely find fault with their food, and they have no problems keeping their slender figures.

Sports are a form of arousal for dogs and keep their minds healthy; there is simply no time for rebellion, disobedience, boredom, and self-absorbed fussing. Athletic training is the best therapy for getting a handle on bad behavior and help get a shaky relationship between master and dog back onto its feet. The only question is who has more fun, the animal or the human.

238

The Sporting Life

Before you get involved in the sporting life, test your dog to see what type of sports are best suited to its qualities, and which ones it likes best. On dog training grounds and in competitions you can get an idea of what it's like to play sports with a dog. Every dog club offers opportunities. Before you get involved in club competitions (→ p.244), a veterinarian should check the dog for health and fitness.

Can My Dog Do It?

▷ **Playfulness.** Your dog must enjoy sports and games. Start with some simple training routines that don't expect too much of it. Praise and recognition will motivate it to participate; pressure to perform will only work against you.

▷ **Obedience.** Only dogs with adequate basic training can take part in group training and dog sports competitions. These are off-limits to rowdies.

▷ **Health.** The veterinarian should decide if dogs with joint or circulatory system disorders should play sports.

▷ **Social Behavior.** A friendly, nonaggressive disposition is the basic requirement for club and group sports.

▷ **Getting Back into Training.** After an illness or an operation, start with movement exercises rather than performance sports. Pregnant and elderly dogs also get light workouts.

Sports with Young Dogs

If you want to engage in sports with a dog, you should choose an active puppy. Young dogs shouldn't be overtaxed up to the age of 12 months (18 months with large breeds) as their physical development (especially bone growth) is not yet complete. Dogs younger than 12 months shouldn't yet take part in dog sports competitions.

A Little Activity Always Helps

Breeds that are susceptible to skeletal and respiratory diseases should participate in sports only if the veterinarian gives them a green light.

▷ **Spine.** Dachshunds, Basset Hounds, and Pekingese are vulnerable to slipped disks. Keep their activity moderate, and avoid jumping as much as possible.

▷ **Respiratory System.** Pugs, English Bulldogs, Pekingese, and other breeds with a short muzzle have breathing problems when excited or hot.

▷ **Joints.** Saint Bernards, Mastiffs, German Shepherd Dogs, Bernese Mountain Dogs, and other large breeds may experience elbow and hip dysplasia. Chihuahuas, Miniature Poodles, and Yorkshire Terriers are susceptible to changes in their hip and knee joints (dislocated knee). Avoid excessive strain, and have the veterinarian check out the dog.

 INFO

The Most Athletic Breeds

▷ The best runners: Dalmatians, Collies, Irish Setters, Airedale Terriers, Afghan Hounds, Border Collies, and Doberman Pinschers

▷ The best Agility dogs: Poodles, Kromfohrlanders, Australian Shepherds, Pinschers, Border Collies

▷ The most athletic pals for children: Bobtails, Beagles, Boxers, Spitzes, Golden Retrievers, Bearded Collies

▷ The most gifted mental gymnasts: West Highland White Terriers, Border Collies, Miniature Schnauzers, Fox Terriers

▷ **Heart and Lungs.** Older dogs of all breeds are vulnerable to chronic heart problems that may lead to edema of the lungs. Stick to mild exercise.

▶ TEST

How Athletic Is My Dog?

Typical breed characteristics, fitness, and individual preferences contribute to what a dog can do in athletics.

	Yes	No
1. Does the dog especially like mental games?	○	○
2. Does it prefer to play little games indoors?	○	○
3. Does it play with its toy all by itself?	○	○
4. Does it prefer to play with people rather than with other dogs?	○	○
5. Does it want to go out and play in all kinds of weather?	○	○
6. Is it happy only when it gets to run and jump a lot?	○	○
7. Does it never tire while running alongside a bike?	○	○
8. Does it get along with other dogs in sports and games?	○	○
9. Is it so fit that it always performs at its peak?	○	○

Solution: If you answered questions 5 through 9 with *Yes* for your dog, you too should have fun testing your own fitness in wind and weather. Your dog will romp and be happy when it is challenged in an Agility course, jogging, or competitive dog sports.

If you checked off only questions 1 through 4, you don't have the right hotshot for a partner, but rather a dog for which playing together and cuddling count for more than anything in the world.

Training Tips for Beginners

▷ Always keep dogs that like to hunt leashed in areas where there is wild game.

▷ Don't let children under the age of ten play sports with a dog without supervision.

▷ Stop training and put the dog on a leash when strange dogs are in the vicinity.

▷ Stop the sports time when the dog is still cooperating enthusiastically. Don't force it to keep playing if it loses interest.

▷ Start endurance training (jogging and cycling) with short stretches, and only during the cool hours of the day in the summer.

Feeding Requirements for Athletes

With normal sports activity the dog gets its normal food ration. Working dogs (hunting and herding dogs) and competitive dogs (sled dogs) are the only ones that have a higher energy need. Drinking water must always be available; for the dog's capacity to perform, this is more important than additional food. Don't begin a session of sports until an hour after feeding; with large breeds wait at least two hours because of the risk of gastric torsion.

Sports Injuries

▷ Limping. Possible causes include a sprain, an injury to footpads or claws, a torn meniscus, or a torn crucial ligament. Check the paws and consult a veterinarian.

▷ Excessive panting. A sign of overexertion; often coupled with restlessness, perhaps also lameness. Stop the exercise immediately.

▷ Shortness of breath. Along with vomiting and restlessness, often a sign that the dog has swallowed something. If possible, remove the foreign body, and get to the veterinarian right away.

With sports you should also watch for the following:

▷ Distance running on a hard surface puts a lot of stress on the bones, especially with young dogs.

▷ Shorten the sports program in the winter with dogs that are susceptible to arthrosis and rheumatism (which is rare).

The Best Types of Sports

Top Speed and Power Play: Lots of dogs want to put the pedal to the metal. They love to run so much that often the owner has to put on the brakes so that the teams don't totally overexert themselves. The best sport becomes even nicer when the dog is paired with a human. And the fun and fitness are free for both of them.

Jogging

A dog doesn't need to learn how to run; however, for jogging with a human it needs some instruction. Basic obedience is a prerequisite; the most important command is *"Heel!"* so that the dog always remains at the same level as you.

At first keep the dog on a leash; with dogs that like to hunt, you'll still need to use the leash later on. With dogs that stop abruptly, cross the road, or pull on the leash, jogging can turn into a nerve-wracking obstacle race. Train the dog to run parallel to you on a slack leash. This works especially well with a special jogging leash (from a pet shop) that fastens around your waist. The advantage is that you have both hands free and can move more naturally as you jog.

Start with short distances (about a mile and a half / 2 km), and then gradually increase the distance and the pace. At first choose a flat course with a soft, springy surface away from busy roads, preferably where not everybody in the neighborhood who owns a dog is already on the move. You can jog with less interference on weekends than during the week. Run long distances only with breeds that like to run, such as the Labrador Retriever and Golden Retriever, Beagle, Afghan Hound, Collie, and Irish Setter. After every run check the feet for injuries and foreign bodies. Even athletic dogs need a break on hot summer days and in extreme cold.

Cycling

When the dog is running next to a bicycle, discipline counts even more than while jogging. The leashed dog must always remain even with the front wheel. That's where you have the most control over it and can react in time if it changes direction without warning.

As in jogging, the dog has to keep pace so that the leash hangs slack. Never wrap the leash around the handlebars while cycling, as, in an emergency, you might not be able to let go in time, and a fall would be unavoidable. Even in meeting other dogs, cats, or wild animals your dog has to stay on track, and it has to be able to resist seductive scent trails. One practical accessory is a leash that clamps to the bicycle frame. The leash attaches to this so that you have both hands free and can concentrate on your cycling.

The start of the season for a new player. Dogs learn to love playing ball even in their infancy.

▽

5

▶ INFO

Summertime Dangers

Dogs are sensitive to heat, as about the only way they can get rid of excess heat is by panting. Bernese Mountain Dogs, Newfoundlands, Landseers, English Bulldogs, Saint Bernards, Shih Tzus, and Huskies, in particular, suffer from the heat. If you suspect that a dog has suffered heatstroke (restlessness, elevated panting and salivating, hanging eyelids), lay the dog in the shade, spray its body with lukewarm water, and alert the veterinarian right away.

▷ **Walks Are Essential.** Jogging is not a replacement for walking. A walk is the dog's only chance to sniff around to its heart's content and make acquaintances. The athletic value of a walk mustn't be underestimated—a dog that's let off-leash continually runs circles around its companion and thus covers several times the distance. It also performs a real interval workout, as it continually changes from a leisurely trot into a sprint.

▷ **Stop for Youngsters.** Endurance training for dogs under the age of 12 months damages the skeletal system, which can't yet take the strain. With large breeds, physical development often doesn't end before age two.

▷ **Training Break.** Avoid long-distance running on asphalt, ice, and crusted snow.

Hiking

Even small dogs such as Dachshunds and Yorkshire Terriers can easily hike long distances. When you hike, try to avoid hot days, and always bring along enough drinking water for the dog.

Mountain Climbing

Powerful medium-sized dogs such as Boxers could make a mountain goat proud. But even if your dog is a zealous climber, don't overdo it in the mountains, avoid dangerous terrain (boulder fields, steep grades, and overhangs) and surfaces where its paws can't gain a purchase or may be injured. Small dogs often ride in style as they take in the mountains from the pack on their master's back.

▷ **Involved in Everything.** This is above all a question of trust. The dog may even accompany its master in sports activities that don't come to it naturally; for example, as a passenger on a surfboard or skateboard, navigator on a paddleboat or canoe, or even as a flying dog on a hang glider. The motto is, Whatever my master does, I do also.

▷ **No Sports.** Fussy dogs and couch potatoes are a minority in canine circles, but we still have to accept their reserved nature. An English Bulldog, for example, is a wonderful dog, but its body is not set up for athletics.

Specialists Want More

Greyhounds, Borzois, and Afghan Hounds don't even get out of breath from a long bicycle tour.

Professional runners such as Greyhounds and sled dogs need regular exertion. Greyhounds should get it on the running track or coursing (chasing a mechanical rabbit on a zigzag course), and sled dogs in the traces in front of a sled, or in front of a training wagon in the summer. Greyhounds are always kept on a leash while jogging and cycling; otherwise they will blindly take after every rabbit or deer that crosses their paths.

Applause for an acrobatic jumper. With regula training, athletic dogs are capable of remarkab performance

A Walk in the City or the Woods

Small joys preserve the friendship. It doesn't have to be a great vacation trip, your dog will be just as excited about a five-minute trip to the nearest newspaper stand. The main thing is to be part of it. So much the better if there is something new to see and sniff. It's easier for both of you if you and your dog know the appropriate conduct in the woods and the city, and for riding a bus or train.

On the Move in Nature

People who always travel the same routes with their dog know where they have to be careful and where the leash is needed—in the vicinity of watchful farm dogs, anywhere near a bitch in heat, and at the edge of the woods, where the dog might find a fresh rabbit trail and get some crazy ideas. The daily monotony really isn't much fun, not for you, and certainly not for your dog. So you find some new routes. This is exciting for the dog. It is all ears, nose, and eyes and ready to react. Many dog owners are sure their dog will stop on command... until it takes off after a deer and disappears into the woods.

▷ **Under Control.** Leash your dog in unfamiliar and unclear situations. The dog must know the most important commands, especially *"Heel!"* Call it back as long as its attention hasn't yet been captured by something else. Here's how to recognize if it's interested in something: its stance becomes tense, it holds its head high, and points its ears; with shorthaired breeds the hackles on the neck will stand up.

▷ **Safety on the Leash.** Usually there are few problems in the woods as long as the dog stays on the trail and within sight of its owner. But in areas where there is a lot of wild game you should still always keep your dog on a leash. Fish and game officers don't have much tolerance for dogs tearing through the underbrush. A loose dog can be especially

harmful in the spring and fall, if birds and animals are trying to raise their young, and in the winter when animals have no energy reserves because there's too little food.

▷ **Only On-Leash.** Dogs that have a strong hunting instinct (such as Greyhounds) must always be on a leash, for they don't respond to commands when they see a wild animal or pick up a trail.

▷ **No Swimming.** In some areas people and dogs are prohibited from swimming, especially when waterfowl are nesting. Watch for signs.

In the City

A dog must be leashed in a city, next to its owner, and away from the street.

▷ **Closed Areas.** In most communities dogs must be leashed in parks and playgrounds.

▷ **Dog Droppings.** The dog owner is responsible for cleaning up droppings. In many places non-compliance can result in fines. Some cities provide disposal locations, and collection bags may be provided.

▷ **Muzzle Requirement.** Vicious dogs must wear a muzzle on public streets and in downtown locations. Different areas may have dif-

5

◁

I have to stay outside. Dogs can't go everywhere on a shopping trip in town. A well-trained dog waits patiently without barking until its owner returns for it. For safety sake, it must always be tied.

ferent determinations of what constitutes a vicious dog (→ p. 34).

Train, Bus, and Taxi

In some areas a train ticket for a dog costs the same as a ticket for a child. Small dogs up to the size of a housecat may travel free if they are kept in a travel cage. Larger dogs must be leashed and wear a muzzle. (An exception is made for Seeing Eye dogs.) Special requirements may apply to overnight coaches. Most dogs have no difficulties traveling by train.

For other public transportation such as a streetcar, city bus, and subway, regulations may vary from place to place. Dogs commonly are welcome in taxis and may even ride for free. If you call to reserve a cab, you should notify the company of your special need, especially in the case of a large dog. Some cities even have animal taxis that specialize in transporting house pets.

Hotels and Restaurants

Some hotels, but few restaurants, welcome dogs. When making reservations it's best to ask if you may bring your dog. If you have trouble finding a hotel that is willing to accommodate dogs in the area where you are going to stay, you might consult a local breed association or club. Chances are that someone in the association or club will be able to give you contact information for lodgings that welcome dogs.

Throughout the United States, dogs are generally not allowed in restaurants for health reasons; however, a few restaurants with outdoor seating may allow you to bring along a dog if local regulations permit it.

If you want to take your dog to a restaurant, you would be well advised to check first with the local authorities and the restaurant in question to find out whether it is permissible to do so. Simply showing up at a restaurant with a dog in tow is not a good idea, as you probably won't be seated.

In Europe, on the other hand, dogs are generally more welcome in restaurants and hotels. Still, if you intend to take your dog to Europe, it would be a good idea to do some research beforehand with regard to lodgings and restaurants. After all, you don't want to have to interrupt your vacation looking for restaurants and hotels that accommodate dogs.

Long Trips and Vacations

If you take a trip, it's good to go by car, at least if the dog is also going along. The car is by far the most common transportation for taking a dog on a vacation trip. Planes and trains are hardly used at all.

A Dog's Travel Baggage

▷ A dog cage or box, plus a blanket.
▷ Collar with address tag (home and vacation address, cell phone number) and leash.
▷ Chew bones and healthy treats.
▷ Favorite toy and blanket to keep the dog occupied and supply a familiar scent.
▷ Canned or dry dog food for the trip, if your dog is used to a certain brand. If you travel to a different country, you may not find the accustomed products.
▷ Dry shampoo in case the dog rolls in some luscious garbage on the trip.
▷ Hand towels and paper towels.
▷ Plastic bags or pouches for droppings in case you need to clean up any "business."
▷ Muzzle for breeds that are required to wear one. In some locations a muzzle may be required for all dogs.

Get the information you need online before you travel, or once you arrive. You don't want to be in violation of any local rules or regulations.

▷ Interstate Health Certificate.

A picnic in the grass. When traveling, both human and dog need a break after two hours. There should be a snack and some fresh water for the dog.

By Car

▷ **By Car.** A small dog can ride on the floor in front of the passenger's seat, but the passenger still needs some leg room. Many dogs become carsick if they can't look out the window. In such cases a small dog can ride in the back. On the backseat dogs should be buckled in. The belt system is made up of the seat belt, shoulder belt, and a chest harness. The safety belt allows some freedom of movement, is available in several sizes, and is appropriate for all kinds of cars (→ photo, p.253).

A safety barrier between the front- and backseats will keep the dog from climbing in front or falling between the seats if the brakes are applied hard. A dog can ride comfortably and safely in the cargo area of a station wagon or van if a grate or net separates it from the passenger compartment. You can find the needed accessories at a car dealership or a pet shop.

Break. Take a break every two hours—more frequently in the summer. Don't open the car door until your dog is on the leash. Give the dog a chance to take a walk and relieve itself, have some water, and maybe even a snack.

Heat Break. Dogs are sensitive to the heat. Air conditioning and draft-free ventilation can help keep the interior cool. Never drive with open windows or in a convertible as the dog could jump out or pick up an eye infection in the wind from driving. Never leave a dog in a parked car.

Careful Driving. Try to avoid braking hard or taking off fast; let up on the gas before reaching curves.

Slow Down. High speed and the noise from the tires bother some dogs.

▶ INFO

A Traveling Canine Drugstore

▷ Bandages and gauze wrap
▷ Wound powder and tincture of iodine
▷ Vaseline
▷ Antihistamine gel (for wasp stings)
▷ Tick collar
▷ Flea spray or powder
▷ Eyedrops (risk of conjunctiva inflammation from wind)
▷ Medicine for travel sickness (when needed, administer before departure)
▷ Stomach pills, plus black tea or chamomile tea

▷ **On a Plane.** Requirements and costs vary among airlines. Small dogs (11–17 pounds / 5–8 kg) in a box or bag may be allowed as carry-on luggage. Important: Book space early because only a limited number of dogs are allowed on board. Larger animals travel in travel cages in the air-conditioned cargo bay and are cared for by employees on stopovers. Some airlines may allow dogs to ride for free on domestic flights; transportation in the cargo area goes by the dog's weight and the flight route. Flights, especially in the cargo hold, are stressful for a dog and should be considered only in cases of extended stays.

▷ If your dog is welcome on a train, you probably will have to buy a ticket for it. Small dogs sometimes can travel for free, and larger dogs must be leashed. Dogs are prohibited from the dining car, and allowed in Pullman and sleeping cars only if the whole section is rented.

International Travel

If you ever travel in Europe with your dog (or cat or ferret), you will need an EU house pet pass. In addition to information about the animal and the owner, it certifies that the animal has a valid rabies shot, which is the only inoculation that all EU countries require for entry. The shot must have been administered at least 30 days before crossing the border and be no older than 12 months. The pet pass also includes the tattoo number (▷TATTOOING, p.273) or the dog's microchip identification (▷MICROCHIP, ▷p.268). In Europe, tattooing will be abandoned in the year 2011, and all animals will be required to have a microchip. For travel to Ireland, Sweden, and the United Kingdom, for the moment, there are additional requirements including, among others, more stringent rabies regulations (blood test for antibodies). Tattoo or transponder identification is required for entry into an EU country such as Andorra, Iceland, Liechtenstein, Monaco, Norway, and Switzerland. For importing a dog from other countries, further requirements must be met, including quarantine under certain conditions. In such cases, request more information from the relevant consulate.

Things to Consider on Vacation

▷ **Accommodations.** Set aside a place in the hotel room or the vacation home for your dog's bed and food and water dishes. Keep the doors shut to keep the dog from running away in an unfamiliar area. The hotel personnel should not come into the room when the dog is there alone.

▷ **Daily Schedule.** To the extent possible, stick to the accustomed times for feeding and going for walks.

▷ **Feeding.** If necessary, bring the usual food from home to avoid problems at the feeding dish.

▷ **Climate.** Southern summers are no picnic for a dog. Save your activities together for the cooler morning and evening hours.

▷ **At the Beach.** Be sure to offer your dog a place in the shade, preferably under an umbrella. It will need regular drinking water. After swimming in the ocean its coat will need to be rinsed with fresh water. Keep the visits to the beach to no more than two hours.

Note: Before leaving for your vacation trip find out about any health risks at your destination. It's a good idea to have pet owner's liability insurance (→ p.34) that's also valid in foreign countries.

Some health insurances (→ Addresses, p.284) offer vacation protection with trip interruption insurance that will cover veterinary costs up to a certain amount for travel to and from the vacation area and some of the costs if the trip has to be abandoned because of accident or illness involving the dog.

▷ **Abandoned Animals.** Every year countless animals are abandoned, nearly half of them in vacation areas during the months of June through August.

The animals include cats, rabbits, and guinea pigs, but most of them are dogs.

Even though pet abandonment is punishable by fines and other means, evidently the penalties aren't enough to deter irresponsible owners.

▷ **Registration.** Things happen more quickly than we realize on trips, vacation, or moves; all of a sudden, the dog has disappeared. The chances of recovering the animal are good only if it is properly registered and identified. Your dog should also be identified by a tattoo or have a microchip (transponder).

If Your Dog Stays Home

Relatives, friends, and neighbors whom the dog knows should be the first choice when your dog has to be cared for at home during your vacation. Animal shelters generally have few rental spaces available but they will gladly provide you with addresses of dog-sitters and boarding kennels. You may also locate people who are happy to take care of a guest pet for a time. You may get leads to such people from your veterinarian or local animal shelter.

Moving

When you move to a different location, you may have a month to register your dog. If you move within the same town or city, don't forget to report your new address.

A dog will generally adapt easily to its new territory, as long as the familiar family pack remains intact.

5

◁
Seat belts first. Dogs should be belted in. There are safety harnesses in various sizes and designs that are made to fit any type of car and still allow the animal some freedom of movement.

Therefore, when you move, try to keep things as stable as you can for the dog's sake. Try to set up your new home in a way that mimics as closely as possible the home that you're leaving. The more continuity there is in the living situations, the better your dog will adjust to new surroundings.

The move itself, however, may well be stressful for a dog, just as it may be stressful for the human members of a family; therefore, you should take care not to ignore your pet during the moving process. See that the dog's basic needs are met, and, if you can find the time and space, you might think about playing a game. If there are older children in the family, they can be given the responsibility of watching out for the dog during the move.

Ten Questions About Sports, Games, and Travel

Every time we go for a walk, I have to throw sticks; my Airedale Terrier is just crazy about it. Unfortunately, he has hurt his gums several times with splinters. How can I keep that from happening?
It's the playing, rather than the object, that's more important for your Airedale. It surely will be just as enthusiastic about a tossing ring. And if you give it a ring to carry, it will treat it like the apple of its eye and will pass right by the most appealing sticks. You can get rings in various sizes and colors in pet shops.

We have been "dog people" for only about six months. We always go to the beach for vacation. Of course, the puppy will come with us. Can it go anywhere it wants on the beach?
Dogs are not welcome on the beach in all vacation areas, but some places have a soft spot in their heart for dogs and have even set up special beaches for dogs. You may be able to do some on-line research to learn of the possibilities before you leave on vacation.

I'm not planning to fly with my Pekingese for the moment, but I have read that flying can harm the dog. Is this correct?
It is indeed the case that certain breeds may be harmed by flying. This affects dogs with a short skull that tend to have difficulty in breathing because of the shape of their head. This includes the Boxer, Bull Mastiff, Pug, smaller spaniels, and Pekingese.

Our Golden Retriever loves to play a ball, especially in the water. Even extreme cold is no obstacle. Should we not let it swim in the winter?
The cold water won't harm your Golden Retriever as long as it remains active. Only in extreme below-zero weather should you keep the dog from swimming. Dry the dog off at home with a towel and let it relax in a warm, draft-free place.

My Spitz is unbeatable at playing fetch— except for the tiny fault of not wanting to give up the "prey." How can I break the dog of this behavior?
This is easiest with double training. It requires two identical objects, preferably your dog's favorite toy in duplicate. Toss one for the dog to retrieve. As the dog is coming back, throw the other toy into the air and start all over. Curiosity wins out; the old toy is quickly forgotten and the dog will drop it without a thought. Now it must fetch the second object. You pick up the first one and use it as before. The cycle continues until your dog automatically drops the object.

Vacation from the family. When the dog can't go on vacation, a boarding kennel is the right choice. Before making a reservation, check to be sure the dog will be well housed.

△

Vacation time. Dogs prove themselves to be good companions as long as we observe the most important rules while traveling and on vacation.

How do I recognize a good boarding kennel?

Here's what to look for: The animals shouldn't be kept in individual cages; they need a chance to move around, preferably in a group. The caregivers regularly take the dogs on walks. The cages, runs, and food dishes are cleaned every day. The noise level is kept within reasonable limits. Dogs that constantly bark are experiencing stress or are bored. What kind of food are the dogs given? There are fewer problems when commercially available feed is used. The owners accept only dogs that have had their shots and ask about the vaccination record and any illnesses. You might also ask what kind of experience and training the operators have.

Is it OK to take a pregnant female on vacation?

A pregnant dog should be spared the stress of travel and unfamiliar places in the last four weeks of pregnancy. Puppies that have not had their shots, and sick animals also should not travel.

How do I get my dog used to a bicycle?

At first push the bicycle and walk the dog on a leash. Keep the dog on the right side of the bike. If the dog pulls or changes sides, pull back on the leash and correct it with the command *"Wheel!"* Later on choose a pace that allows the dog to go at an easy trot and stay abreast of you.

We like herding competitions more and more. These seem to attract Border Collies more than any other breed. What happened to the German Shepherd Dog and other breeds?

The old German herding breeds include the Fuchs, Schwarzer, Gelbbacke, Tiger, Rauhbärtel, Stumper, and Strobel. They all have a strong herding instinct; they have a good disposition, are calm, and weather-resistant. There is an association dedicated to breeding the old German herding dogs (the Arbeitsgemeinschaft zur Zucht Altdeutscher Hütehunde, ❍HERDING DOGS, p.265). It has taken over the tasks of registering, maintaining, and breeding these herding dog varieties, some of which are threatened with extinction. Shepherds, sheep owners, and private dog owners have come together in the AAH. The dogs that concern them are pure working dogs that are used primarily for herding sheep, but also for other herd animals such as cows, pigs, goats, and geese. Since 1990 a breed registry has kept track of the offspring of all strains of the old German herding dogs.

◁

Always active. A dog's need for exercise depends on age, size, and breed—but they all love to run.

The daily exercise is usually specified as two to three hours. How much ground should a dog cover in that time?

There is a great difference in the NEED FOR EXERCISE (❍p.263): a Chihuahua is happy with 700–800 yards (700 or 800 m); a Westie needs about twice that much, and Collies and Labrador Retrievers can easily cover 6–9 miles (10–15 k). A dog off leash covers a lot of distance on a walk because it continually runs back and forth.

5

Quick Finder
from A to Z

From A as in *aggressiveness* to Z as in *zoonoses*, the Quick Finder contains all the terms that are important for dog owners (and for people who want to become dog owners). Each term provides you with practical data and interesting background knowledge. If you want more complete information, follow the references to the appropriate chapters and sections.

GREETING RITUAL　　　　Quick Finder Term

③ Scent Signals and Smell Check, *Page 145*　　Circled numbers, title, and page number refer to chapter and sections that deal with the Quick Finder term.

ANAL SNIFFING (Page 258)　　Reference to further Quick Finder terms

⊙ AGGRESSIVENESS

The aggressive behavior of a family dog can be directed toward unknown people, owners and family members, and other dogs and house pets. The causes of the problem behavior range from inadequate socialization while a puppy and extreme fixation on one person to dominance, excessive anxiety, and jealousy. In stubborn cases behavior therapy is often required.

③ **Warning and Preparation for Attack,** *p. 148*

⊙ AGILITY

Agility is a type of dog sport in which the dog must negotiate the obstacle course as quickly and as error-free as possible. Agility obstacles include a dog walk, A-frame, seesaw, pipe tunnel, weave poles, table, and various jumping obstacles. In competitive dog sports there are three Agility classes of increasing difficulty. Mini-Agility (also with three degrees of difficulty) is for dogs under 16 inches (40 cm) at the shoulder, and the obstacles are smaller in size. The dogs with the best traits for Agility are Border Collies, Shelties, Collies, PONs, and other nimble herding dogs, plus lots of terriers. Less appropriate are the heavy, large breeds and Greyhounds and sled dogs. The jumping may cause disk problems in Dachshunds and other breeds with a long back; short-nosed dogs experience shortness of breath rather quickly in athletic exertion. Dogs that are in heat or pregnant should not take part in Agility; overweight animals should shed some pounds before starting training. Dogs at least 15 months old are eligible to participate in Agility.

⑤ **Agility,** *p. 246*

⊙ AGING

Depending on the breed, the first signs of aging appear between the ages of six and eight. Older dogs require more attention, more intensive care and health measures, as well a special lighter food that's tailored to the decreasing efficiency of stomach and intestines. Smaller breeds live longer than larger ones. The aging process also begins significantly later in small dogs. Breeds with a life expectancy of 15 years and longer include the Affenpinscher, Australian Terrier, Bichon Frise, Brussels Griffon, Cairn Terrier, Chinese Crested, Eurasier, Havanese, Italian Whippet, Japan Chin, Canaan Dog, Medium-sized Poodle, Kromfohrlander, Lakeland Terrier, Pharaoh Dog, Puli, Saluki, Schipperke, Schnauzer, Scottish Terrier, West Highland White Terrier, Whippet, Miniature Poodle, and Pomeranian. The Australian Silky Terrier and Chihuahua can live up to 20 years.

③ **The Older Dog,** *p. 137*

⊙ ANAL SNIFFING

This is part of the GREETING RITUAL (⊙p.264); it involves mutual sniffing of the area under the tail where the anal sacs are located, which give off an individual scent. Another part of greeting involves touching noses.

③ **Anxiety-free Meetings,** *p. 157*

⊙ ANXIETY BITING

Anxiety biters are usually dogs whose social and communication behavior are disturbed. This is typical of dogs that have been shielded excessively by their owners. Aggression caused by anxiety can also stem from inadequate socialization when the dog was a puppy. Punishment only heightens the will to attack in an anxiety biter. Therapy succeeds only when every peaceful behavior is reinforced and every aggressive action is ignored. Anxiety aggression is more common in dogs than domineering aggressiveness. There are intermediate forms of body language between a self-confident dog and one that threatens from anxiety, and it is not always easy to evaluate a dog's behavior.

③ **Fraidy Cats,** *p. 176*

▶ BEHAVIOR PROBLEMS

Among dogs the most common behavior problems include aggression directed toward strangers or the family, excessive anxiety, loss of control, extreme timidity, destructiveness, and compulsive licking or nibbling its own body. Causes of the neurosis may be inappropriate living conditions, inadequate socialization, or traumatic experiences during puppyhood.

③ Help with Behavior Problems, *p. 164*

▶ BIRTHING PROBLEMS

With some smaller dog breeds birthing seldom comes off without a hitch, as with the Norwich and Sealyham Terriers and the Pekingese. The small pelvis and the large puppy head cause problems with the Pug and the French Bulldog.

① If Things Don't Go as Planned, *p. 81*

▶ BOARDING

A boarding kennel is the right choice for dogs that don't travel with their owners. Here's what to watch for: The dog must be sheltered properly, cared for in a knowledgeable fashion, and get adequate attention, regular exercise, and contact with other dogs. You should inspect the kennel before making your first reservation. You can get addresses from veterinarians and DOG TRAINING SCHOOLS.

① Dog Ownership Takes Time, *p. 22*

▶ BODY LANGUAGE

A dog's body language is very important in communicating with other dogs and with humans. Dogs have a broad spectrum of different body signals that are combined and reinforced with VOCALIZATIONS (▶p.274) according to the situation.

③ The Silent Language of the Body, *p. 143*

▶ BREED BOOK

The PEDIGREE (▶p.270) contains the breed book numbers of a puppy and its preceding generations. The breed book number is used to record a purebred dog in the breed registry of the breed association. The signatures of breeder and registry office personnel attest to the accuracy of the data in the pedigree.

① A Personal ID for Purebred Dogs, *p. 84*

▶ BREED STANDARD

The breed standard (often abbreviated to *standard*) specifies the ideal characteristics of a breed. It is established and accepted by the FCI as the overseeing body of breeders of purebred dogs. With a new standard, the breed's country of origin retains the exclusive right to specify changes the breed description. One recently recognized breed is the White Swiss Shepherd (formerly the American-Canadian White Shepherd), with Switzerland as the country of origin.

① Today's Dog Breeds, *p. 40*

▶ BREEDER

A person who wants to breed a purebred dog and participate in shows and trials must buy the dog from a breeder who belongs to a club recognized by the dog breeders' association. Major dog breed associations include the AKC and the FCI, the international umbrella organization of purebred associations. There is also a Canadian Kennel Club (▶Addresses, p.284). All breeders must meet certain conditions of a recognized purebred association. The BREED STANDARD (▶p.259) defines the breeding goals. Puppies are sold only with breeding papers.

① **Breeders Need a Breeding Permit,** *p. 84*

▶ BREEDING SUITABILITY EVALUTION

In selective breeding, breeders seek animals that come closest to their breeding goals and the qualities and traits encouraged by the BREED STANDARD (p.259). A breeding suitability evaluation also seeks to avoid passing on hereditary defects and illnesses. The process involves assigning a breeding score to a dog's genetic disposition. If the breeding scores for a mating pair exceed the breed average, the risk of passing on a genetic disease, or the susceptibility to it, is higher than normal; the danger is less with lower breeding scores.

① **Breeders Need a Breeding Permit,** *p. 84*

▶ BREEDS

Dog breeds are distinguished by specific physical characteristics, natural abilities, and skills. The phenotype and DISPOSITION (p.261) are the result of selective breeding. The BREED STANDARD describes the breed-specific characteristics. The various breed clubs and national or international organizations such as the FCI and AKC ensure compliance

with the standards. Of the more than 400 existing dog breeds, about 330 are officially recognized.

① **The Most Beloved Dog Breeds,** *p. 38*

▶ CANIDS

From a zoological viewpoint, dogs belong to the canid or doglike family. This family also includes wolves, coyotes, jackals, foxes, and wild dogs such as the Löffel, Dhole, and Raccoon Dog. All are capable endurance runners; the larger types live and hunt in packs. The largest family member is the wolf; the smallest is the Fenneck or desert fox.

③ **Of Wolves and Humans,** *p. 127*

▶ CLICKER TRAINING

With clicker training a dog learns through positive reinforcement. The clicking sound is given simultaneously as a secondary reinforcement along with a food reward. The dog links the two experiences, and after a few repetitions the clicker provides positive reinforcement of the desired behavior, even in the absence of the additional stimulation from food or praise. Clicker training makes it possible to encourage and reinforce desirable behavior.

③ **Research and Practical Application,** *p. 177*

▶ COLOR PERCEPTION

There are light-sensitive cells in the retina of mammals; the so-called rods perceive differences in light and dark; and the cones are used for color perception. There are different types of cones for the basic colors red, green, and blue.

Our eye is rich in cones, and distinguishes some 200 color tones. The rods dominate in a dog's eye; the proportion of cones doesn't exceed 20 percent. A dog's eye is thus more sensitive to light, but not as adept at perceiving colors as the human eye. Whereas we have three types of cones and see trichromatically, dogs have only two types. Their dichromatic color perception is limited to blue and yellow; a dog can't distinguish red and orange objects from one another.

① The Dog's Eye—Better Than It's Cracked Up to Be, *p. 18*

▶ COLOR TYPES

In one and the same breed there frequently are a variety of fur colors. In some dog breeds the color varieties are judged separately at shows.

① Hovawart Breed Portrait, *p. 58*

▶ COMFORT BEHAVIOR

Comfort behavior refers to behaviors related to metabolism, relaxation, and body care. In dogs this includes yawning, lounging about, and stretching, scratching, shaking, and nibbling the fur, as well as twitching while sleeping.

③ Behavior Basics, *p. 141*

▶ CONDITIONING

This is a learning process in which behavior is directed in such a way that a link is produced between a stimulus and a response. In classical conditioning a conditioned reflex is triggered by a stimulus; for example: before feeding a dog hears a bell. After a while, only the bell is rung. Since the dog has made the connection between the sound and the food, it salivates at the mere sound of the bell, even though the feeding doesn't follow. Operational or instrumental conditioning helps a dog learn successfully; for example, every time a dog pushes the correct lever among several choices, it gets a food reward. After a short time the dog activates only the lever that produces the food.

③ How Dogs Learn, *p. 153*

▶ DISPLACEMENT BEHAVIOR

Displacement behavior is the term used by behavior researchers to indicate a reaction that's inappropriate at a given moment. Such actions are triggered by conflict situations when it's difficult to determine the appropriate behavior. A dog that's uncertain whether it should flee or attack frequently starts to eat grass or scratch its head in "displacement." Typical displacement behavior includes shaking objects, urinating, digging, yawning, and licking the snout; this last behavior can also be a gesture of submission.

③ Behavior Basics, *p. 141*

▶ DISPOSITION

The term indicating a dog's nature is multi-layered, but it pertains to inborn and hereditary tendencies, characteristics, and abilities. A dog's disposition is expressed by its ability to learn, its temperament, and its readiness to bond with a human. Researchers estimate the hereditary portion of a dog's disposition at 10 to 30 percent.

② Questions about Ownership and Acclimatizing, *p. 122*

▶ DOCKING

Some BREED STANDARDS (p.259) used to prescribe docking the ears of certain breeds (such as the Boxer) and the tails of others (such as the Miniature Schnauzer and Rottweiler). This practice is now prohibited in many places.

① The Standard Defines the Breed, *p. 83*

▶ DOG HANDLER'S CERTIFICATION

Training courses for dog handlers lay the groundwork for rewarding and trouble-free dog ownership. Every dog owner can take special courses to get ready for a certification exam. The test covers theory and practice, and is based on a course that lasts several weeks. The best way to find out about educational opportunities related to dog ownership is to contact local and national dog associations, or search on line for opportunities close to home.

① A Certificate for Dog Handlers, *p. 34*

▶ DOG TRAINING SCHOOL

Dog training schools offer training and development courses for dogs of any age—from basic training to special courses for dogs with behavior problems and schooling for guide dogs. In earlier times negative reinforcement was used as a training tool, but today the material is transmitted through gentle training methods based on positive reinforcement. Many dog training schools offer PUPPY PLAY DAYS (p.271).

③ School for Every Dog, *p. 160*

▶ DOMESTICATION

The oldest discovery of bones proven to belong to a domesticated dog dates back some 14,000 years; it is associated with a late Ice Age grave in northern Germany. A dog footprint in a southern French cave is 10,000 years older. Genetic analyses date the beginning of domestication even farther back; people evidently succeeded in getting wolves used to them as early as about 135,000 years ago. Gene researchers distinguish four genetically independent strains of dogs. The evidence is that there were several domestication sites that functioned independently of one another, where early humans and early dogs tried out their new partnership. One emblem of the dog's domestication is its skull, which is smaller than that of the wolf; the size of the bones and teeth in dogs has also diminished. Because of the variety of forms among today's dog breeds, this phenomenon, which also applies to other domesticated animal forms, is no longer obvious. At first a dog's usefulness as guardian of house and yard, defender of the herds, and hunting companion and draft animal was the main consideration; however, in subsequent breeding, appearance played an increasingly important role. Today there are about 400 dog breeds, from dwarfs such as the Chihuahua and Pekingese to the huge Mastinos, Mastiffs, and Wolfhounds.

① The Dog Is Our Oldest House Pet, *p. 13*

▶ DOMINANCE

In the pack, dominant dogs take over the leadership role. With faulty or insufficient training a dog also tries to accomplish the same relative to the owner or family. When grown animals demonstrate pronounced dominant behavior, frequently the help of DOG TRAINING SCHOOL (▶p.262) or a behavior therapist is required to restore obedience and subordination.

③ Basic Training for the Puppy, *p. 151*
③ Disobedience, *p. 167*

▶ EATING BEHAVIOR

Many large dog breeds still display the typical eating behavior of their wolf ancestors and gulp down their food as fast as possible. Smaller dogs are much more demanding than their larger colleagues in matters of food; they

FACIAL EXPRESSION

In the communication by dogs, facial expressions play a central role, even though dogs have fewer optical signals than wolves do. Facial expression makes it clear if a dog is confident, timid, or fearful, if it is bored or is watching something attentively, whether it is serious or playful in its threat. A signal from a facial expression is comprised of several components. The placement of the ears and muzzle, the shape of the eyes, and the corners of the mouth, the lips, and the wrinkling behind the nose and the forehead all carry significance.

③ The Vocalization Dictionary, *p. 144*

FALSE PREGNANCY

An unfertilized female may experience a false pregnancy around six to eight weeks after coming into HEAT (⊙p.266). The dog exhibits all the typical behaviors of a pregnant animal—it is restless, it carries around and hides toys and treats them like puppies, it builds nests for its imaginary offspring, and usually acts withdrawn or even aggressive with strangers that come too close. A dog that's experiencing false pregnancy has a greater appetite, its teats swell visibly, and it even produces milk. A false pregnancy may last for several weeks. Dogs that repeatedly experience significant milk production with false pregnancy are more susceptible to mammary tumors. Spaying should be considered for such dogs. A spayed bitch will experience no further false pregnancies.

④ Kidneys and Reproductive Organs, *p. 213*

---

don't accept everything that's offered, and eat rather more reservedly and with enjoyment.

④ The Eating Habits of Dogs, *p. 189*

EXERCISE NEEDS

Some very tiny dogs need only a little exercise, but regular, ample exercise is important for most dogs. In contrast to cats, which run quickly only when they have to, dogs love high gear, and for many breeds, such as Greyhounds, a trot is the normal pace. In a pack, a dog adjusts its running speed to the pace of the leader. This applies also to the animal-human pack—at least as long as the dog recognizes the owner's authority.

⑤ Questions About Sports, Games, and Travel, *p. 255*

EYE COLOR

The iris of most puppies is blue, other pigments don't appear until later on. With many breeds the eye color is prescribed in the BREED STANDARD (⊙p.259). Structural changes in the lens often leave the eyes of older dogs with a blue-gray sheen.

① Everything in Full View, *p. 18*

FERAL DOGS

Feral dogs are descended from domestic dogs. They include the Pariah Dogs (Tamil: pariah, outcast) in many regions of Asia and North Africa. Pariah Dogs don't constitute any particular breed and vary greatly in size and coloration. The best-known feral dog is the Australian Dingo, which arrived on the fifth continent with the original settlers and is related to the Indonesian domestic dog. Since for several thousands of years there were no other dogs in Australia with which the Dingos could intermix, they are generally considered the purest breed.

① Info: Dingos, *p. 13*

▶ FETCHING

Picking up and carrying objects or prey is part of dogs' behavior. Through selective breeding hunting breeds have been developed into perfect retrievers. These are usually easily trained dogs like the Golden and Labrador Retrievers, which will reliably bring back downed game undamaged to their master. Retrievers belong to breed group eight (→ p.40) of the recognized breeds.

⑤ Fetching Games, *p. 232*

▶ FIGHTING DOGS

Dangerous dogs that have an elevated potential for aggressiveness are considered fighting dogs. There are special regulations that govern their ownership and breeding. In some places such dogs must be kept on a leash and identified with a microchip. Fees for registering fighting dogs may be higher than for other dogs.

① Leash and Muzzle Requirements, *p. 34*

▶ FUR TYPE

The original double coat is comprised of a tough, water-resistant topcoat and a thick undercoat. This all-weather fur is found on the German Shepherd Dog and the Nordic breeds. In general there are five types of fur that occur on dogs: long-hair (Bobtail, Bernese Mountain Dog, and Collie); smooth hair (Boxer, Basset, German Mastiff); rough hair (West Highland White Terrier, Cairn Terrier, Schnauzer); silky hair (Pekingese, Afghan Hound, Maltese); and curly or frizzy hair

(Poodle, Bedlington Terrier). In addition, there are breeds with exceptional fur, such as the Chinese Tufted, the nearly bald Mexican Hairless, and the Hungarian herding dogs Puli and Komondor, whose hair hangs down in ropes.

① A Magic Coat for All Types of Weather, *p. 17*

▶ GENETICS

Genetics or the science of heredity focuses on the laws and basis for forming hereditary traits and passing them on to successive generations. In addition to classical genetics, molecular genetics plays an important role today. It examines hereditary phenomena through molecular structures that carry the hereditary information.

① Breeding Dogs Takes a Lot of Experience, *p. 28*

▶ GREETING RITUAL

When two unfamiliar dogs meet, it's the scent that determines if they will get along. They approach one another until their noses nearly touch. After nose contact each one sniffs the other's hind end (◑p.258). There are anal glands beneath the tail that also produce a dog's scented business card. Confident dogs lift their tail and thus communicate that they have nothing to hide; fearful dogs often hang their tail low. The greeting ritual almost

always goes peacefully, with wagging tails. Usually there are problems only with strong dogs with which you don't want to show any weakness.

③ Scent Signals and Smell Check, *p. 145*

▶ HEAT REGULATION

People sweat all over their bodies when the weather is too hot. The evaporation of the sweat keeps our body temperature relatively stable. Dogs have sweat glands only between their toes, and their mouth and tongue are important in controlling their body temperature. With heat and physical exertion a dog breathes with short, powerful breaths; it pants. Its tongue hangs far out of the open mouth and is continually moistened to conduct away excess heat. The paws sweat primarily when a dog is excited or under severe stress.

① Dogs Prefer Things Cool, *p. 16*

▶ HERDING DOGS

Herding dogs are distinguished by an enthusiasm for work and a patient disposition. The recognized breeds are classified by the FCI in Group I with the sheepdogs and cattledogs. Examples include the Bearded and Border Collie, Puli, Australian Shepherd, German Shepherd Dog, Malinois, Briard, and Kuvasz. The old German herding dogs, including the Kuhhund, Gelbbacke, Harzer Fuchs, Rauhbärtel, Tiger, Stumper, Strobel, and others, have become rare.

③ When Humans Settled Down, *p. 129*

▶ HEREDITY

The parents pass on a series of traits to their offspring. That affects both the phenotype and certain behavior and performance characteristics. Breeding deals with this inheritability. The appearance of a characteristic is

determined by genes that are located on the chromosomes in the nucleus of every cell in the body. The genes don't mix, but they are passed on partially concealed so that they don't appear in the next generation. Since environmental factors also play a decisive role in revealing characteristics, many hereditary factors can't be predicted. In BREEDING SUITABILITY EVALUATION (▶p.260), breeders now have a method that makes it possible to assess fairly accurately how genetic defects and HEREDITARY DISEASES (▶p.265) are passed on.

① The Standard Defines the Breed, *p. 83*

▶ HEREDITARY DISEASES

With changes in the genetic material caused by illness, the specific hereditary tendencies are passed on to the offspring. Depending on how the hereditary disease is expressed in the parents, the disease may be more pronounced in successive generations (and may occur early), or appear only in diminished form. The hereditary disposition is thus present when the heightened susceptibility to certain diseases is inherited. Many dog breeds or individual breeding lines are susceptible to specific diseases: Cavalier King Charles Spaniels, for example, to heart problems, Samoyeds to deafness, and Miniature Poodles to retinal atrophy. Hereditary skeleton and joint diseases such as hip and elbow dysplasia are more common in large, heavy breeds. Through BREEDING SUITABILITY EVALUATION (▶p.260), breeders attempt to avoid passing on hereditary defects

① The Standard Defines the Breed, *p. 83*

▶ HOUSE PET PASS

If you ever travel with a dog inside the European Union, you will need to have a house pet pass. It is required by all EU member states. The house pet pass must include the dog's ID number—either the tattoo or microchip number until the year 2011, and thereafter, only the microchip number will be accepted. The pass also confirms the valid rabies vaccination, which must be at least 30 days but no more than 12 months old at the time of the border crossing. For Ireland, Sweden, and Great Britain there are special requirements. The house pet pass is issued by veterinarians.

⑤ International Travel, *p. 252*

HOWLING

Howling is very important for wolves as a means of staying in touch with one another. The howling, which can be heard at great distances, maintains contact with the pack, and communal howling strengthens the group consciousness. Even dogs howl when they are separated from their human pack; however, in communicating with humans barking has become more important. A male dog that gets wind of a female in heat and can't get to her communicates his location by howling.

③ Characteristics of Wolves, *p. 138*

IMPOSING BEHAVIOR

In demonstrating imposing behavior, a dog tries to make itself as large as possible; it stands on straightened legs, stares at its antagonist, and shows itself broadside. The head is held high, the ears erect, the neck, back, and tail hairs held erect, and the tail points upward. If this display impresses the other dog, the threatened squabble is usually avoided.

③ Dictionary of Body Language, *p. 143*

IN HEAT

Most bitches come into heat twice a year—between January and March, and between August and October. During this phase they are ready to mate at the height of the rut. The

scents that a female in heat gives off attract male dogs over great distances.

① The Scent of Love, *p. 77*

INBREEDING

Breeding closely related animals may eventually cause genetic defects to come to light. Good breeding should be free of such inbred pairings for several generations.

① The Standard Defines the Breed, *p. 83*

INFECTIOUS DISEASES

The most dangerous infectious canine diseases include rabies, leptospirosis, distemper, hepatitis, and parvovirus. The only sure protection is inoculation before exposure.

④ The Most Dangerous Infectious Diseases, *p. 204*

INTELLIGENCE

Dogs learn through both linking actions and situations (association) and trial and error. The highly developed adaptability of dogs and the ability to distinguish between natural laws and training are signs of their mental agility.

③ Intelligence and Learning, *p. 140*

KENNEL CONFINEMENT

If dogs are kept in a kennel for a long time, they lack the vitally important contact with a pack. The result is severe BEHAVIOR PROBLEMS (⊙p.259). When you buy a dog you must be sure that the owner's animals have regular contact with the family and that the mother dogs and puppies were kept in a kennel for only a short time.

① What Difference Does a Good Breeder Make? *p. 28*

KENNEL NAME

Purebred dogs have a regular and a kennel name. The names of all puppies in a litter have the same first letter. In successive litters the names begin with the next letter of the alphabet.

① **A Personal ID for Purebred Dogs,** *p. 84*

KNEADING

In the first couple of weeks of life a puppy is totally helpless. In addition to finding its mother's teats, one of its inborn abilities is kneading. The pup kneads the mother's body with its paws as it drinks and squeezes more out of her. The kneading stimulates the mother to give milk. The movement pattern survives beyond puppyhood as the gesture of giving the paw.

① **Mother's Milk and Lots of Sleep,** *p. 81*

LIABILITY INSURANCE

The dog owner may be legally liable with assets and income for all damage caused by a dog, even if not under the owner's direct influence (for example, while straying). The owner should have comprehensive personal and liability insurance. Animal owners' liability insurance is the only insurance that will help in a serious case involving high costs. Such insurance is now available from many carriers.

① **Liability Insurance for Animal Owners,** *p. 34*

LITTER

After successful mating, a female dog gives birth after about 63 days. A litter contains an average of six puppies, or more with large breeds and fewer with smaller ones; sometimes just one pup is born. The littermates can come from different fathers, if the bitch was mounted by several males while in heat.

① **A Normal Birth,** *p. 79*

MARKING

A dog's SCENT MARKING (◖p.272) notifies other dogs in the vicinity who they have to deal with and what its territory is. Males, in particular, but also dominant females, mark especially where other dogs have already left their scent message behind. The male lifts his leg as high as possible to mark over his predecessor's scent mark and deposits a little urine. Marking is also accompanied by scratching the ground with the hind paws, which deposits scent from the sweat glands on the paws.

① **Typical for Dogs,** *p. 22*

MARKINGS

Colored markings and splotches in the fur of predominantly one-colored dogs. With many breeds certain markings are desired or encouraged by the breed standard (◖p.259). Even the mask (◖p.267) is a marking. The white markings on the head, chest, and paws of the Bernese Mountain Dog, for example, along with the black fur and red blaze, are part of this breed's tricolor fur.

① **Pinscher Breed Portrait,** *p. 67*

MASK

A usually dark, clearly defined marking on a dog's face, as with the Pug, Mastiff, Boxer, Leonberger, and Malinois.

① **Boxer Breed Portrait,** *p. 48*

MICROCHIP

A microchip is a dog's personal ID. The tiny chip is injected under the skin of the shoulder region by the veterinarian. It contains the identification that can be read by a special device. Just as with TATTOOING (○p.273) the code is entered into a pet registry (→ Addresses, p.284) so that the dog can be identified if it becomes lost. In the European Union, the ID must be entered into the house pet pass; after 2011 only the microchip number will be used.

⑤ International Travel, *p. 252*

MOTION DETECTION

A dog's eye reacts more sensitively to movement and light than a human's eye. A dog can recognize its owner even at a great distance from the familiar manner of movement and gesture; however, they may overlook motionless people or animals even at short distances. Since dogs have a wide field of vision (○VISION, p.274), scarcely a movement gets by them.

① Origin and Meaning, *p. 85*

MUZZLE GRIP

Among wolves and dogs a superior animal reprimands a subordinate pack member with a meaningful bite on the muzzle. A handgrip over the top of the muzzle is thus an appropriate method of scolding a dog for bad behavior. The muzzle grip should be used only in serious situations.

③ How Should Bad Behavior Be Punished? *p. 164*

MUZZLE LAW

Dangerous dogs are often required by law to wear a muzzle (○FIGHTING DOGS, p.264). Depending on size and weight, other dogs in many areas must also wear a muzzle as soon as they leave their home property. Local ordinances may also prescribe the use of a muzzle in public places.

① Leash and Muzzle Requirements, *p. 34*

NEUTERING

In neutering a female dog, the veterinarian removes the ovaries and sometimes the uterus; with a male, the testicles are removed. In contrast to sterilization, which is no longer widely practiced, a female dog cannot be made fertile again after the operation. Neutering prevents unwanted pregnancies, uterine infections, and false pregnancies, and it reduces the risk of mammary cancer. Neutered male dogs generally are less aggressive and less prone to straying.

④ Info: Neutering, *p. 214*

OFFERING A PAW

Offering a paw is an inborn begging gesture. It can be observed even in puppies, when they

instinctively knead the mother's teats to stimulate milk production. With people, giving the paw is a friendly way to establish contact. Depending on the situation, the dog wants to attract attention, beg, soothe, or invite play.

③ An Atlas of Dog Language, *p. 147*

▶ ORIGIN

The domestic dog is descended from the wolf. Even though dogs have lived with humans for thousands of years, they still show a lot of resemblance to their ancestors, especially in their social behavior and in communicating with one another. It's been only in recent years that the origins of dogs have been proven incontestably through molecular genetic research. Analysis of genetic material has yielded a difference of just 0.2 percent between wolf and dog; however, the difference between wolf and coyote and jackal, which had long been considered possible ancestors of dogs, amounts to four or five percent.

① Searching for Ancestors, *p. 13*

▶ PACK

Dogs are pack animals and need a solid place in their community. In the relationship between human and dog, the human takes on the function of the leader, and thus the place of the top or alpha dog. A dog expects authority and leadership qualities from its pack leader; only then does it demonstrate obedience and follow orders. Attempts at "anti-authoritarianism" and partnership invariably lead to rebelliousness and disobedience.

① How the Wolf Turned into the Domestic Dog, *p. 14*

▶ PARASITES

Worms are the most significant internal parasites in dogs. Even puppies become infested with roundworms inside their mother's womb, so regular worming starting at the age of two weeks is important. Roundworms and tapeworms can be communicated to humans; our health is also at risk from canine and vulpine tapeworms, in addition to hookworms and roundworms. The external parasites that infest dogs include fleas, ticks, mites, and lice, which cause damage to skin and fur.

④ Other Infectious Diseases, *p. 207*

▶ PECKING ORDER

In a wolf or dog pack every member has an established rank and submits to the leader of the pack. The lead animal doesn't necessarily assert itself through size and strength; self-assertion, superiority, and experience are much more important. The dog requires similar leadership qualities from its owner. Especially with confident male dogs there is always a problem with hierarchy if the person bends to the dog's wishes and lets it make the decisions.

③ Adolescence and Puberty, *p. 137*

▶ PEDIGREE

A purebred dog's pedigree indicates its origins and the characteristics that were bred into it. The form is signed by both the breeder and the manager of the association's breed book, in which the female's litter is recorded. The pedigree goes along with a purebred dog. It describes the dog and the previous generations. The purchaser always gets the pedigree directly from the breeder rather than from the association.

① A Personal ID for Purebred Dogs, *p. 84*

▶ PET CEMETERIES

Some people prefer to bury a deceased dog on their own property. People who don't have that opportunity can bury their dogs in a pet cemetery. These can be found in many locations; an Internet search will lead to some, and animal shelters may have further information. Some people also have their dogs cremated; many veterinarians can provide this service.

④ What to Do If..., *p. 211*

▶ PLAYING

Playing is vitally important to dogs. Playing teaches a puppy what's permitted and what's not. Playing works off aggression, keeps a dog physically and mentally fit, and is the best way to prevent boredom. Playing with the owner strengthens the relationship. Like cats, dogs are animals that regularly play as adults, and even into advanced age. Boxers, terriers, and spaniels are particularly fond of playing.

⑤ Playing Makes Dogs Strong, *p. 228*

▶ POISONOUS PLANTS

Among common plants, the following are poisonous to dogs: laurel, daffodil, delphini-

um, meadow saffron, lily of the valley, tomato, box tree, oleander, mistletoe, yew, laburnum, azalea, lupine, and others. With many plants the poisonous effect is increased by or exclusive to certain parts, such as blooms, leaves, stems, seeds, or fruit. With laurel the leaves and stems are poisonous; with mistletoe the berries are especially poisonous, and with the yew it's the needles, seeds, and the bark.

② Operation "Safe House," *p. 110*

▶ POISONS

Dogs are curious. They lick tentatively at spilled liquids or chew up packages of medicine. All chemical compounds should be beyond the reach of a dog. That includes household cleansers, polishes, paints and varnishes, disinfectants, insecticides, fungicides, oils and gasoline, antifreeze, snail repellant, plus all medications in a human medicine cabinet. Aspirin, for example, is highly poisonous to dogs.

② Operation "Safe House," *p. 110*

▶ PREGNANCY

A canine pregnancy lasts from 59 to 65 days—an average of 63 days. In the first couple of weeks there usually are no visible changes in the dog's body or behavior. Starting in about the third week, however, a veterinarian can determine if a bitch is pregnant. The size of the litter depends on body size and breed; large breeds such as the Saint Bernard deliver an average of eight puppies; a Miniature Poodle, four or five. With large breeds there are significantly more stillbirths than with small ones, and that tendency increases with the mother's age.

① Pregnancy Symptoms, *p. 78*

⊙ PROBLEM DOGS

There are many causes for problems with dogs. The most common ones include incorrect or insufficient training, a lack of hierarchy, excessive demands by the owner, too much attention, anthropomorphizing, and neglect. Behavior incidents can also be triggered by illnesses (such as tumors), chronic complaints (declining eyesight, bone problems) and age-related problems. There may also be a genetic disposition to problem behavior. Major disturbances must be treated by experts (⊙DOG TRAINING SCHOOL, p.262).

③ Therapy for Problem Dogs, *p. 160*

⊙ PROTEST BEHAVIOR

Changes in the pack structure, disturbances to the accustomed routine, jealousy, a sudden change in food, frequent absence by the owner, and a lack of attention can lead to protest behavior by a dog. Depending on the dog's nature, it may be expressed through refusal to eat, uncleanliness, apathy, or rebelliousness, and even through aggressive behavior toward its own family. One common protest reaction among dogs that feel neglected or demoted is STRAYING (⊙p.273). Effective treatment is possible only when the causes of the protest are identified.

③ Lack of Control, *p. 166*

⊙ PUBERTY

Depending on the breed, a dog reaches puberty starting about age five months. During this "bratty" stage, which can last until the age of 12 months, the dog keeps flexing its muscles and testing its owner's authority, ignoring commands, and acting rebellious. Frequently the dog will even try to take over the leadership role in the pack.

③ Adolescence and Puberty, *p. 137*

⊙ PUPPY PLAY DAYS

Puppy play days offer a puppy the best opportunity to playfully try out all forms of social interaction with other dogs of the same age. With the rest of the group it meets unfamiliar people and learns to approach unknown situations without fear. Puppies are welcome to participate between the ages of 9 and 20 weeks, but the dogs must be healthy and up to date on their shots. The director also makes the group (usually six to eight dogs) familiar with the first playful obedience exercises.

③ Puppy School, *p. 160*

⊙ PUREBRED

The term *purebred* refers to dogs that pass on their physical and personality traits as intact as possible to their offspring. With the recognized dog breeds these traits must conform to the BREED STANDARD (⊙p.259). The PEDIGREE (⊙p.270) that describes a dog

and lists several preceding generations belongs with a specific dog.

① **Raising Purebreds,** *p. 83*

● REGISTRATION

A dog's tattoo or microchip number can be entered in a pet registry (→ Addresses, p.284). An animal that's lost and then recovered can be positively identified in the registry data bank and returned to the owner.

⑤ **Things to Consider on Vacation,** *p. 252*

● REPORTING REQUIREMENT

In some areas, people who buy dangerous dogs are required to report them to the authorities (●FIGHTING DOGS, p.264). In the case of a move, the dog must be removed from the records in the former location and added in the new one within a specified time (for example, a month). There is also a reporting requirement for contagious diseases that can be transmitted from dogs to humans (such as rabies, canine and vulpine tapeworm, and toxoplasmosis under certain conditions).

④ **Tip: Infections That Must Be Reported,** *p. 208*

● SCENT MARKING

Dogs live in a world of smells. Around the territory and on walks male dogs, and some females, deposit small amounts of urine. A dog uses this MARKING (●p.267) to leave behind a personal scent mark and let other dogs know that it was here. This happens especially when it finds the mark left by another dog, which it covers over with its own scent; males also mark places that smell of a female in heat. At home there is only the familiar "house smell" of the family. There a dog will put down a scent marking only if the scent of a strange dog reaches its nose. Female dogs mark much less frequently than males, and usually only where other females have already left their scent.

③ **Ambassadors of Scent,** *p. 140*

● SENSE OF HEARING

Dogs hear better than people and perceive tones in the ultrasound range. People make use of this hearing ability when they use silent (to us) dog whistles. The lower hearing threshold is about the same in dogs and humans, but a cat reacts to even lower-frequency tones. Dogs can perceive sounds from four times farther away than we can. Dogs that have the original erect ear shape (German Shepherd Dogs and Bull Terriers, for example) hear best and are better at local-

izing tonal signals. Breeds with drop ears don't hear as well.

① Nothing Escapes a Dog's Ears, *p. 18*

SENSE OF SMELL

The chemical composition of scents communicates lots of information to the canine nose. The sense of smell is central to hunting, MARKING (⊙p.267), sexual behavior, and the GREETING RITUAL (⊙p.264). The smelling surface of a dog's nose is 30 times greater than that of humans. In breeding tracking dogs and scenthounds a lot of value is placed on high-performance scent perception.

① Always Ahead by a Nose, *p. 18*

SHEARING

In shearing the fur the hairs are trimmed with shears or clippers (⊙TRIMMING, p.274). The most familiar clip is the one seen on Poodles. The standard allows several shapes such as new clip, old clips, and English Saddle Clips. The new clip replaced the Lion Clip in the middle of the last century.

④ The Most Important Care Measures, *p. 193*

SOCIALIZATION PHASE

Starting no later than the age of four weeks a puppy becomes increasingly interested in its surroundings. Its ability to learn is now exceptionally strong. In the socialization phase, which lasts until the age of 14 weeks, or up to 20 weeks with some breeds, the groundwork for sociability is laid. Dogs that have no opportunity to have positive experiences with humans in this time remain insecure and difficult even in adulthood.

① Curious About Life, *p. 82*

STEREOTYPIES

Behaviors that are continually repeated in a pattern are known as stereotypies. Examples for such compulsive actions are continuous running back and forth in a cage and monotonous barking. The behavioral disturbances are often pathological in nature.

③ Behavior Basics, *p. 141*

STRAYING

Male dogs are particularly prone to straying, but even females will try to get away when they are in heat. Straying involves major risks such as traffic, getting lost, picking up an infection such as rabies, or capture by dogcatchers. Temporary confinement helps with females in heat; for stubborn wanderers a course in a DOG TRAINING SCHOOL (⊙p.262) is the right choice. With male dogs, neutering also frequently helps.

③ Straying, *p. 171*

TATTOOING

A runaway dog can be identified by its tattoo and returned to its owner. Tattooing is carried out on the ear or the inner thigh of a young dog. Travel within the EU requires entering the tattoo or microchip number (⊙MICROCHIP, p.268) in the house pet pass. Starting in the year 2011 only the microchip number will be permitted.

⑤ International Travel, *p. 252*

TEETHING

Puppies get their milk teeth starting at the age of four weeks. Teething begins in the third month and ends with the appearance of the back molars at the age of six or seven months. With large dog breeds with a short life expectancy, the new teeth erupt sooner than with small breeds that live longer. If the second dentition grows in before the milk teeth fall out, the first set has to be pulled to prevent problems with the bite.

③ Time for Teeth, *p. 136*

▶ TERRITORY

Every dog instinctively guards and defends its pack (the family) and its home. The desire to defend the home territory varies in intensity with breed. Excessively strong territorial behavior can complicate living with the dog, if for example, it refuses to allow strangers onto the property. A dog also considers objects that the human pack regularly uses to be part of the territory, such as the garden plot and the family car.

③ The Home Territory As a Source of Strength, *p. 138*

▶ TOOTH CARE

Tooth care is important even for puppies. Chewing and gnawing on chew bones and dog biscuits strengthens their teeth and cleans them mechanically. Dogs that are made comfortable with teeth cleaning early on accept the toothbrush without resistance. Unlike our toothpaste, dog toothpaste must be edible, as the dog swallows it. Special chew snacks help prevent tartar, and thus tooth problems and gum infections. Dogs are not very susceptible to tooth decay, as pieces of food rarely get packed into their scissors bite.

④ Teeth and Gums, *p. 197*

▶ TRIMMING

In particular the more than 30 terrier breeds, plus Affenpinschers and Schnauzers, require trimming. The fur is shortened and shaped with a stripping knife or plucked by hand; at the same time, dead hairs are removed. Pup-

pies must learn to stand still while they are being trimmed on a trimming table, preferably right from the beginning. Proper trimming according to standard is a time-consuming procedure, especially with large dogs such as the Airedale Terrier. Experts in breed associations are happy to give beginners some help.

④ Info: Trimming and Shearing, *p. 193*

▶ VISION

A dog's eye is flatter than a human eye. Since its focal length is thus restricted, it can't see clearly at all distances. Dogs see objects up close only indistinctly. The canine eye has a limited capability of perceiving colors (▶COLOR PERCEPTION, p.260), but it picks up movement (▶MOTION DETECTION, p.268) better than static objects. The field of view of short-nosed dogs (such as a Boxer) covers 200 degrees; with breeds that have longer, thinner snouts (Afghan Hounds, Greyhounds), it covers up to 270 degrees. (A human's field of view is 100 degrees.) Since the fields of view of long-nosed dogs scarcely overlap, they have three-dimensional vision in only a limited range. Three-dimensional vision is a prerequisite for judging distances.

① Everything in Full View, *p. 18*

▶ VOCALIZATION

There are many sounds used by dogs in their vocalizations. Barking is of particular significance in communicating with humans, but it is scarcely used in communicating with other dogs. Every vocalization corresponds to a specific FACIAL EXPRESSION (▶p.263) and BODY LANGUAGE (▶p.259).

③ Language and Communication, *p. 143*

WITHERS

The physical size of a dog is measured at its withers. The withers are seen as an extension of the legs, up to the point where the neck transitions to the back. Among all mammals, dogs exhibit the greatest diversity of heights at the withers, from 5 inches (13 cm) in a Chihuahua to over 31 inches (79 cm) in an Irish Wolfhound. Many male Wolfhounds reach heights at the withers that exceed 39 inches (100 cm). Almost every BREED STANDARD (◐p.259) encourages adherence within close tolerances to specific heights at the withers.

① Raising Purebreds, *p. 83*

WORKING DOGS

The working dogs include the Rottweiler, German Shepherd Dog, Hovawart, Boxer, Airedale Terrier, Giant Schnauzer, Bouvier des Flandres, Doberman Pinscher, and Malinois. In character, disposition, stature, and physical strength they come equipped with the best characteristics for helping humans in many different areas.

③ Specialists on the Rise, *p. 131*

ZOONOSES

Zoonoses are infectious diseases that can be transmitted from animals to people and from people to animals. An annual shot protects the dog—and thus humans—from rabies. Regular worming minimizes the transmission of worms. Careful hygiene in daily dealings with a dog also prevents infestations of dermal fungi.

④ Are Dogs a Threat to Our Health? *p. 203*

Breed Index

Helpful Addresses

American Field
542 South Dearborn Street
Chicago, IL 60605
312-663-9797

American Kennel Club
260 Madison Avenue
New York, NY 10016

American Rare Breeds Association
9921 Frank Tippet Road
Cheltenham, MD 20623
301-868-5718

American Society for the Prevention of Cruelty to Animals
242 East 92nd Street
New York, NY 10128

American Veterinary Medical Association
930 North Meacham Road
Shaumburg, IL 60173

Canadian Kennel Club
180-89 Skyway Avenue
Etobicoke, Ontario M9W 6R4 Canada
416-675-5511

Lost Dog Recovery
AKC Animal Companion Recovery
5580 Centerview Drive, Suite 250
Raleigh, NC 27606-3394
1-800-252-7894

Microchip Pet Identification System
For a complimentary Home-Again
Information kit, call
1-800-2Find-Pet;
visit the Web site at
http://www.spanimalhealth.com/ha.htm

National Bird Dog Museum
505 West Highway 57
P.O. Box 744
Grand Junction, TN 88039
901-764-2058

Orthopedic Foundation for Animals, Inc.
Hip Registry
2300 East Nifong Boulevard
Columbia, MO 54201-3856

Pet Sitters International
418 East King Street
King, NC 27021-9163
336-983-9222

United Kennel Club
100 East Kilgore Road
Kalamazoo, MI 49002-5584

▷ DOG REGISTRY

You can protect your dog from animal thieves and death in a research laboratory by entering it into a dog registry. Entry and computer-assisted search upon report of a missing dog are free. An Internet search will put you in contact with dog registries. Also see the Web sites below.

▷ HEALTH AND LIABILITY INSURANCE

Check with your preferred insurance carrier; some companies offer insurances for pet owners. An online search will also lead you to sources of coverage.

▷ WEB SITES

AKC home page: *www.akc.org*

AKC Online Services:
www.akc.org/online_services/index.cfm

Canine Search and Rescue Organizations:
*http: dir.yahoo.com/Health/Emergency_*

Services/Search_and_Rescue/
Canine_Search_and_Rescue_Organizations/
CAR: Companion Animal Recovery:
www.akccar.org

Dog Club Listings;
dmoz.org/Recreation/Pets/Dogs/Clubs

FCI breeds and nomenclature: *www.fci.be/
nomenclatures.asp?lang=en&sel=0*

Specific Dog Breed Associations:
*http://dir.yahoo.com/science/biology/
zoology/animals_insects_and_pets/mam-
mals/dogs/organizations/specific breeds*

Useful Books

Alderton, David. *The Dog Care Manual.* Hauppauge, New York: Barron's Educational Series, Inc., 1984.

American Kennel Club. *The Complete Dog Book.* New York, New York: Howell Book House, 1992.

Baer, Ted. *Communicating with Your Dog.* Hauppauge, New York: Barron's Educational Series, Inc., 1989.

Bailey, Gwen. *The Well-Behaved Dog.* Hauppauge, New York: Barron's Educational Series, Inc., 1998.

Davis, Kathy Diamond. *Responsible Dog Ownership.* New York, New York: Howell Book House, 1994.

Frye, Frederic I. *First Aid for Your Dog.* Hauppauge, New York: Barron's Educational Series, Inc., 1987.

Hegewald-Kawich, Horst. *My Dog and Me.* Hauppauge, New York: Barron's Educational Series, Inc., 2002.

Kiever, Ulrigh. *The Complete Book of Dog Care.* Hauppauge, New York: Barron's Educational Series, Inc., 1989.

Ludwig, Gerd. *Sit! Stay! Train Your Dog the Easy Way.* Hauppauge, New York: Barron's Educational Series, Inc., 1998.

Rice, Dan. *The Dog Handbook.* Hauppauge, New York: Barron's Educational Series, Inc., 1999.

Schlegel-Kofler, Katharina. *Dalmatians. A Complete Pet Owner's Manual.* Hauppauge, New York: Barron's Educational Series, Inc., 1999.

Smith, Cheryl S. *Pudgy Pooch, Picky Pooch.* Hauppauge, New York: Barron's Educational Series, Inc., 1998.

Smith, Cheryl S. and Stephanie J. Tauton. *The Trick Is in the Training.* Hauppauge, New York: Barron's Educational Series, Inc., 1998.

Vine, Louis, L., D.V.M. *Your Dog, His Health and Happiness.* New York: Prentice-Hall, 1986.

Whitney, Leon, D.V.M. and George Whitney, D.V.M. *The Complete Book of Dog Care.* New York: Doubleday, 1984.

▶ PERIODICALS

AKC Gazette
Subscriptions: 919-233-9767

Dog Fancy
P.O. Box 53264
Boulder, CO 80322-3264

Dog World
29 North Wacker Drive
Chicago, IL 60606

Off-Lead
204 Lewis Street
Canastota, NY 13032
800-241-7619

Important Notice

The guidelines in this advisory book refer to normally developed dogs of good breeding, thus to healthy animals of irreproachable character. People who adopt an adult dog must realize that such a dog has already had its disposition shaped by experiences with humans. Such people must observe the dog very closely, including its behavior toward other people, and they should consider the previous owner. If the dog is from an animal shelter, the shelter may be able to provide information about its personality traits and origins. There are dogs that have had bad experiences with people and may even be prone to biting. Such dogs should be adopted only by experienced dog owners. Even with well-trained and carefully supervised dogs there is a chance that they will cause damage to other people's property or even cause an accident. In either case, adequate insurance protection is strongly recommended.

Acknowledgments

The author and publisher thank Mr. Horst Hegewald-Kawich for his expert advice and Mr. Reinhard Hahn, Esq., for checking the text of the legal passages.

The Author

Dr. Gerd Ludwig is a freelance journalist and zoologist. He has written several advisory books about dogs and cats for Grafe and Unzer Publishing.

The Translator

Eric A. Bye, M.A., is a freelance translator working from German, French, and Spanish. He lives and works in Vermont and is a lifelong dog owner. He has translated dozens of books for Barron's.

Photographers

Pictures Pur/Steimer: page 52 left; Cogis/Alexis: page 70 left; Cogis/Kd: page 46 left; Cogis/Hermelind: page 55 left; Cogis/Lanceau: page 65 right, 71 left; Giel: pages 29, 40, 78, 106, 123 bottom, 150, 162, 180, 182, 184, 195, 200, 221, 235, 251, 269; IFA/Nakamura: Cover 1; Juniors/Botzenhardt: page 49 right, 71, right; Juniors/Essler: page 56 right; Juniors/Farkaschowsky: page 73 left; Juniors/Hütter: pages 36, Cover 4 middle; Juniors/Köpfle: page 75 right; Juniors/Krämer: page 48 left, 49, left, 67 right; Juniors/Prawitz: page 74 left; Juniors/Schanz: page 80; Juniors/Steimer: page 191; Juniors/Wegler: page 5 top, 45 right, 54 right, 61, right, 68 left, 72 right, 123 top, 207; Juniors/Wegner: page 43 right; Krämer: page 47; Kuhn: page 122, 194, right, 199 bottom, 230 (Chart 3 picture), 271; Layer: page 60 left; Masterfoods: page 231, 243; M4GMBH/more4dogs: page 103; photonica/KO.FUJUWARA: page 121; photonica/McDonough: page C4 left; photonica/Neleman: page 5 bottom; photonica/New Vision: page 8; Prawitz: page 128; Reinhard: page 45 left, 62 right; Roth: page 238; Schanz: page 50 left, 51, 57 right, 64 left, 69 right, 79, 94 (chart), 95, 96, 108 middle, 199 top, 230 (chart 1 picture), Cover 4 right; Silvestris online/Lenz: page 72 left; Steimer: pages 4, 6, 7 bottom, 25 top, middle, 37, 42 left, 44, 48 right, 59 right, 61 left, 64 right, 65 left, 67 left, 70 right, 74 right, 108 top, bottom, 132, 155, 161, 177, 189, 194 left, middle, 215, 216, 223, 246 right, 248, 249, 253, 255 bottom; Wegler: pages 2, 7 top, 10, 12, 14, 15, 17, 20, 22, 25 bottom, 26, 31, 32, 33, 35, 38, 39, 41, 42 right, 43, left, 46 right, 50 right, 52 right, 53, 54 left, 55 right, 56 left, 57 left, 58, 59 left, 60 right, 62 left, 63, 66, 68 right, 69 left, 73 right, 75 left, 76, 81, 83, 85, 86, 87, 88, 90 , 91, 94 top, 97, 98, 101, 104, 112, 115, 116, 117, 119, 126, 127, 130, 134, 136, 137, 139, 142, 145, 147, 149, 152, 145, 158, 153, 164, 165, 166, 167, 169, 172, 173, 174, 178, 179, 186, 192, 197, 201, 204, 209, 211, 212, 219, 224, 225, 226, 228, 229, 230 top, (Chart 2, 4-6 picture), 233, 234, 237, 241, 245, 246 left, middle, 154, 155 top, 256, 259, 262, 263, 264, 268, 272, 275.